The Spirit of Mourning

How is the memory of traumatic events, such as genocide and torture, inscribed within human bodies? In this book, Paul Connerton discusses social and cultural memory by looking at the role of mourning in the production of histories and the reticence of silence across many different cultures. In particular he looks at how memory is conveyed in gesture, bodily posture, speech and the senses – and how bodily memory, in turn, becomes manifested in cultural objects such as tattoos, letters, buildings and public spaces. It is argued that memory is more cultural and collective than it is individual. This book will appeal to researchers and students in anthropology, linguistic anthropology, sociology, social psychology and philosophy.

PAUL CONNERTON is a research associate in the Department of Social Anthropology at the University of Cambridge, and an honorary fellow in the Institute of Germanic and Romance Studies at the University of London. His recent publications include *How Modernity Forgets* (Cambridge, 2009).

The Spirit of Mourning

History, Memory and the Body

Paul Connerton

CAMBRIDGE
UNIVERSITY PRESS

CAMBRIDGE UNIVERSITY PRESS
Cambridge, New York, Melbourne, Madrid, Cape Town,
Singapore, São Paulo, Delhi, Tokyo, Mexico City

Cambridge University Press
The Edinburgh Building, Cambridge CB2 8RU, UK

Published in the United States of America by
Cambridge University Press, New York

www.cambridge.org
Information on this title: www.cambridge.org/9781107648838

First published 2011

Printed in the United Kingdom at the University Press, Cambridge

A catalogue record for this publication is available from the British Library

Library of Congress Cataloging-in-Publication Data

Connerton, Paul.
The spirit of mourning : history, memory and the body / Paul Connerton.
    p.   cm.
  ISBN 978-1-107-01139-7 (Hardback) – ISBN 978-1-107-64883-8 (Paperback)
  1. Bereavement–Psychological aspects.   2. Memory–Social aspects.   I. Title.
  BF575.G7C648 2011
  155.9′37–dc22

                                                           2011012437

ISBN 978-1-107-01139-7 Hardback
ISBN 978-1-107-64883-8 Paperback

To my sister

Contents

Preface

This book is about the inscription of memory within human bodies, and about the many ways in which memories are incorporated in institutions, histories and traditions. The inner dialectic of the book is that between what lived bodies undergo, retain and express pre-linguistically and the explicitly verbal language that acts to conceptualise and specify what is happening in bodily experience. The book argues that the semiosis that occurs at the bodily level has its own articulateness, history and purposes.

The arrangement of the book is organised in two broad clusters: a first, Chapters 1–3, is concerned with the relationship between narrative and cultural memory; while a second, Chapters 4–7, treats the relationship between the body and cultural memory.

The first three chapters set the stage. The first, on 'The birth of histories from the spirit of mourning', recounts the dark times of genocide, world war and totalitarian regimes that characterised the last century and whose shadows reach deeply into the present, while it also contains substantial forays into earlier history. A second chapter reminds the reader that the topic of forgetting is itself forgotten in most discussions of memory; I argue here that there are at least seven ways to forget, three of which are constructive and even necessary, while four of them are forced upon human beings against their will or interest. In 'Silences', the third chapter, I acknowledge the widespread resort to reticences in its many practices and across many cultures. This chapter is strategically placed, since by its very topic it brings to a halt the glib and verbose tendencies of late modern life, and incidentally much of its scholarship, in order to dive under the chatter down to a core of what matters most in human experience.

The first chapter in the second half of the book, on spatial orientation, seeks to establish that what is conventionally called 'cultural memory' occurs as much, if not more, by bodily practices and postures as by documents and texts. This memory *takes place* on the body's surface and in its tissues, and in accordance with levels of meaning that reflect human sensory capacities more than cognitive categories. Here I seek to show that culture happens as and in the lived body.

The fifth chapter offers a deconstruction of Gadamerian hermeneutics as failing to take account of the corporeal roots of interpretation and understanding, showing this approach to be a sophisticated but insistent logocentrism of verbal language and text. Here I seek to demonstrate that long before the level of 'tradition' in Gadamer's sense is reached, the body must be operative in the dynamics of oral speech and the actual pronunciation of words: building on the pioneering work of Parry and Havelock, I here stress the importance of the continual re-enactment of certain basic motions of tongue, lips and hands.

In 'Tattoos, masks, skin', I extend my thesis by taking a careful look at tattoos, scarifications and the use of masks as these arise across a multitude of cultural settings, seeking to demonstrate that these skin signs are not merely decorative, but highly expressive of certain cultural interests and values: they literally embody, on the surface of the skin, matters that are normally considered to exist at the level of institutions, governments and family genealogies.

A last chapter on 'Bodily projection' brings my thesis about bodily actions and traces into the realm of the habitats that surround the human subject: buildings and public spaces, as well as natural environments. I argue that these are not, as is too often assumed, simply prior in status but can be considered as projections of bodily states and attributes in three major forms: empathic, mimetic and cosmic. This brings my book full circle, showing the full scope of my thesis and its wide applicability to architectural, social and natural dimensions; each of which must henceforth be construed as expressions and outcomes of a profound bodily memory that precedes them.

The illustration on the front cover of this book exemplifies at once cultural remembering and cultural forgetting. It is taken with permission from Johannes Fabian's distinguished work, *Remembering the Present: Painting and Popular History in Zaire* (University of California Press, 1996). Fabian there describes the ambition of the Congolese painter Tshibumba Kanda Matulu to paint the entire history of his country; thanks to Fabian's foresight anyone wishing to do so may see a collection of some one hundred of Tshibumba's paintings in Amsterdam. Not least of Fabian's merits is to have rescued Lumumba, represented here by Tshibumba in prison, from relative oblivion. Only Africanists and those who lived through those times will easily recognise the portrait of Lumumba, although in 1960 he was sufficiently important and highly regarded for his African political rivals and the CIA to collude in his murder. As it happens, the author of the present book remembers seeing on Pathé News a filmed sequence of Lumumba shortly before his death; he was a prisoner in the African jungle, sitting on a chair with his hands tied behind his back. Patrice Lumumba was a man with a memorably beautiful and noble face, and I still recall vividly my revulsion on witnessing how his captors wrenched his chin from side to side in derision.

Acknowledgements

A number of friends have read earlier drafts of this book in whole or in part, and I am grateful to all of them for making this a better book than it would otherwise have been. They are: Peter Burke, David Forgacs, Russell Keat, Michael Minden, Yael Navaro-Yashin, Graham Pechey, Marilyn Strathern and Martin Thom. I am grateful to the two anonymous readers from Cambridge University Press for their particularly helpful comments on the penultimate version of my manuscript. I owe an enormous debt of gratitude to Graham Pechey for his indefatigable patience and kindness in making available to me a vast body of research material which, without his help, I would have found far more difficult of access. Clare Campbell has typed the entire volume efficiently and uncomplainingly. My copy-editor, Fiona Sewell, exhibited a capacity for rigorous reading that was beyond praise. Finally, I should acknowledge that an earlier version of Chapter 2 appeared in *Memory Studies*, Volume 1 (2008), and a much abbreviated variant of the same chapter was published in *Proceedings of the British Academy* (2009); a shorter version of Chapter 4 appeared in the *Journal of Romance Studies*, Volume 3 (2003).

Acknowledgements

1   The birth of histories from the spirit of mourning

Why do we produce histories?

The answer frequently given in reply to that question is that histories seek to legitimate a present order of political and social power. That answer has usually taken one of two possible forms. The first form might be called the affirmative version, while the second form might be called the critical version, of the legitimation thesis.

The affirmative version of the legitimation thesis consists essentially in the claim that to speak of historical narratives as justifications of a current political order is to point to a cultural universal. This is what Hegel is asserting in his *Lectures on the Philosophy of History* when he declares that, whereas family memorials and patriarchal traditions have an interest confined to the family and the clan, the uniform course of events that such a condition implies is no subject of what he calls serious remembrance; 'it is only the state which first presents subject-matter that is not only adapted to the prose of History, but involves the production of such history';[1] by which he means to say that the existence of a political constitution, enshrined in a system of laws, implies both the ability and the necessity to set down an enduring record, because a system of laws cannot be thoroughly understood without a knowledge of the past. Malinowski would diverge from Hegel in the sense that he sees that narratives of past actions can justify a present social order even when archival state records are lacking; but he joins Hegel when, in his study of *Myth in Primitive Psychology*, he says that myth, as the form which those narratives originally took, is 'the dogmatic backbone of primitive civilisation' because, by providing an account of origins, it 'contains the literal charter of the community'; on this view, myth, no less than written records, serves principally to establish 'a retrospective model of behaviour'; it is a 'justification by precedent' which endows tradition 'with a greater value and prestige by tracing it back to a higher, better, more supernatural reality of initial events'.[2]

The critical version of the legitimation thesis consists essentially in the claim that historical narratives seek to justify a current political order, and that they do so by duplicitous strategies which exclude what will not fit into their

1

narrative schema. This is the gist of Lyotard's concept of metanarrative. In *Instructions païennes*,[3] his first extensive critique of metanarratives, what he calls the 'masters of metanarrative' serve the Communist will to power; in *La Condition postmoderne*,[4] his better-known work, they serve the narcissism of the West. Metanarratives are institutionalised, canonical and legitimating; they pretend to represent an external object and then they pretend not to be a narrative; they issue from what he calls 'the grand institutionalised narrative apparatus'; they are 'official'; they are the 'legitimations of theorists'; they tell the stories 'which are supposed to rule'. Against this type of narrative Lyotard counterposes the 'petit récit' and the 'petite histoire'. In their name he first came to align himself with the narratives of dissent coming from Peking, Budapest and the Gulag; later he was to say that little stories, local narratives, have, as their typical narrators, prisoners, appellants, prostitutes, students, peasants – in short, subalterns who do not claim omniscience.

Some of Foucault's work a little later in *L'Archéologie du savoir* [5] features notions very close to what Lyotard means by 'petit récit' and 'petite histoire'. To Lyotard's alignment with 'local histories' against 'ruling metanarratives' corresponds Foucault's quest for ruptures and discontinuities as against the credence in the linear schema of what he calls 'total history'. In *L'Archéologie du savoir* Foucault argues the need for concepts like threshold, rupture, break, mutation, which enable us to conceive of discontinuities; he urges the necessity of investigating scales that are distinct from one another and which 'cannot be reduced to the general model of a consciousness that acquires, progresses, and remembers'; he pleads for the recognition of different historical series that are juxtaposed to one another and that overlap and intersect 'without one being able to reduce them to a linear schema'. Just as Lyotard rejects the justifications of metanarratives, so Foucault rejects the justifications of what he calls total history: that concept of a total history which supposes that one and the same form of historicity operates upon economic structures, social institutions, political behaviour, technological practices and mental attitudes, subjecting them all to the same type of transformation; that concept of a total history which is interested above all in how continuities are established, how a single pattern was formed and preserved, how evolutionary curves might be tracked, how origins might be sought, how one might push back further and further the line of antecedents – how, in other words, legitimating histories might be written.

It was above all the opening of state archives that made history the memory, and so the legitimation, of the state.[6] It is true that before the opening of state archives in the nineteenth century, those who wrote the history of their own age had for hundreds of years produced the original narrative which their successors were for a long time happy to copy in broad outline; in this way they produced for their own lifetime legitimating histories which later generations of historical writers would adhere to, handing on in their turn the legitimating narrations which they had themselves received.[7] And even before the opening of state archives much later, lay and ecclesiastical lords and corporations who were possessors of property rights and jurisdictions had deposited in archives charters and other documents designed to substantiate their claims to authority, and these documents became the objects of erudite scrutiny.[8] Donald Kelley has singled out law, and the Roman civil law in particular, as being filled with descriptions of past social practices, values and relationships, which subsequent historical study might try to reconstitute.[9] Law and religion, between them, furnished the foundations on which could be grounded nearly all forms of authority. Adam Smith believed that the crucial difference between ancient historiography and modern historiography lay in the fact that the latter, unlike the former, reconstituted past states of authority and constructed narratives around them with the intention of substantiating contested claims to authority in the present.[10]

In the remarkable connection between the development of historical writing and the occurrence of warfare we come across a proliferation of legitimating histories.[11] The relationship between these two phenomena was evidently a lively one in the case of Guicciardini's *Storia d'Italia*. But it was particularly in the aftermath of the First World War that politicians and men of action wrote memoirs in order to justify their past actions. Attention was focused in a number of countries on the question of the origin of the Great War. The Germans in particular, affronted by the 'War Guilt Clause' at the Paris Peace Conference, claimed that the issue could not be properly judged except by neutral historians; to this end they devoted a special periodical, *Die Kriegsschuldfrage*, which appeared between 1923 and 1928, to the topic.[12] When the *History of the Peace Conference of Paris* appeared between 1920 and 1924, its editor, Harold Temperley, stressed the importance of a work which conveyed accurately the atmosphere of the discussions; while the most notable British achievement in the sphere of contemporary history after 1919 was the publication, finally completed in 1938, of the *British Documents on the Origin of the War*, edited by G.P. Gooch and Temperley. This official documentation published not only the formal correspondence, as well as some of the private correspondence, of the most important participants, but also included important minutes attached to despatches after their receipt by the Foreign Office.[13]

Whether in this critical version or in the affirmative version, the legitimation thesis is persuasive because all institutional authority needs firm and reliable accreditation. It needs that retrospectively, and it needs it prospectively. Retrospectively, authority needs to be able to point to a proper descent; like the chief protagonist in *The Importance of Being Earnest* it must be able to justify its existence by reference to legitimate ancestors, and it should at least be able to muster something like the twenty-generation genealogies claimed by the Tallensi or the king-lists of the Sumerians and Egyptians. Prospectively, authority needs to be remembered appropriately; like the young child whose survival depends upon not being forgotten, rulers have an overriding wish to outwit the threat of oblivion and they will seek to usurp the future as well as the past, with narrations of their famous actions, documents in their archives, buildings to affirm their glory and memorials to their deeds.

Who would argue with that? In fact, some might; and to give a preliminary indication of why they might, I cite an etymological fact and an anecdote.

The etymological fact relates to the verb 'to care', which used to have a meaning now declared obsolete, namely, 'to mourn'; so caring was once connected to memory through the idea of mourning.

The anecdote is related by the Russian poet Anna Akhmatova. In her famous poem 'Requiem', which contains the lines 'I stand as a witness to the common lot, survivor of that time and place', she refers to the Stalinist reign of terror, exercised by the secret police under the direction of Nikolai Ivanovich Yezhov, in 1937–8. She prefaces her poem with an anecdote. 'In the terrible year of the Yezhov terror', she recalls,

I spent seventeen months waiting in line outside the prison in Leningrad. One day somebody in the crowd identified me. Standing behind me was a woman with lips blue from the cold, who had of course never called me by name before. Now she started out of the torpor common to us all and asked me in a whisper (everyone whispered there) 'Can you describe this?' and I said 'I can'. Then something like a smile passed fleetingly over what had once been her face.[14]

It would be well now to investigate in some detail a text that has good reason to be considered a historical narrative of legitimation but equally good reason to be thought a historical narrative of mourning. This text is Aeschylus' *Oresteia*.

The *Oresteia* centres upon a sequence of constantly repeated transgressions. All those who exact retributive justice in the first part of the trilogy, in *Agamemnon*, claim that they are acting in order to bring about a just retribution, yet the chain of murder which they set in motion is self-perpetuating; eventually, it seems that the acts of retribution no longer issue from some personal purpose or motive, but that they are generated rather by some impersonal force, from the inexorable action of a curse. There is a cascade of crimes. Social violence mechanically pursues a devastating course of action; a first murder, or a first offence, is followed by a second murder, or a second offence, to avenge the first, and then that in turn by a third to avenge the second.

The tragic action of *Agamemnon* takes place, as Richmond Lattimore has observed, at three interlocking levels: it is a tragedy of the *oikos*, a tragedy of warfare and a tragedy of politics.[15]

Agamemnon is at the most obvious level a domestic tragedy. The dominant figure in this, the first part of the trilogy, is Clytemnestra, a wife estranged from her husband Agamemnon on account of the grievous wrong he had inflicted upon their daughter, Iphigenia, by sacrificing her. Clytemnestra seeks revenge for the sacrifice of Iphigenia. Clytemnestra's paramour and partner, Aegisthus, is Agamemnon's cousin. Then, behind these relationships, stands the figure of Helen, Clytemnestra's sister, and the wife of Agamemnon's brother; it is Helen's treachery that caused the Trojan war, and then, in turn, the sacrifice of Iphigenia, and all the ensuing entanglements and acts of broken faith that follow on from this. This domestic aspect of the tragic action is underscored when Agamemnon, on his return from victory at Troy, describes himself as proof against all flatterers; yet, even as he does so, he is about to be trapped by flattery. For when Clytemnestra tells Agamemnon of all the torments which, she says, she was forced to endure during the period of his ten years' absence at Troy, what is she doing but misleading him by flattering him? This domestic feature of the tragic action is further highlighted in the second part of the *Oresteia*, the *Choephori*; there Clytemnestra speaks of her son, Orestes, as a serpent; in a dream she sees him hanging like a snake from her breast (*Choephori*, 527–34); and Orestes, in his turn, picks up the imagery of the snake and endorses it; 'It is I', he says, 'who, becoming a snake, shall kill her' (*Choephori*, 549–50). Yet is Orestes truly a snake? Surely, it is Clytemnestra herself who deserves the epithet. Clytemnestra has been compared to a number of animals – a lioness and, once (*Agamemnon*, 1233), a serpent that can move both ways – and it is she who is the viper that has killed the young of the eagle (*Choephori*, 246–9); when it is said that she is a 'sting-ray or viper' (*Choephori*, 994), the inevitable conclusion is that it is she, Clytemnestra, who is the real serpent.

Then again *Agamemnon* is a tragedy of warfare. Agamemnon was besotted not so much with Helen as rather with the idea of Helen. For the sake of this idea of Helen, Agamemnon was prepared to drain Greece of its manhood and to involve scores of innocent men in a military campaign lasting ten years. The Trojans themselves welcomed Helen and her captor; the punishment for their guilt was the total destruction of their city, their temples and their men, and the enslavement and defiling of their women and children. Neither Troy nor Greece deserved what the idea of Helen had led Agamemnon to do to them. He destroyed Troy and his own country as well. Many men died in the years of bitter siege before Ilium; the survivors were drowned or scattered during a great storm on their return journey; and in the end Agamemnon returned home with something utterly paltry, the crew of a single ship. The moment when Agamemnon, tempted by Clytemnestra, sets foot on the carpet with which she seduces and entraps him, we know, as we could perhaps not have known definitively at an earlier point, what the sacrifice of Iphigenia, his daughter, really meant for him. At the time, Agamemnon had represented the act of murder as his necessary obedience to the orders of Artemis, in order that his fleet might secure a fair wind as it set out to conquer Troy. We now know, however, that the sacrifice of Iphigenia betrayed above all the weakness of a passionately ambitious man. And we know, too, what the capture of Troy really meant: the sacrilegious destruction of an entire city. What Agamemnon had earlier declared to be religiously permissible, the sacrifice of his daughter, was not an action he was compelled to commit despite himself; rather it demonstrated his passionate desire to do anything within his power so that he might open the way for the onslaught of his army on Troy. It was the violence of Agamemnon's passion and ambition that caused him to rush headlong into action. The particular quality which dominates the first half of *Agamemnon* is a constant change of mood, a perpetual pendulum swing; again and again joy changes into apprehension. The prologue of *Agamemnon*, with its intense mood-swings, expressed in scarcely more than forty verses, is proleptic: it anticipates the curve of the entire drama. The third choral incantation in particular sings simultaneously of victory and of defeat. This precipitates the distinctive rhythm of *Agamemnon*, a rhythm in which every tone of joy is undercut, again and again, by a tone of apprehension.

Then, finally, *Agamemnon* is a political tragedy. The chorus, who represent the elders of Argus, have seen that Agamemnon's war against Troy was wrong, and they have told him so (*Agamemnon*, 799–804). As the reports of fallen Greek soldiers and the return of urns bearing their ashes come back from the front, the people at home begin to mutter against Agamemnon and to ask why the war, which has cost so much in Grecian manhood, was fought.

If there are three levels to the tragic action of *Agamemnon*, there are three dominant leitmotifs in the trilogy of the *Oresteia*. There is the leitmotif of the hunt, the leitmotif of entanglement and the leitmotif of ritual sacrifice. These three intersect and are reciprocally enriching.

Throughout *Agamemnon* the imagery of animal hunting is dominant.[16] A hare with young is said to be devoured by eagles, an image in which the vanquished beast represents Troy, which will be caught in a net from which neither grown men nor children will escape (*Agamemnon*, 357–60). The chorus describes 'these countless hunters armed with shields' who 'rush in pursuit of the vanished trace' of Helen's ship (*Agamemnon*, 694–5). Again, the same characters, Agamemnon and Orestes, play the role first of the hunter and then of the hunted. Agamemnon hunts Troy and later is hunted by Clytemnestra. Orestes, the hunter in the *Choephori*, becomes in the *Eumenides* the quarry when the Erinyes are the huntresses (*Eumenides*, 231).

More elaborately worked out than the imagery of the hunt is that of the net and of entanglement.[17] This dominant image is expressed in various forms of speech. A 'curb' is forged in order to subdue Troy (*Agamemnon*, 132);

Iphigenia is gagged by a 'bit' (*Agamemnon*, 234); Agamemnon is said to be impelled to his crime by the 'yoke' of circumstance, just as the yoke of slavery is forced upon Troy (*Agamemnon*, 529); and a 'yoke' is forced also upon Cassandra (*Agamemnon*, 953, 1071, 1226); Agamemnon is said to capture Troy with the 'snare' of his huntsmen (*Agamemnon*, 358, 821), just as he in his turn is captured in a 'snare' (*Agamemnon*, 1375, 1611). The robe in which Clytemnestra entraps Agamemnon in order to strike him down is later displayed on stage as a murder exhibit by Orestes in the *Choephori* (980–4, 997–1004). When Clytemnestra tells of her dreams and of her imaginings of terror during the course of Agamemnon's ten years' absence at Troy, she says that 'had Agamemnon taken all the wounds the tale whereof was carried home to me, he had been cut full of gashes like a fishing net' (*Agamemnon*, 866–8). And once more returning to the image of the net as the device of entrapment, she says that just as 'fishermen cast their huge circling nets, I spread deadly abundance of rich robes and caught him fast' (*Agamemnon*, 1382–3). Then again, at the climax of Clytemnestra's revenge, she intones:

An endless net, like a fish-net, I throw around him, an evil wealth of dress, and I strike him twice; and with two cries there on the spot he lets his limbs go slack; and then, when it is done, I add a third stroke, a welcome prayer-offering to the Zeus beneath the earth. So he belches out his own life as he lies there, and blowing forth a sharp wound of blood, he strikes me with a darksome shower of gory dew; and I rejoiced no less than the crop rejoices in the rich blessing of the rain Zeus bestows when the sheath is in labour with the ear. (*Agamemnon*, 1390–2)

Orestes later kills Clytemnestra in the same net in which Agamemnon was murdered (*Choephori*, 557–8); and, foretelling the murder of Aegisthus, he envisages himself 'enmeshing' his adversary 'in supple bronze' (*Choephori*, 576), the point of the epithet 'supple' here being that the pliability of a net can be used for enmeshing, whereas bronze, because of its inflexibility, is well adapted to fighting. Orestes says that 'having killed a revered hero by treachery', Clytemnestra and Aegisthus 'must themselves be caught and perish in the self-same snare' (*Choephori*, 556–7).

The third leitmotif of the *Oresteia* is that of ritual sacrifice.[18] The language of ritual sacrifice is a guiding thread throughout *Agamemnon*. Near the beginning of the drama, the choral song announces the portent of two eagles ripping to pieces a pregnant hare (*Agamemnon*, 137); this anticipates the demand of the goddess for 'another sacrifice' (*Agamemnon*, 151), a demand fulfilled when Agamemnon comes to sacrifice his own daughter (*Agamemnon*, 224). When news arrives of Agamemnon's victory at Troy, Clytemnestra makes preparations for a great sacrifice (*Agamemnon*, 83, 261, 587). Within the palace, as if in preparation for such a sacrifice, herds of sheep stand ready to be slaughtered (*Agamemnon*, 1056ff.). Later, after she has murdered

Agamemnon, Clytemnestra boasts that she has slain her husband as a sacrifice (*Agamemnon*, 1433, 1415 ff.), while Cassandra is yet one more sacrificial victim, going to her destruction with full knowledge: 'like a heifer driven on by a god, you go unafraid to the altar' (*Agamemnon*, 1126). Agamemnon, however, is said to have been slaughtered like a bull (*Agamemnon*, 1126). The sacrilegious nature of his murder is conveyed by the fact that, whereas all possible efforts are made to strike down a sacrificial animal with a single blow, and so to execute the act as painlessly as possible, Agamemnon is struck down three times (*Agamemnon*, 1384–6). We should notice at this point that Greek sacrificial rites displayed a marked ambivalence of feeling. When people made sacrifices in accordance with the will of a god, they still needed to overcome their reluctance to kill. They showed their deep respect for life by expressing feelings of guilt and remorse in the very process of carrying out ritual sacrifice. Whereas, therefore, the ritual of Greek sacrifice is designed to exhibit the destruction of a life as a sacred action, many complex preparations for the act of sacrifice are designed to underscore just how unnatural and just how shocking the act of sacrifice is felt to be. In this way, the opening phases of a sacrificial rite are shown to be harmless. A vessel containing water and the basket with the sacrificial barley are brought to the place of sacrifice by a virgin; and the participants in the ceremony wash their hands and sprinkle water upon the sacrificial victim. Such preparations for sacrifice demonstrate, by the contrast they offer, how sacrilegious are the ritual sacrifices in *Agamemnon*.

The imagery of ritual sacrifice in the *Oresteia* should alert us to the role played in the trilogy by the actions of the gods. The clash of human wills and desires in the trilogy is shown to be interlinked with the further fact that the universe of the gods is also in a condition of profound conflict. The gods are grouped into violently contrasting categories between whom agreement is difficult, perhaps even impossible, to achieve. That is because these different categories of gods belong to different levels of being.

The tradition of thought in which the universe of the gods is conceived to be in a condition of profound conflict continues to co-exist side by side in the *Oresteia* with the emergence of legal values and the development of a new legal terminology, even though the boundaries between the respective domains of religious terminology and legal terminology are as yet not clearly drawn and even though the indeterminate nature of that boundary itself is intrinsic to the tragic action. With the advent of law and the institution of the city courts the older religious conception of what constitutes a misdeed begins to wane. A new idea of crime is emerging. It is the particular merit of Gernet to have shown how, in this process, the role of the individual in the attempt to think about crime becomes more clearly defined, and how individual intention now begins to appear as an element that is constitutive of criminal action, particularly in the case of homicide.[19] The development of a sense of subjective responsibility, and the fact that it now becomes possible to distinguish between an action that is performed despite oneself and an action that is carried out of one's own volition, is an innovation of which Aeschylus is aware and which he actively builds into the dramatic action of his trilogy. The historical advances which were brought about by the development of these distinctions had a profound effect on the concept of the person as a social agent. It changes the understanding of the individual's relationship to his actions. Yet, although Aeschylus employs technical legal terms in the *Oresteia*, that terminology remains ambiguous and incomplete. Legal terms are used, but they are employed imprecisely, their meanings change, and incoherencies remain in their application. Internal tensions remain within the system of Greek legal thought to such an extent that the question arises as to whether it can appropriately be described as a system; it never achieved the highly elaborated form of Roman law.

Tragic action in the *Oresteia* therefore occupies an intermediate terrain between the concept of defilement, on the one hand, and the concept of intentionality, on the other. Human error, which is still perceived to be an assault upon the religious order, is caught up in the throes of a malignant power that is understood to be far more extensive than that within which the human agent operates. The individual who commits error is perceived to be as it were swept up by a force that he has unleashed. The action does not issue, therefore, from an agent as from a source, but rather envelops that individual, engulfing him in a power beyond himself, a power that extends beyond the range of his own person and his personal actions. Rather than being its author, the individual is so to speak comprehended within a more all-encompassing action. Tragic guilt, therefore, is located between, on the one hand, the ancient religious concept of defilement, *hamartia*, a kind of delirium visited by the gods upon humans that necessarily generates crime, and, on the other hand, a new concept in which the one who is guilty, *hamarton*, is defined as someone who has deliberately chosen to commit a crime. The law, even if still in a hesitant manner, places the emphasis upon the ideas of intention and responsibility, because the individual is coming to be seen as someone who is more or less autonomous in relation to the religious powers which hold sway over the universe. This historical development is expressed in the tragic action: we see it at work when Orestes in the *Choephori* deliberates upon the intended act of retributive justice which he is to enact on his mother, Clytemnestra. This issues in a process of anxious self-questioning with respect to the relation of the agent to his actions.

The tragic action of the *Oresteia* must necessarily be located in an intermediate zone between a condition of religious defilement on the one hand and a condition of legal intentionality on the other because the ancient Greek language is deficient in terms with which to express what might be called decisional density: deficient, that is to say, in terms adequate to describe how the individual comes to make a choice, comes to form a decision, becomes an agent, establishes the solid ground upon which it is possible to speak of the individual becoming an autonomous subject.[20] Indeed, it is precisely this deficiency, and the linguistic struggle to transcend that deficiency, which explains much of the force and poignancy in the tragic action of the *Choephori*. Orestes, it might be said, is struggling, together with his sister Electra, to constitute in his own person the category of the will, where by 'will' we mean the capacity to perceive the person as an agent, as a self seen as the source of actions for which it can be held responsible. But a fully elaborated category of the will was absent in Greek ethical thought; and, along with this, the ancient Greeks lacked a term corresponding to our concept of duty, and they possessed only a vague idea of obligation as we would now understand it.

It is possible to argue, as Bruno Snell has done, that in the *Choephori* Orestes arrives at 'a proud awareness of his freedom, a sense of autonomous action, which necessarily frees him of his old religious and social shackles'.[21] Since Orestes is obliged to avenge the death of his father, he must do so, and can only do so, by murdering his mother. This retributive act he achieves only after experiencing the cruel difficulty of his impasse. It is in this process that he discovers the contrast between fate and freedom. Standing as he does between divine commands, an obligation to his father and an obligation to his mother, his personal conflict issues in the final act of the trilogy, the *Eumenides*, in a struggle between the two hostile groups of gods: the Erinyes, who wish to punish Orestes for the murder of his mother, and Apollo, who clears him from guilt. When, in the *Choephori*, two deities make irreconcilable claims upon him, Orestes is obliged to fall back on his own resources. Becoming irresolute and incapable of spontaneous action, he finds that he is impelled by the conflicting demands made upon him to reflect, in his own terms, upon the question of right and wrong action. It is by this route that Orestes arrives, according to Snell, at a proud sense of his capacity for autonomous action.

In opposition to Snell's interpretation, which has of course audible Hegelian overtones, André Rivier has argued that the emphasis placed by Snell on the decision made by Orestes underestimates the superhuman forces at work in the *Choephori*, and elsewhere in the *Oresteia*, forces that go far to explain the tragic dimensions of the action in the *Oresteia*.[22] For, as Rivier interprets the matter, all that Orestes' deliberations achieve is to make him aware of his impasse. Rather than Orestes 'choosing' between the possibilities, he 'recognises', according to Rivier, that there is only one option open to him. In that sense he is still internally 'compelled' even in the process of making his 'decision'.

Yet, for all that the *Oresteia* is a tragedy which centres on a sequence of constantly repeated transgressions – acts of retributive justice in a self-perpetuating chain of murders in which it seems that the acts of retribution no longer issue from a personal purpose, but are precipitated rather by an impersonal force, by the impersonal working-out of a curse – the *Oresteia* is also, and no less emphatically, a tragedy of transformation. That impulse to transformation is felt most profoundly at two points, in the *Choephori* and in the *Eumenides*.

In the *Choephori* Orestes and Electra are the only protagonists in the trilogy to approach the act of retribution with clean hands. Before brother and sister approach the act of vengeance upon their mother Clytemnestra for the murder of their father Agamemnon, as they are doomed to approach it, Electra addresses the spirit of her father in a prayer, asking that he should not wipe out the seed of his house, even though she and her brother are about to wipe out their mother, Clytemnestra, by murder. In offering this final prayer, Electra invokes the image of the net, as has so often been done by protagonists in the *Oresteia*, and by implication too she invokes the image of blood drenching the ground through so much killing, not only in acts of personal retribution, but also, and above all, in the ten years' military campaign in which so much blood has been shed in the conflict between Greece and Troy. But now the image of the net, which elsewhere figures the process of deception and entanglement in which protagonists throughout the trilogy have been brought down to their doom, is invoked in a quite different sense; the net, which is said to have drenched meshes, conjures up a quite different possible future, since it has become an image which now represents not the deadly process of dragging down protagonists to their doom, but rather one of holding them up so that they might survive. This is the sense in which Electra concludes her prayer. Therefore, she says,

though you died, you shall not yet be dead, for when a man dies, children are the voice of his salvation afterward. Like corks upon the nets, these hold the drenched and flaxen meshes, and they will not drown.

Again, in the *Eumenides* the Erinyes, who have been hunting Orestes in order to exact vengeance for the murder of his mother, are finally accommodated within the city of Athens, once Athena has acquitted Orestes of his alleged crime. When she acquits Orestes, Athene, which is to say the city of Athens, declares that 'In all things save wedlock, I am for the male with all my soul, and am entirely on the father's side' (*Eumenides*, 737–8). Nevertheless, she is successful in persuading the female Erinyes, the divine avengers of bloodshed, to settle in Athens. '[You] have not been vanquished', she tells them, since 'the trial resulted fairly in ballots equally divided without disgrace to thee' (*Eumenides*, 795–6). Even feminine values, it would appear, may form a constituent element in the operation of the new institution of civic honour. When they become incorporated in the city of Athens and its judicial proceedings, the 'Erinyes', which means 'Furies' or 'Avengers', change their name; they now become 'Eumenides', which means 'Kindly Ones'. No longer the deities of blood and wild nature, they become the protectresses of vegetation, of agriculture and of stock-breeding. Athene prays now that 'the waft of gentle gales wash over the country in full sunlight, and the seed and stream of the soil's yield and of the grazing beasts be strong and never fail our peoples as time goes, and make the human seed be kept alive' (*Eumenides*, 905–9).

In the *Oresteia* Aeschylus has represented the tragic decision as being grounded in two types of reality: on the one hand, there is character, *ethos*; on the other hand, there is divine power, *daimon*. The origins of action are shown to lie at one and the same time *in* and *outside* humanity; it follows that the same characters – Agamemnon or Clytemnestra or Orestes – appear now as agents, as the cause and source of their actions, and now as acted upon, as engulfed by a force that is beyond them.

Aeschylus' tragedy may be seen, therefore, as a particular phase in the development of the categories of the agent and of human action; it is a turning point in the history of the ancient Greeks' understanding of the idea of the will.

By the way in which the dilemma of Orestes is presented in the *Choephori*, and by the way in which that dilemma is shown to have been finally resolved in the *Eumenides*, the tragic history of the House of Atreus is represented by Aeschylus as a parable of historical progress. But in concluding that the trilogy is a parable of progress we cannot possibly be understood to be saying that the *Oresteia* narrates a history that is a form of legitimation, a justification for the existence of that particular form of political and social order that is shown finally to hold sway in Athens at the end of the trilogy. Too much blood has been shed, too much pain suffered, too excruciating an impasse has been encountered by Orestes and Electra for us to be able to speak of the *Oresteia* as a narrative of legitimation. Above all, Orestes and Electra have been shown struggling, in their language and in their actions, with an aporia, an impasse: we have seen them struggling to restructure the quality of motivation they bring to the inevitable act of retributive justice, an act of retribution which is visited upon them just as much as they visit it on Clytemnestra. Aeschylus has brought us to understand the sheer accumulation of pain entailed in the process of historical transformation and enlightenment. We must conclude, therefore, that the process of historical change which he portrays for us is one in which there has been a costly purchase, in which wisdom has been learned only at the cost of suffering. The *Oresteia* is simultaneously a parable of *progress* and a tragedy of *lament*. If it is indeed a narrative of legitimation, it is just as much, if not more, a narrative of mourning.

We might consider, in the light of this, the extraordinary dance floor which visitors can find in Charleston in the United States.[23] It is the product of a collaborative enterprise by the artist Houston Conwill, the poet Estella Conwill Majozo and the architect Joseph de Pace. Much of the building space in which the dance floor is situated has been left sparsely furnished. The wooden roof is supported by three wooden columns, the windows are uncurtained, the walls are of bare brick. Architectural reticence directs attention towards the floor. Unlike in most large public buildings where great care has gone into the overall design, the floor, not the walls or the ceiling, is the dominant element. The brown wooden floor is the site of an artwork, painted with indigo blue and white made from local oyster shells. Here you will find a detailed map of places that have been important for centuries in the lives of African Americans. The map represents an elaborate narrative, a *lieu de mémoire*.

This map is a cosmogram of mourning. It depicts an image of a water journey, retracing the trajectory of a horrible itinerary: from the waterways along which the slaves travelled from the Rokel River in Sierra Leone, across the Atlantic Ocean, through the Caribbean Sea, and into Charleston harbour. It depicts many sites of suffering in Charleston itself: the houses on Sullivan's Island which provided the initial quarantine holding places for enslaved Africans; the Slave Market where thousands of enslaved Africans had to endure the indignity of the auction block; Boone Hall Plantation, the site of enslaved Africans' living quarters; the Hanging Tree where many enslaved African Americans were executed; Middleton Place Plantation, the burial site of enslaved African Americans. But the cosmogram also represents, as iconic places, the sites of the slaves' resistance: the site on Sullivan Island of Cato's Insurrection, one of the earliest occasions of resistance among enslaved Africans; Charleston harbour, where Robert Smalls commandeered a transport steamer and carried his family north to freedom; Emmanuel church, built by the congregation of Denmark Vesey, who, inspired by the revolution in Haiti, masterminded an unsuccessful insurrection; Fort Sumter, where the first shot of the Civil War was fired; Morris Island, the burial site of Colonel Robert Gould Shaw and the 54th Massachusetts Regiment, the first African American military unit to fight in the Civil War; Jenkins Orphanage, founded by the Reverend Daniel Jenkins in 1893 to help African American young men, a site which later became famous for its jazz band; and the Avery Normal Institute, established initially for the education of African American children and now the Avery Research Center for African American History and Culture. So the artwork on the dance floor is double-layered in meaning. As a dance floor it is a site of celebration. As a visual narrative it is a site of remembered grief.

As the representation of a subaltern group's shared grief the memorial dance floor in Charleston invites comparison with another collective enterprise, the AIDS Memorial Quilt Project.[24] It was Cleve Jones who conceived the idea for the project, which was launched in the 1980s. He had asked participants in the annual march in honour of Harvey Milk to make some placards bearing the name of someone they knew who had died of AIDS, and the sight of the massed placards, all hung on the façade of the federal building, reminded him of a patchwork quilt handed down within his family and used to console those who were ill. Formally organised on 21 June 1987, the NAMES Project was displayed a week later in San Francisco's Lesbian and Gay Freedom Day Parade. It consisted of some forty panels, each one 3 feet by 6 in size, corresponding approximately to the size of a body or coffin. In October 1987, when the NAMES Project was displayed for the first time on the Mall in Washington, panels extended over an area the size of two football fields. Five years later, at the display of October 1992, the official count exceeded 20,000 panels, and two years after that the NAMES Project began the task of photographing every quilt panel in existence. Only seven years separated the invention of this ritual and its archivalisation. Although the Quilt Project has no public funding and no fixed location in Washington, those who are in charge of it, by occupying the Mall for a weekend at a time, lay claim to the traditional site both of governmental authority and of civil protest against that authority.

The opening ceremony of folding and unfolding the panels inevitably recalls the military procedure of folding and unfolding the American flag and so is designed to evoke the idea of a second imagined community on a national scale. The choice of white clothing for those who unfold the Quilt panels has come to take on a symbolic significance. Symbolically charged too is the roll call of the names of the dead at all Quilt displays, when community leaders, family members, lovers, friends and AIDS volunteers read the names aloud. The reading of names, the signing of signature panels, the ceremonial walk through the display, all are ritually orchestrated. But nothing is more heavily impregnated with symbolism than the material out of which the Quilt panels are constructed. Diverse materials are often drawn upon: cloth, leather, items of clothing, photographs, wedding rings, teddy bears, dolls, cowboy boots, credit cards, computer-generated graphics, cremation ashes. The AIDS Quilt comprises not only quilting but also appliqué, embroidery and spray paint. The era of the AIDS Quilt, you could say, is the second great age of collage. Malleability is a presiding motif and informality is insistent. If in many cases the name of the deceased is noted 'legally', as on a birth certificate or tombstone, often the names inscribed are private rather than public, first names and nicknames. Cloth is the privileged material because it is yielding, because it is not stone or bronze or steel. When a memorial is made of stone or bronze or steel the rhetoric of the material implicitly claims that the memory of the dead recorded there will last forever. Cloth carries no such illusions of enduring witness. It is fragile, it fades and frays, it needs mending. It remembers the dead by sewing together mere fragments of their lives. Cleve Jones pointedly drew attention to this material contrast at the 1988 Washington display. 'Today', he said, 'we have borne in our arms and on our shoulders a new monument to our nation's capitol. It is not made of stone or metal and was not raised by engineers. Our monument was sewn of soft fabric and thread, and it was created in homes across America.'

What Cleve Jones did not say, but could have said, was that cloth and thread are traditionally materials worked by women, who, within the private sphere of their homes, have, particularly in America, used quilting as a way to remember lives. Excluded from most recorded history, women turned to the art of quilting to create an art of memory. Quilting, you might even say, has been in North America a distinctively female form of historiography. But it would be misleading to overemphasise the gender-specific features of cloth. In the Jewish tradition mourners wear a torn piece of cloth to symbolise the torn fabric of life. During the plague in Europe churches displayed banners with the names of the victims. In the western migration of Euro-Americans a quilt often stood in for a coffin when someone died on the Great Plains. In opting for the quilt as the material of mourning Cleve Jones was drawing on a long and broad historical connection between cloth and mourning.

That there should be such an insistent linkage of mourning and cloth seems curious only to a post-Cartesian mentality.[25] It is only in the Western post-Cartesian world that we frequently speak of the life of matter as the life of what is 'merely' matter; it is as if consciousness, and therefore memory, were about minds rather than about material things, as if the real can reside only in the purity of ideas rather than in the impurity of what is material. But the richly cultivated connection of cloth and mourning, above all in Oceania, but also in Madagascar and the Congo, should teach us otherwise. In Oceania cloth is a powerful economic and cosmological resource symbolising the abilities of individuals to transcend time, loss and death; precisely because cloth can be made to last for generations, it exhibits some semblance of immortality.[26] In Samoa, and elsewhere in Polynesia, certain cloths are thought to be endowed with sacred qualities, such that they can represent the histories and legends associated with important ancestors and mythical deities. In Sakalava, when a person dies, the cleaned body is wrapped in cloth and placed in a coffin, and the coffin is then covered with another piece of white cloth.[27] In Kodi, the tying, binding and dressing of the corpse with a textile shroud is understood to be a preparation for a later rebirth, the textiles that wrap the body providing, it is thought, a splendid costume for the deceased in a new life.[28] In Kuba, the concern that the deceased should be properly dressed at burial is so insistent that to be buried in anything other than traditional attire is considered tantamount to being buried nude.[29] Each time someone dies in the Trobriands, the circulation of cloth marks the current state of relationship between members of one matrilineage and those related primarily through spouses and fathers; skirts are distributed in seventeen different categories, all of them being defined by the specific characteristics of these relationships.[30] And indeed until the seventeenth century in England in funeral ceremonies cloth expressed the continuity of the groups with ancestral authority and their reproduction through time.[31]

The dance floor at Charleston and the AIDS Quilt exemplify a particular kind of mourning; or rather, to be more precise, they illustrate a form of mourning whose distinctive feature lies in its antecedent circumstances, those of a historical catastrophe. My subject is histories and mourning. But I exclude from the outset many particular occasions of mourning; specifically, I rule out of account all the mourning customs which have been so extensively studied by social anthropologists, who have shown that, while cultural patterns differ greatly in what they encourage and what they forbid, and in the extent to which the ceremony of mourning should be elaborated or curtailed, in virtually all cultures rituals and rules exist regarding the way in which the grief attendant upon the death of loved ones is expressed: for determining how a relationship with the dead person should be conducted; for prescribing how blame should be assigned and anger expressed; and for stipulating how long mourning should last. The kind of mourning I have in mind has to do not with bereavement customs of this kind but with historical traumas: that is to say, with those circumstances of mourning where the benefit of rituals and rules do not obtain and cannot be drawn upon as a repertoire of practices and an emotional resource.

The historical traumas I am referring to may entail one of two broad types of suffering. There is, first of all, the suffering that results from extreme conditions: this would be exemplified by survivors of the Holocaust, or of the atomic bombs dropped on Japanese cities, or of the depredations of the Chinese Cultural Revolution. And then there are more routinised forms of suffering, against which certain categories of persons are relatively protected but to which others, the poor and the defeated, are especially exposed: experiences of deprivation, of exploitation, of degradation, of oppression. Sufferings of this type might be exemplified by the losses endured under apartheid, or by the enforced migration suffered by political refugees, or by the chronic unemployment to which particular social classes are exposed. The examples I have cited already suggest that these two categories of suffering, those resulting from extreme conditions and those of a more routinised nature, are not really so easily distinguishable, that at the margins the one type tends to blend into the other, and that we ought therefore to think of both types as exemplifying a broad category, that of historical catastrophe or trauma: those large-scale events so widely recurrent in the histories of peoples that pose questions of identity and call for ways of coming to terms with the losses they impose and the legacy they leave. Mourning customs can sometimes be invented in response to these catastrophes, as the sites of mourning that proliferated in the wake of the First World War show. But it is a distinctive feature of such historical catastrophes and traumas that they precipitate cultural bereavement for which mourning customs are often difficult to find or invent, or which are widely felt to be scarcely adequate to the immensity of the bereavement, and where the emotional responses of the bereaved lack the formalised channels which might, to some extent, ritualise and contain those responses of loss and grief.

My suggestion is that, in the absence of bereavement customs, people turn to histories in order to cope with an otherwise uncontainable experience of loss, and that both the dance floor at Charleston and the AIDS Memorial Quilt are examples of such histories. These, I would say, are not legitimating histories but histories of mourning. Could it be, then, that the legitimation thesis is less persuasive than it is often assumed to be?

Recent developments in historiography suggest this. In the past two generations historical research has undergone a sea-change, shifting its attention from the stories of elites to the histories of everyday life. Everyone has always known, of course, that effective agency and knowledge have been hierarchically limited throughout history; but by displacing the focus of their attention historians have recently held up to extensive scrutiny the continuous victimisation of large segments of humanity along the lines of class, gender and race. In seeing all unequal relationships as somehow in this sense 'political', recent historiography has subjected earlier historiography to the criticism that it was complicit in the knowledge practices used to justify the exclusion or subordination of the working class, or of women, or of conquered peoples.

The culture of public apology which became so prominent in the closing decades of the twentieth century belongs to the same mental universe as that occupied by this recent historiography. In replacing the victorious history of elites with the lives of the poor, the conquered and the victimised other, historians laid history bare as a terrain of injustices. If many nations throughout the globe extended public apologies to specific groups of people – South Africa, to the victims of apartheid; Britain, to the Maori people; Australia, to the Aborigines; the United States, to Native Americans, African Americans and Japanese Americans – it is difficult to believe that this international proliferation of requests for forgiveness for past wrong-doing would have occurred without the sea-change in historiography which had directed attention so insistently, as earlier historiography had not, to the continuous victimisation of large segments of humanity along the axes of class, gender and race discrimination.

With this change of orientation in mind, we may briefly pass in review a set of histories which fully justify the epithet 'histories of mourning'.

In Bachofen's lament for the lost legal system of *Mutterrecht* we have one of the most remarkable of all histories of mourning.[32] Bachofen's concept of *Mutterrecht*, and his decision to write its history, is explicitly conceived as a polemic against Mommsen's great *History of Rome to the Death of Caesar* (1854–6).[33] Mommsen celebrated Rome as the force that succeeded in unifying Italy by combining state power and legal administration. Bachofen argued that, despite the enormous erudition of Mommsen's undertaking, Rome and the Romans were not his primary concern. If Mommsen wanted to produce a legitimating history, it was not Rome that was being legitimated. The core of Mommsen's book, where he speaks endlessly of Roman power, is in reality the boundless radicalism of nineteenth-century Prussia. The true legitimation is in the subtext. It was in opposition to Mommsen's Rome, that power-hungry state, that Bachofen excavated another Italy. Building his historical account on the study of myths and funerary sculpture, he presented a pre-political Italian antiquity, characterised above all by a different force of law, represented by the Etruscans, and also by the Sabines, which sought to channel chaotic libidinal instincts; this form of law was that of *Mutterrecht*.

Bachofen showed that the peoples of Asia had come to be in possession of the entire Italian peninsula, from the fertile fields of Campania to the foothills of the Alps; that the Etruscans exerted great influence, especially on the city of Rome; and that the Sabines, who were closely related to the Etruscans, held sway in the mountains of central Italy. In these pre-political societies, Bachofen argued, it was women, the only visible source of new biological life, who established the first system of law, *Mutterrecht*. This was a system of law grounded in lineage and in the family, and enforced by codes of blood vengeance. Matriarchy, which succeeded to hetaeric promiscuity, sublimated natural love into the idea of sacred and elevated procreative instincts which became a form of marital bonding. The fundamental service of women to humankind, Bachofen argued, lay in a form of culture which refined our nature, whereas the male, at a later historical stage, created the political state to rule over nature.

This matriarchal form of society, Bachofen was forced to concede, was eventually defeated by the power of Rome. Through his great epic, the *Aeneid*, Virgil had represented Aeneas and Dido, both of whom had their roots in the Orient. Dido was the oriental king-woman, who planned to enslave her man by her harlot's wiles; she sought to dominate Aeneas as Omphale dominated Heracles, as Semiramis dominated Ninus and as Delilah dominated Samson. She strove to embody the power which Asia gave the hetaeric queen over the life and throne of her husband. The central thought in Virgil's entire epic is that Oriental culture, defeated in the East, will come to fulfil a higher destiny in the West. Rome, built on Asiatic foundations, becomes the ultimate conqueror of Asia. This, Bachofen argues, is the essence of the *Aeneid*.[34] Then, too, with Pompey, Brutus and Cassius, and above all with Mark Anthony, the East succumbed to the West. The imperial Rome that Caesar built came to be identified with the West for two thousand years. Everything that could not be assimilated to the idea of Rome was to be swept from the face of the earth; a single year saw the destruction of Corinth, crossroads between the two worlds. Bachofen sees the fall of Carthage and of Jerusalem, above all, as 'tragic episodes' in the drama of Roman history.[35] While Scipio's death guaranteed for all time the political emancipation of the West from the East, the Flavian triumph liberated the religion of the future from Mosaic Orientalism. It was not Byzantium or Antioch or Alexandria but Rome that took the place of Jerusalem. Christianity became Occidental. Bachofen had to concede that in the course of this gigantic historical process the culture of *Mutterrecht* yielded to the might of the Roman state. He was able to produce only an elegy, his lifetime of scholarly polemic against the more overpowering scholarship of Mommsen issuing at last in resignation and lament. But his sympathies remained with the vanquished. Bachofen had produced one of the most memorable of all narratives of mourning.

The sense of cultural bereavement also animated the efflorescence of historical studies which began a quarter of a century after the Norman Conquest and continued until about 1130. The dates are not coincidental. Historical studies were a response to a crisis in national affairs. No aristocratic society in Europe, between the rise of the barbarian kingdoms and the twentieth century – with the possible exception of that which fell victim to the French Revolution – had undergone so radical a change so rapidly as England experienced after 1066. The old English aristocracy had disappeared; the English language, until recently the medium of a large area of religious life, was no longer in use among the upper strata of society; the literature, prayers, rituals and legal procedures which had employed this language were becoming unintelligible. The only people who were in a position both to observe and to express their reactions to these changes were Benedictine monks in monasteries sufficiently old and wealthy to have an acute sense of the difference between the present and the past. They were the only members of the old community who could understand the documents in which much of the evidence of the past was preserved, and the only ones with any hope of marshalling resistance to further depredations. To do that they needed to reanimate the image of the pre-Conquest past. These were the circumstances which forced scholarly monks to become historians.

The imaginative reconstruction of the monastic past grew out of the impulse to regain lost lands and to preserve those that remained. Canterbury, Malmesbury, Worcester, Evesham and Durham were the outstanding places in the movement. Eadmer, Wulfstan, John of Worcester, Symeon of Durham and, above all, William of Malmesbury were the outstanding names. They collected charters, transcribed documents, studied monastic buildings and inscriptions, and wrote the histories of estates and biographies. William of Malmesbury used the materials of every monastery he could visit in the course of his extensive journeys, or from which he could get information, to make a survey of the entire kingdom. He, like all the other monastic scholars, found a common thread for his work in the memories of small communities accumulated over several centuries. It is hardly an exaggeration to say that, out of their local knowledge and their local materials, these historical scholars were responsible for bringing the entirety of Anglo-Saxon history into existence.[36]

There is at least another moment in the history of historiography which is entirely dominated by the sense of cultural bereavement. That distinction belongs to Jewish historiography in the sixteenth century. This is hardly surprising. If one is searching for a discourse of historical mourning it is surely to Jewish culture, if anywhere, that one should look. In the Jewish literature of the Middle Ages much thought is, indeed, devoted to the meaning that might be discovered in the long story of Jewish tribulation and the prolonged exilic status of the Jews. But the desire to find some meaning in the sufferings of the Jewish people was insistently schematic rather than strictly historical. For many centuries Jews displayed no more than a superficial interest in the historical events themselves. Their meditations on past tribulations never issued in historiography as a distinct genre of writing. For many centuries after Josephus no Jewish writer called himself a historian. Even major events were to be understood, so it was thought, by being subsumed under familiar archetypes. If Jews composed chronicles of the Crusades they were less concerned with the investigation of any particular historical episode than with emphasising the overarching image of Abraham's preparedness to slaughter Isaac. The response to historical catastrophe was not to chronicle events but to compose penitential prayers. Ritual, not chronicle, was the pre-eminent channel through which the memory of the group was transmitted. Always the leitmotif was provided by a schematic contrast in Jewish historical experience, a contrast structured around the polarity of two great historical 'departures' marked by the terms Jerusalem/Egypt; Exodus/Exile.

It might seem puzzling, in the light of this, that the flourishing of Jewish historical writing in the sixteenth century was precipitated by two later departures: the Spanish Expulsion of 1492, and the flight from Portugal when,

with the coming of the Inquisition to that country during the reign of King
Joao III (1522–57), Jews still living in the Iberian peninsula were left with no
alternative but to take refuge in a more hospitable country, with all the
sufferings of refugees on land and at sea which that entailed. The magnitude
of these traumas shifted the shape of Jewish responses to catastrophe. That the
Jews perceived the Spanish Expulsion as one of the pivotal events of world
history is evident from the fact that sixteenth-century Jewish calendars
ascribed to it a special status, along with the creation of the world, the exodus
from Egypt, and the destruction of the Temple. That Jewish historiography
did in fact receive its main stimulus from the Iberian catastrophe cannot be
doubted once we recognise that, within the span of a hundred years, ten major
historical works were produced by Jews – Solomon ibn Verga, Abraham
Zacuto, Elijah Capsali, Samuel Usque, Joseph ha-Kohen, Gedaliah ibn Yahia
and Azariah de'Rossi – and that, of these eight historians, five were either
exiles from Spain or Portugal or descendants of exiles, and one of them,
Elijah Capsali of Crete, was greatly influenced by Spanish refugees who had
come to live on that island.

After the early Crusades, after the expulsions from France, after the perse-
cutions in the wake of the Black Death, after the massacres of 1391, after the
wholesale enforced conversions of 1412, the expulsions from Spain and
Portugal had concluded a cascade of tribulations and precipitated among the
Jewish people a profound spiritual disturbance and a prolonged self-
questioning. Was their suffering to be endless? Was there any discernible
purpose in it? Some Jews now came to think that an answer to those questions
was to be found not in ritual penitence but in historical inquiry. Among those
who sought that type of answer perhaps the most prominent were Solomon
ibn Verga and Samuel Usque, not because they told tales of woe, but because
they told them in a distinctive way. Solomon ibn Verga's book *The Scepter of
Judah*, published in 1554, was the earliest sociological treatise on the Jewish
question; Samuel Usque's *Consolation for the Tribulations of Israel*, published in 1553 and addressed 'to the people of the Portuguese exile', is notable
for its historical meticulousness. Solomon ibn Verga wants to understand why
it was that the Jews were singled out as the target of persecution; and he
concludes that they were so regarded not by the pope, who appeared rather as
their friend and protector, or by the kings of France and Spain, or by other
men of prominence, or by the educated classes, all of whom were friendly to
the Jews, but by the populace, whose credulity and jealousy were goaded by
the priests. Samuel Usque assembles an account of what he calls the 'calam-
ities' that had befallen the Jewish people, from 317 to 1553, in England,
France, Germany and Bohemia; but it is especially when he comes to write
about the Iberian expulsions that he produces work which is recognisably that
of a historian, citing sources in Hebrew, Latin and Italian, and describing

events from personal observation and from the accounts of eye-witnesses. So it was that a specifically historical awareness, dormant among the Jews for some fifteen hundred years after Josephus, was reawakened, and that historical writing came to be viewed as a guide for the perplexed.[37]

The work of mourning pervades yet another significant body of texts whose defining feature is their desire to bear witness to the holocaustal events of the twentieth century. It has been said that if the Greeks invented tragedy, the Romans the epistle and the Renaissance the sonnet, the generation of the mid-twentieth century invented a new literature, that of testimony.[38] The genre of testimony is animated by a historian's impulse. Survivors need to tell the truth about a historical catastrophe. What is the origin of that need? Elie Wiesel and Primo Levi have provided the two most persuasive answers to that question. For Wiesel it resides in a sense of indebtedness, for Levi in a fear of annihilation. The survivor's sentiment of indebtedness means that, however much they may feel the tug of a voice within them telling them to stop mourning the past, they find themselves visited by an even more compelling sense of obligation to serve as the emissary of the dead. The survivor's fear of annihilation has nowhere been more poignantly conveyed than in Levi's account of his recurring nightmare in Auschwitz, in which he is telling the story of his incarceration but his listeners, his sister included, are entirely indifferent to his story; when he repeated this dream to a fellow-inmate he discovered that many others who were incarcerated with him had to endure the same nightmare, the same ever-repeated scene of the unlistened-to story. For Wiesel, not to transmit the history of their disappearance would be to betray the dead. For Levi, not to transmit the history of his annihilating experience would be the ultimate annihilation.

Albert Camus could have been speaking for all the writers of testimony when, in his Nobel Prize acceptance speech, he said that the writer cannot serve today those who make history; he must serve those who are subject to it. In other words, he cannot serve those who seek to justify the historical events they have precipitated, but only those who must mourn their consequences. It is not only the ravages of contemporary history, it is the complicity of those who would minimise the enormity of its depredations, or who would even be silent about them, that demands redress.[39] La Peste is not, of course, a work of history; it is an allegory about the trauma of a Europe 'quarantined' by German occupation. But the narrator of that allegory speaks of himself as a historian: as someone who must 'play the part of a historian' who feels obliged to 'chronicle' the 'grave events' of a catastrophe; to 'bear witness in favour of those plague-stricken people, so that some memorial of the injustice done them might endure'. He must labour to produce that memorial because, after the plague was over, his contemporaries who had lived through the experience of the plague entered upon a conspiracy of silence; 'they denied, in the teeth of the evidence, that we had ever known a crazy world in which men were killed off like flies'; 'they denied that we had ever been that hag-ridden populace a part of which was daily fed into the furnace and went up in oily fumes'.[40]

Much the same words could have been used of himself by Alexander Solzhenitsyn. He too is driven by the need to play the part of a historian, to bear witness, to leave behind a memorial of injustice, to chronicle the events of a grave catastrophe. *The Gulag Archipelago* is not the best work, but it is the best-known work, in that body of narrative discourse devoted to Stalin's purges and the rise of the Soviet Gulag system, and like some other specimens of the genre it cannot be strictly categorised either as history or as fiction because it hovers somewhere in between the two. His text lacks many of the conventionally accepted distinguishing features of the historian's discipline. His unremittingly polemical tone is at variance with that common in historical writing; his references to sources are sparse; he often accepts rumours as documentation if they support his argument; he concedes from time to time that his text lacks the quantitative, statistical component which a large-scale historical account would require if all its claims were to be empirically verifiable; he acknowledges at the outset that he is writing an unusual kind of history when he subtitles the work 'An Experiment in Literary Investigation', rather than 'A History of' the camp system. But a kind of history it is, nonetheless: a work dedicated to chronicling, to perpetuating the memory, of the vast and tragic experience of the Soviet camp system.

Alongside the genre of testimony there is another new literary form which seeks to give expression to a generational sense of cultural bereavement. This is an exclusively German genre. It is a blurred genre, consisting in part of autobiographical narratives and in part of extended obituaries. These two elements are woven together to shape what might be called historical reports. The reports do what the psychoanalysts Alexander and Margarete Mitscherlich claimed the Germans of their generation appeared incapable of doing. In 1967 the Mitscherlichs argued in their book *The Inability to Mourn* that, on the evidence of the two decades that had elapsed since 1945, the Germans, though capable of an economic miracle, seemed incapable of any sustained emotional confrontation with the legacy of the Nazi past.[41] Perhaps this was because that past was buried but not dead. In any event, the Mitscherlichs' point is that the Germans were unable to cope with the damage to their narcissistic identification with Hitler as father figure and that they could not mourn their own, immense losses. The argument is not entirely convincing. To a degree it is undermined by the marvellously elegiac writing of Günter Grass in *The Tin Drum*, published in 1959, and, in addition, by the huge success of that novel. But if, with this major exception, the generation who experienced the humiliation of total defeat as adults produced no tradition of mourning texts, their children certainly did. The new type of literature they created, commonly referred to as 'Vaterliteratur', is, you might say, a reply to the claim made in the title of the Mitscherlichs' book, *The Inability to Mourn*. 'Vaterliteratur' does nothing but mourn. Its practitioners mourn the wounds inflicted on the psyche of the author by the fact of the father's defeated condition and by their emotional response to that defeat.[42]

This is the burden of Paul Kersten, in *Der alltägliche Tod meines Vaters* ('The everyday death of my father'); of Ruth Rehmann, in *Der Mann auf der Kanzel: Fragen an einer Vater* ('The man in the pulpit: Questions for a father'); of Sigfrid Gauch, in *Vaterspuren* ('Traces of a father'); of Heinrich Wiesner, in *Der Riese am Tisch* ('The giant at the table'); of Peter Härtling, in *Nachgetragene Liebe* ('Love in the aftermath'); of Brigitte Schwaiger, in *Lange Abwesenheit* ('Long absence'); of Ludwig Harig, in *Ordnung ist das ganze Leben: Roman meines Vaters* ('Order is the essence of life: Novel of my father'); of Christoph Meckel, in *Suchbild: über meinen Vater* ('Image for investigation about my father'). Christoph Meckel speaks for them all when he writes of his father: 'His self-confidence had collapsed after the war and had to be produced anew every day, violently, at the expense of his family . . . His brokenness tormented the children [who] did not know that his fatherhood . . . was characteristic of a whole generation.' That generation had been broken by the totality of their military defeat, by the gigantic futility of their sufferings and losses, by the destruction of the values for which they had supposedly fought, by the humiliation of being subjected to occupying powers and undergoing a programme of re-education at the hands of those powers. About all these matters the defeated were silent. They were silent about the pogroms, the deportations, the executions during the Polish and Russian campaigns which the fathers had participated in or observed. They were silent, and feigned ignorance, about the political and economic roots of German fascism. They were silent about the mounting resentment they harboured against the conquering powers. Nothing spoke more eloquently than this massive silence. It was the admission of a toxic inheritance. Helmut Dubiel once wrote that 'people relate to the national past as they do to a nuclear power station for whose radioactive waste no final destination has been found'.[43]

The toxicity of that legacy was palpable during the German student movement of 1968 which seethed with a virulence present nowhere else in Europe. In France and in Italy there were sharp political conflicts at that time between fathers and sons, but those conflicts rarely resulted in an actual break in the emotional relationships between parents and children. But they did in West Germany. There students seldom spoke of their parents affectionately; more commonly they spoke of them with indifference or even with open contempt. When they were approaching the middle of their lives and had children of their own, a decade or so later, the generation of Germans born during the last years of the war or shortly after its ending were impelled by an urgent curiosity concerning the prolonged psychological damage left in the wake of National Socialism. That was when a flood of books, articles, films, television programmes and public debates about German history began to inundate West Germany. That was when, following the example set by Oskar Matzerath in *The Tin Drum*, children came to occupy a central role as figures of identification in German cinema, in Sanders-Brahms' *Germany Pale Mother*, in Syberberg's *Hitler*, in Edgar Reitz's *Heimat*. That was when the focus of women's oral history was directed upon the reconstruction period after 1945. And that was the time of explicit mourning in Vaterliteratur.

Not all texts of mourning have a literary form; some have a legal status. This is the bequest of retributive justice.[44] A criminal trial is often felt to be the most appropriate procedure for rectifying the injustices perpetrated in the course of large-scale administrative massacres; these trials provide a ritual framework which family members and a sympathetic public find necessary and helpful in mourning the victims of such massacres. The official records of criminal trials try to give a voice where before there was only erasure and silence: the erasure of the perpetrators and the silence of the dead. A salient feature of such records is the demand for factual accuracy. The basic facts about who did what to how many, when and in what way, must be set right. What is wanted is the military lists, detailing who kidnapped which person, at what date, for what reason, where that person was taken, where they were killed, where they were buried. The procedure of legal rectification must be as precise as was the administrative massacre. Positivism comes into its own. A mass of flatulent rhetoric and empty abstractions must be replaced by a bedrock of basic facts, for only if this bedrock is securely put in place can the foundation be laid for any legitimate future public discussion of these traumatic events. The effect of a trial is to express the horror and help to expunge the repressive silence which preceded it. And the bedrock of facts must be established authoritatively. It is not enough that the facts about past injustices be generally known, they must be officially acknowledged. Thomas Nagel has defined this process of institutional accreditation as 'what happens and can only happen to knowledge when it becomes officially sanctioned, when it is made part of the public cognitive scene'.[45]

Mourning channelled through retributive justice can be observed when criminal culpability for crimes assigned to the category of the unjustifiable was brought to public prominence and submitted to judgment at Nuremberg and Tokyo, in Paris, Lyon and Bordeaux, and before the International Criminal Court at the Hague. It has been widely operative elsewhere when, in the aftermath of administrative massacres, there has been a call for the recovery of facts previously erased from collective memory: in Russia, in the former Soviet bloc societies, in Argentina, in Chile, in El Salvador, in Guatemala.

And that too, of course, was the animating impulse behind the South African Truth and Reconciliation Commission, which sat from January 1996 to July 1998 and remitted its report in five thick volumes in October 1998. In providing a forum for the voices of certain victims who were being heard for the first time in the public sphere, in making available a public space for the naming of criminals and the telling of past sufferings, the most striking feature of the Truth and Reconciliation Commission was the attempt to engage in a collective ritual process of mourning past losses so that the conditions might be created for a more liveable society and a more desirable future. Compared with the relative moral vacuum in Germany in the post-war period and the later flourishing of Vaterliteratur, the Truth and Reconciliation Commission permitted the making of a public apology and, to that extent, of amends.

Mourning for historical catastrophes extends beyond the sphere of legal and literary texts. It is dispersed across a wide spectrum of genres: in newspapers, in cinema, in video, in painting, in photographs, in songs, in plays and festivals. We might chance upon it in newspapers. Under pressure from Memorial – a movement founded in 1987, which has over a hundred branches in Russia and the other republics of the former Soviet Union, whose members are dedicated to laying bare the history of the Gulag system – the KGB has released photographs of purge victims, and, when this has happened, newspapers in many cities usually published black-bordered columns every day, with photographs and thumbnail sketches of some ten secret police victims, almost all shot in the late 1930s; gradually, over the course of months and years, the newspaper would work its way through thousands of victims. We might chance upon mourning in the cinema: most obviously in Claude Lanzmann's *Shoah*, a film not directly about catastrophe but about the witnessing of catastrophe, made up of first-hand testimonies by participants in the experience of the Holocaust. We find it in video form: as in the Fortunoff Video Archive for Holocaust Testimonies at Yale, an archival collection of filmed accounts, given to professionally trained inter-viewers, mostly psychoanalysts and psychotherapists, by Holocaust survivors, many of whom were enabled to tell their story in its entirety for the first time in their lives.

Paint too has its texts of mourning: as in the great painting by Anselm Kiefer, *Shulamite*, which wholly transforms Wilhelm Kreis' originally cele-bratory fascist design of 1939 for the Funeral Hall for the Great German Soldier in the Berlin Hall of Soldiers into a memorial which evokes the terror perpetrated by Germans on their victims, a cavernous space blackened by the fires of cremation which reminds the viewer unmistakably of a gigantic brick oven. Or one might think, on a more extensive scale, of the account given by Johannes Fabian in his marvellous book *Remembering the Present*,[46] of the way in which the Zairean painter Tshibumba embarked in the 1970s on the project of painting the entire history of his country, and of how he claimed to be not only a painter but also a historian, insisting on showing and telling what truly happened, as opposed to what is said to have happened. In his vast pictorial series of some hundred paintings, which can now be seen in Amsterdam, he depicts the killings and executions of African rulers: how Banza Congo of the lower Congo is poisoned; how Msiri of Katanga is beheaded and his severed head carried all over the country until finally it is lost; how Lumpungu of the Basongye is hanged; while the story of Patrice Lumumba is dramatically emplotted as another 'Passion', as the suffering of Christ. Loss is not limited here to the forfeit of sovereignty; everything perishes, including all possessions, knowledge of the ancestors, traditional languages, medicines and charms; and, though Tshibumba concentrates on the wielders of power – kings, warlords, politicians, prelates – women too play important roles: they suffer the indignities and cruelties of colonisation; they are among the victims of postcolonial strife; and as mourners they bear the brunt of bereavement.

Photography too can tell of a generation's cultural bereavement. In 1920 Atget sold 2,621 negatives, the result of two decades of dedicated work, to the Département des Monuments Historiques. Simply to list the Parisian subjects Atget photographed in his massive enterprise of artistic salvage is to catalogue a whole city and civilisation half-erased by Haussmann's rebuilding of Paris: a half-forgotten sense of place mourned and located in an ambience of old streets, courtyards, squares, fountains, kiosks, cafés, bars, markets, junk shops, horse-drawn tramways, wagons, bridges, barges, the quays of the Seine. Folk song too can be a way of passing on the oral tradition of mourning, as in the lament for the Highland Clearances and the Irish depopulation and the remembrance of the resulting diaspora. Mourning for historical catastrophe can be found long after the moment of that catastrophe has passed: as in Latin American plays and festivals, where the persistence in the collective consciousness of a trauma suffered four hundred years ago, at the time of the Spanish Conquest, still reached into the Native South American folklore of the twentieth century – in Mexico, where in the play of the 'Great Conquest' Moctezuma and Cortés once more take the stage; in Guatemala, where the most popular folk spectacle is the 'Dance of the Conquest' in Peru and Bolivia, where every year peasants gather in the village square to perform 'The Tragedy of the death of Atahuallpa'.

It would be an error to imagine that narratives of mourning and narratives of legitimation belong to easily separable categories. We would be alerted against any such misunderstanding if we remembered how often national groups have reinforced their internal cohesion by telling stories about the injustices done to their ancestors by other nations. Hitler, for one, was spectacularly successful in rejuvenating a German sense of legitimate identity in the aftermath of the First World War by reminding Germans of the memory of their humiliation represented by the Versailles Treaty. Both Peter Sloterdijk in *Critique of Cynical Reason*[47] and Klaus Theweleit in *Male Fantasies*[48] have demonstrated the intertwinement of legitimation and mourning in Germany in the twenties and thirties: the former by reading Weimar cynicism as the expression of a fundamental crisis of male identity after the defeat of 1918; the latter by showing how the fear of emasculation, and the concomitant attempt to bolster a sense of intact bodily identity, figured so prominently in the imaginary of the fascist warrior. The massed military rallies and gymnastic displays of German fascism were a belated response to the traumatic experience of 1914–18: the legitimating display of fit bodies choreographed in the form of a mass ornament depended for the persuasion of its bodily rhetoric on the never acknowledged but unmistakably present collective memory not only of the many war dead but also, and perhaps even more, of the many mutilated bodies of those who had survived the lost war but who would no longer be able to form component elements in a mass ornament shaped out of human bodies.

Nowhere are narratives of legitimation and narratives of cultural bereavement more explicitly or more intricately entwined than in the case of the state of Israel. The building of memorials to the Holocaust in Israel was understood as a foundational event. Zionists had for long claimed that without a state and the power to defend themselves which only a state could guarantee, Jews in exile would always be vulnerable, and if any single event proved the validity of that claim it was the Holocaust. Nachum Goldman, former president of the World Jewish Congress, drew that inference when he said that, if the state of Israel came into being, that 'was not only by virtue of the blood spilt by those who fell in battles for its existence . . . but also, indirectly, because of the millions murdered in the Holocaust'.[49] For most Israelis in 1948, when only three years separated the liberation from the camps and the foundation of the state of Israel, the link between the Holocaust and national independence was self-evident. That link was spelt out by Abba Eban and David Horowitz when, in order to persuade the UN Commission appointed to study the proposed partition of Palestine into Jewish and Arab states, they spent much of their time reminding the delegates of the details of the Holocaust. And it was spelt out again when, on 19 April 1955, posthumous citizenship was officially bestowed on all the Jewish victims of the German administrative massacre, so effectively creating an ever-present shadow population of martyrs.

If legitimation and mourning are frequently imbricated that fact should be attributed not so much to this or that particular set of circumstances as rather to a general circumstance: namely, to the fact, to which Derrida drew attention, that the application of law is always the operation of a form of authorised force.[50] Some linguistic idioms disclose this fact more directly than do others; the French term which speaks of 'appliquer la loi' might be thought more hypocritical in this respect than the English usage which speaks of 'enforcing the law'. The interconnection between force and law is at once prospective and retrospective. It is prospective, in the sense that all revolutionary discourses, whether of the right or of the left, justify their recourse to violence by alleging the founding, currently in progress or anticipated in the foreseeable future, of a new law. And it is retrospective, in the sense that the legal foundation of all states can be shown after the event to have taken place in a context of violence. For there surely exists no historical community which has not been born in an original context of violence; what come later to be celebrated as founda-tional acts are violent acts subsequently legitimated by the institutional machinery of a state that is considered legitimate. From this it follows that a strong interest in historical narratives seems frequently to arise, whether in literate or in preliterate cultures, where rights and claims are acknow-ledged, but where there is also a widespread feeling that these rights and claims need to be defended against real or possible hostile accounts. Contradictory assertions about the 'same' event – about the Norman Conquest of England or the French Revolution, for instance – are attribut-able not so much to lapses of memory as to the contradictory interests of different social groups within a culture. It follows that the same events signify glory for some and humiliation for others. Behind the foreground narratives of justification, real or symbolic wounds are stored in the archives of cultural memory.

Admittedly, those defending the affirmative version of the legitimation thesis do not always claim that it is an exhaustive and exclusive account of the production of histories. More importantly, many proponents of the critical version of the thesis, such as Foucault and Lyotard, are far from being blind to the frequent intertwinement of legitimation and mourning, and have acknowledged the existence of real or symbolic wounds in narra-tives of the past. We may conclude, therefore, that the legitimation thesis remains persuasive only in so far as it can co-exist with an acknowledge-ment that many histories are generated also by a sense of loss, grief and mourning. The emphasis on painful pasts, in other words, is a supplement to, rather than a replacement for, the legitimation thesis. Moreover, histories that are driven by a sense of loss, grief and mourning may differ significantly in the degree of their explicitness. In some cases, as in that of the AIDS Quilt, the origin and extent of the narrative are transparent. But there are other cases – for example, in Latin American plays and festivals concerning the persistence in the collective consciousness of a trauma suffered some four hundred years earlier, at the time of the Spanish Conquest – where observers or other participants need not know much factual detail about the historical references of the narrative of mourning.

The claim that histories legitimate a contemporary order of political and social power is a persuasive one. But it suffers from at least one significant deficiency. It is blind to the birth of histories from the spirit of mourning.

NOTES

1 G.W.F. Hegel, *Lectures on the Philosophy of History* (tr. J. Sibree, New York, 1956), pp. 60–3.
2 B. Malinowski, *Myth in Primitive Psychology* (London, 1926).
3 J-P. Lyotard, *Instructions païennes* (Paris, 1977).
4 J-P. Lyotard, *La Condition postmoderne: rapport sur le savoir* (Paris, 1979).
5 M. Foucault, *L'Archéologie du savoir* (Paris, 1969).
6 J.G.A. Pocock, *Barbarism and Religion. Vol. 2: Narratives of Civil Government* (Cambridge, 1999), p. 7.
7 H. Butterfield, 'Some Trends in Scholarship 1868–1968, in the Field of Modern History', *Transactions of the Royal Historical Society*, fifth series, 19 (1969), p. 183; and 'Delays and Paradoxes in the Development of Historiography', in K. Bourne and D.C. Watt, eds., *Studies in International History: Presented to W. Norton Medlicott* (London, 1967), pp. 2–3, 12–13.
8 Pocock, *Narratives of Civil Government*, p. 15; and 'Narrative History and the Spade-Work Behind It', History, liii (1968), pp. 169–70, 176–8.
9 D.R. Kelley, *The Human Measure: Social Thought in the Western Legal Tradition* (Cambridge, 1990).
10 Pocock, *Narratives of Civil Government*, p. 15.
11 Butterfield, 'Some Trends in Scholarship 1868–1968', p. 178.
12 *Die Kriegsschuldfrage* (1923–8), continued as *Berliner Monatshefte* (1929–39).
13 G.P. Gooch and H. Temperley, eds., *British Documents on the Origins of the War* (London, 1938); F.H. Hinsley, 'Reflections on the History of International Relations', in M. Gilbert, ed., *A Century of Conflict: Essays for A.J.P. Taylor* (London, 1966), pp. 24–5.
14 A. Akhmatova, 'Instead of a Preface' (tr. S. Kunitz and M. Hayward), in C. Forche, ed., *Against Forgetting* (New York, 1993), pp. 101–2.
15 R. Lattimore, 'Introduction', in *Aeschylus: Oresteia* (Chicago and London, 1947), pp. 9–10.
16 See P. Vidal-Naquet, 'Hunting and Sacrifice in Aeschylus' *Oresteia*', in J-P. Vernant and P. Vidal-Naquet, *Myth and Tragedy in Ancient Greece* (New York, 1990), pp. 141–59.
17 See in particular P. Vidal-Naquet, 'Aeschylus, the Past and the Present', in Vernant and Vidal-Naquet, *Myth and Tragedy in Ancient Greece*, pp. 261ff.
18 See F. Zeitlin, 'The Motif of the Corrupted Sacrifice in Aeschylus' *Oresteia*', *Transactions and Proceedings of the American Philological Association*, 96 (1965), pp. 463–508; W. Burkert, 'Greek Tragedy and Sacrificial Ritual', *Greek, Roman and Byzantine Studies*, 7 (1966), pp. 87–122; J-P. Guépin, *The Tragic Paradox: Myth and Ritual in Greek Tragedy* (Amsterdam, 1968); J. Rudhardt,

Notions fondamentales de la pensée religieuse et actes constitutifs du culte dans la Grèce classique (Geneva, 1958); J. Casabona, *Recherches sur le vocabulaire des sacrifices en grec* (Aix-Gap, 1966); P. Stengel, *Opferbraüche des Griechen* (Leipzig and Berlin, 1910).

19 L. Gernet, *Recherches sur le développement de la pensée juridique et morale en Grèce* (Paris, 1917).

20 J-P. Vernant, 'Intimations of the Will in Greek Tragedy', in Vernant and Vidal-Naquet, *Myth and Tragedy in Ancient Greece*, pp. 49–84.

21 B. Snell, *The Discovery of the Mind* (Oxford, 1953), pp. 102–12.

22 A. Rivier, 'Remarques sur le "nécessaire" et la "nécessité" chez Esychyle', *Revue des Études Grecques*, 81 (1968), pp. 5–39.

23 D. Hayden, *The Power of Place: Urban Landscapes as Public History* (Cambridge, MA, 1995), pp. 69–72.

24 M. Sturken, *Tangled Memories: The Vietnam War, the AIDS Epidemic, and the Politics of Remembering* (Berkeley, Los Angeles and London, 1977), pp. 183–219.

25 P. Stallybrass, 'Worn Words: Clothes, Mourning, and the Life of Things', *Yale Review*, 81.2 (1993), pp. 35–50.

26 A.B. Weiner, 'Why Cloth? Wealth, Gender and Power in Oceania', in A.B. Weiner and J. Schneider, eds., *Cloth and Human Experience* (Washington, DC, 1989), pp. 37–72.

27 G. Feeley-Harnik, 'Cloth and the Creation of Ancestors in Madagascar', in Weiner and Schneider, *Cloth and Human Experience*, pp. 75–116.

28 J. Hoskins, 'Why Do Ladies Sing the Blues? Indigo Dying, Cloth Production and Gender Symbolism in Kodi', in Weiner and Schneider, *Cloth and Human Experience*, pp. 142–73.

29 P. Darish, 'Dressing for the Next Life: Raffia Textile Production and Use among the Kuba of Zaire', in Weiner and Schneider, *Cloth and Human Experience*, pp. 118–40.

30 Weiner, 'Why Cloth? Wealth, Gender and Power in Oceania', pp. 37–72.

31 Stallybrass, 'Worn Words: Clothes, Mourning, and the Life of Things', pp. 35–50.

32 For a summary of Bachofen's study of the nature of matriarchal society and the transition to Roman patriarchy, see J.J. Bachofen, 'Introduction to The Myth of the Tarquil', in *Myth, Religion and Mother Right: Selected Writings of J.J. Bachofen*, Bollingen Series, lxxxiv (Princeton, 1973), pp. 211–46.

33 T. Mommsen, *History of Rome to the Death of Caesar* (1854–56; Eng. tr. London, 1860).

34 Bachofen, 'Introduction', p. 228.

35 Bachofen, *ibid.*, p. 235.

36 R.W. Southern, 'Aspects of the European Tradition of Historical Writing. 4: The Sense of the Past', *Transactions of the Royal Historical Society* (1973), pp. 243–63.

37 Y.H. Yerushalmi, *Zakhor: Jewish History and Jewish Memory* (Seattle and London, 1989), pp. 53–76; A.A. Neuman, *Landmarks and Goals* (Philadelphia, 1953), pp. 82–129.

38 E. Wiesel, 'The Holocaust as a Literary Inspiration', in *Dimensions of the Holocaust* (Evaston, 1977), p. 9.

39 S. Felman and D. Laub, eds., *Testimony: Crises of Witnessing in Literature, Psychoanalysis and History* (London, 1992), p. 96.
40 A. Camus, *The Plague* (tr. S. Gilbert, New York, 1972), pp. 276–7.
41 A. Mitscherlich and M. Mitscherlich, *The Inability to Mourn: Principles of Collective Behavior* (New York, 1975).
42 See M. Schneider, 'Fathers and Sons, Retrospectively: The Damaged Relationship Between Two Generations', *New German Critique*, 31 (1984), pp. 3–51.
43 Quoted in I. Buruma, *The Wages of Guilt* (London, 1994), p. 205.
44 M Osiel, *Mass Atrocity, Collective Memory, and the Law* (New Brunswick, NJ, 1997).
45 Quoted in Osiel, *Mass Atrocity*, p. 269.
46 J. Fabian, *Remembering the Present: Painting and Popular History in Zaire* (Berkeley, Los Angeles and London, 1996).
47 P. Sloterdijk, *Critique of Cynical Reason* (London and New York, 1988).
48 K. Theweleit, *Männerphantasien*, 2 vols (Frankfurt, 1977).
49 Quoted in J.E. Young, *The Texture of Memory: Holocaust Memorials and Meaning* (New Haven and London, 1993), p. 245.
50 J. Derrida, *Force de loi: le fondement mystique de l'autorité* (Paris, 1994).

2   Seven types of forgetting

Coerced forgetting was one of the malign features of the twentieth century. Forgetting as repressive erasure appeared in its most brutal form in the history of totalitarian regimes where, in the words of Milan Kundera, the struggle of man against power is the struggle of memory against forgetting. The testimonies of Primo Levi and Elie Wiesel, of Alexander Solzhenitsyn and Nadezhda Mandelstam, were written in defiance of that threat of forgetting. Their testimonies were at once political acts and therapeutic acts. Political acts: because to write was to denounce the injustice which they had survived or escaped. And therapeutic acts: because for them to write was a way of making sense of a destructive, violent past, one in which they had been victims, and of triumphing over that experience, of turning it into a motivation for living and working. Germany after Hitler, France after Pétain, Spain after Franco, Chile after Pinochet, Greece after the colonels, Argentina after the generals, South Africa after apartheid, the post-socialist states of central and eastern Europe – all these societies had a difficult past and needed to take up some explicit position with regard to that past.

We may, therefore, say that there was an ethics of memory at the end of the twentieth century, in the sense that there had not been an ethics of memory at the end of the nineteenth or eighteenth or seventeenth centuries. This structure of feeling has cast a shadow over the context of intellectual debate on memory, in the shape of the view, widely held if not universal, that remembering is usually a virtue and that forgetting is necessarily a failing.

So widespread and emphatic is the current conviction that remembering has both private and public virtue that the opinion is sometimes expressed that even victims of traumatic experiences must be helped to speak the horrifying truth about their past, to 'speak the unspeakable',[1] as Judith Herman has put it, because telling the truth about the past is held to be both a personal therapeutic value and a public value of overwhelming importance. It is precisely because personal testimony regarding the past is thought to be inherently political that the narration of remembered trauma is believed to be so important. As Herman summarises her position, 'remembering and telling the truth about terrible events are prerequisites both for the restoration of social order and for the healing of individual victims'.[2]

Is it necessarily the case that the recuperation and retelling of past experiences have an inherent ethical-political value? Neither William James nor Nietzsche thought so. William James wrote that 'if we remembered everything, we should on most occasions be as ill off as if we remembered nothing';[3] while Nietzsche, who was, as is widely known, a famous advocate of the value of forgetting, claimed that even a happy life is possible without remembrance, as the beast knows, but that for humans life in any true sense is absolutely impossible without forgetting.[4]

A number of lesser figures are on record as registering agreement with William James and Nietzsche. French psychiatrists in the late nineteenth century in particular often took this view.[5] Ribot, the founder of the *Revue Philosophique de la France et de l'Étranger*, who aimed to make psychology and philosophy more scientific; Guillon, whose thesis on hyperamnesia reflected some important trends in nineteenth-century French psychiatry; Azam, a clinician at Bordeaux who was well known throughout French scientific circles: all agreed with Nietzsche's high valuation of forgetfulness, while they expended much effort trying to specify just how much forgetting conduced to a 'normal' life and how much forgetting was a sign of disease. In their high estimate of forgetting they were joined by a figure of greater stature. Pierre Janet believed that the faculty of memory was much overvalued and he was fond of quoting Taine's dictum to the effect that one must know how to forget. 'How could it be', he asked, 'that our own minds, our poor attention, could fix itself constantly on the innumerable perceptions which register in us? We must . . . forget in order to learn. Forgetting is very often a virtue for individuals and for a people.'[6] In 1884, in *Névroses et idées fixes*, he observed that one of the most valuable discoveries of pathological psychology would be a reliable method of helping us to forget.[7]

It may be the case, then, that forgetting is not always a failure, and it is not always something about which we should feel culpable. Perhaps indeed the thought that forgetting is necessarily a failing is not really so widely held. It is doubtful if this applies to folk psychologies in many distinctive cultural contexts, and many practitioners and theorists alike have always acknowledged that forgetting can sometimes be a success. I want to distinguish three types of forgetting which are successful, in the sense that they establish and enhance social bonds.

The first type is what I would call *prescriptive* forgetting. This is precipitated by an act of state and is believed to be in the interests of all the parties to the previous dispute; it can therefore be acknowledged publicly. Its aim is to prevent a chain of retribution for earlier acts from running on endlessly.

The ancient Greeks provide us with a prototype of this type of forgetting. They were acutely aware of the dangers entailed in remembering past wrongs because they well knew about the endless chains of vendetta to which this so often led. And since the memory of past deeds threatened to sow division in the whole community and could lead to civil war, they saw that not only those who were directly threatened by motives of revenge but all those who wanted to live peacefully together in the polis had a stake in not remembering. This thought was famously expressed in 403 BC. In that year the Athenian democrats, after having suffered defeat at the hands of the dictatorship, re-entered the city of Athens and proclaimed a general reconciliation. Their decree contained an explicit interdiction: it was forbidden to remember all the crimes and wrongdoing perpetrated during the immediately preceding period of civil strife. This interdict was to apply to all Athenians, to democrats, to oligarchs and to all those who had remained in the city as non-combatants during the period of the dictatorship. Perhaps more remarkable still was the fact that the Athenians erected on the acropolis, in their most important temple, an altar dedicated to Lethe, that is, to forgetting. The installation of this altar meant that the injunction to forget, and the eradication of civil conflict which this was thought to promote, were seen as the very foundation of the life of the polis.[8]

Ernest Renan shared the same sentiment. In his essay *What is a Nation?* of 1882 he argued that a shared amnesia is at least as essential for the development of what we now consider a nation as is the ability to invoke common memories. He cited as his example the fact that every French citizen must have forgotten the anniversary of St Bartholomew. He saw no necessity to explain to his readers what 'St Bartholomew' meant; any French reader could be assumed to know that it referred to the anti-Huguenot pogrom launched on 24 August 1572 by Charles X and his Florentine mother. To remember that event vividly would be to recall that the French body politic was once riven by murderous hatred. Better instead to remain in a paradoxical position; Renan's readers were being told to 'have already forgotten' what Renan's words assumed they naturally remembered.[9]

Nor was Renan alone in this conviction. Whether at the resolution of civil conflict or after international conflict, the formulation of peace terms has frequently contained an explicit expression of the wish that past actions should be not just forgiven but forgotten. The Treaty of Westphalia, which brought the Thirty Years War to an end in 1648, contained the injunction that both sides should forget forever all the violence, injuries and damage that each had inflicted on the other. After Charles II ascended the English throne in 1660 he declared 'An act of full and general pardon, indemnity and forgetting'. And when Louis XVIII returned to occupy the French throne in 1814 he declared in his constitutional charter that he sought to extinguish from his memory all the evils under which France had suffered during his exile, that all research into utterances of opinion expressed before his restoration was to be forbidden, and that this rule of forgetting was enjoined upon both the law courts and the citizens of France.[10]

Or to cite a twentieth-century example: Paloma Aguilar contrasts what she calls the pathological amnesia of the Spanish regarding the civil war in the political sphere with the many representations of the same topic in the fields of film and literature.[11] The prolonged period of political repression under Franco had brought about a generational break. Veteran *mujeres libres*, who had been militants in the organisation founded by anarchist women in 1936, and young ones, who took up the name of the organisation when they began to mobilise themselves after the death of Franco, found that they were unable to work together or even to speak to each other without their exchanges degenerating into mutual recriminations and misunderstandings. The protracted repression of the Franco regime was responsible for this generational rupture. But for this loss there was a compensating gain. In the period of transition after Franco's death in 1975 there was a widespread feeling in Spain that it was essential in political life to forget the rancour of the past if democracy was to be consolidated. The silence about the Franco period, while it was the site of a generational break, made it possible to avoid the use of the past as a weapon in contemporary struggles.

This demonstrates that sometimes at the point of transition from conflict to conflict resolution there may be no explicit requirement to forget but the implicit requirement to do so is nonetheless unmistakable. Societies where democracies are regained after a recent undemocratic past, or where democracy is newly born, must establish institutions and make decisions that foster forgetting as much as remembering. Not long after the defeat of Nazism, it became evident that West Germany could not be returned to self-government and civil administration if the purge of Nazis continued to be pursued in a sustained way. So the identification and punishment of active Nazis had become a forgotten issue in Germany by the early 1950s, just as the number of convicted persons was kept to a minimum in Austria and France. For what was necessary after 1945, above all, was to restore a minimum level of cohesion to civil society and to re-establish the legitimacy of the state in societies where authority, and the very bases of civil behaviour, had been obliterated by totalitarian government; the overwhelming desire was to forget the recent past.[12]

A second type of forgetting is that which is *constitutive in the formation of a new identity*. One ingredient in a sense of identity is the feeling of being committed to certain patterns of action. Specific narratives sometimes play a role in shaping people's dispositions to act in certain ways, whether directly or by giving rise to stereotypes of right action; and socially shared dispositions which function in this way are likely to be connected with narratives preserved by collective memory. The narratives preserved by collective memory may play a causal role in influencing people's dispositions; or they may play a normative role, by providing criteria by which models of action can be shaped.

When a new identity is in process of formation some of these older narratives may fall into abeyance. We might think of this as a loss but it is not necessarily so. The forgetting which is entailed in the formation of a new identity is not so much the loss involved in being unable to retain certain things as rather the gain that accrues to those who know how to discard memories that serve no practical purpose in the management of one's current identity and ongoing purposes. Forgetting then becomes part of the process by which newly shared memories are constructed because a new set of memories is frequently accompanied by a set of tacitly shared silences. Many small acts of forgetting which these silences help to enable over time are not random but patterned. There is, for instance, the forgetting of details about grandparents' lives which in some cases are not transmitted to grandchildren whose knowledge about grandparents might not conduce to, but rather detract from, the effective implementation of their present intentions; or there is the forgetting of details about previous marriages or sexual partnerships, which, if attended to too closely, could impair a present marriage or partnership; or again there are the details of a life formerly lived within a particular religious or political affiliation which has been superseded by embracing an alternative affiliation. Not to forget might in all these cases provoke too much cognitive dissonance. So pieces of knowledge which are not passed on come to have a negative significance by allowing other narratives of identity to come to the fore. They are, so to speak, like pieces of an old jigsaw puzzle which if retained would prevent a new jigsaw puzzle from fitting together. Or to put the matter in another way, unlike prescriptive forgetting this second type of forgetting is unmarked.

The cognatic societies of South East Asia exemplify the way in which this type of forgetting provides living space for present projects. Ethnographic studies of these societies, in Borneo, Bali, the Philippines and rural Java, frequently remark upon the absence of knowledge about ancestors. Knowledge about kinship stretches outwards into degrees of siblingship rather than backwards to predecessors; it is, as it were, horizontal rather than vertical. It is not so much a retention of relatedness as rather a creation of relatedness between those who were previously unrelated. The crucial precipitant of this type of kinship, and the characteristic form of remembering and forgetting attendant upon it, is the high degree of mobility between islands in the South East Asian area. With great demographic mobility it is no longer vital to remember ancestors in the islands left behind, whose identity has become irrelevant in the new island setting, but it becomes crucial instead to create kinship through the formation of new ties. Newcomers to islands are transformed into kin through hospitality, through marriage and through having children. The details of their past diversity, in the islands they have now left, cease to be part of their mental furniture. Forgetting them may be unacknowledged, it is probably only gradual and implicit, and no particular attention is drawn to it. But it is necessary nevertheless. Forgetting is here part of an active process of creating a new and shared identity in a new setting.[13]

In much the same sense, no narrative of modernity as a historical project can afford to ignore its subtext of forgetting.[14] That narrative has two interrelated components, one economic, the other psychological. There is, first, the objective transformation of the social fabric unleashed by the advent of the capitalist world market, which tears down feudal and ancestral limitations on a global scale. And there is, second, the subjective transformation of individual life chances, the emancipation of individuals increasingly released from fixed social status and role hierarchies. These are two gigantic processes of discarding. To the extent that these two interlocked processes are embraced, certain things must be forgotten because they have to be discarded. This long-term forgetting, this casting into forgetting, in the interests of forming a new identity, is signalled by two types of semantic evidence, of which one is the emergence of a new type of vocabulary, while the other is the disappearance of a now obsolete vocabulary. On the one hand, certain substantives, which refer at once to historical movements in the present and to projects for the future, enter the currency: History, Revolution, Liberalism, Socialism, Modernity itself. On the other hand, certain words previously employed by writers in English cease to be used and are no longer easily recognisable: memorous (memorable), memorious (having a good memory), memorist (one who prompts the return of memories), mnemonise (to memorise), mnemonicon (a device to aid the memory).[15] Could there be a more explicit indication than that signalled in these two semantic shifts of what is thought desirable and what can be cast into oblivion?

A third type of forgetting might be called *annulment*. This is a possible response to a surfeit of information. Paradoxically we live in a throwaway society and in one where memory is archival. No epoch has deliberately produced so many archives as ours, with our museums, libraries, depositories and centres of documentation.

Nietzsche gave famous expression to the cultural nausea of this surfeit in *The Use and Abuse of History* when he directed his polemic against historical writing, more particularly against the kind that he called antiquarian historical scholarship, under the weight of whose remembrance the elementary ability to live and act, as he saw it, was crushed and withered.

In the excess of this historical consciousness he saw nothing more than 'the repugnant spectacle of a blind lust for collecting; of a restless gathering up of everything that once was' so that 'man envelops himself in the odour of decay'.[16] Long before this Rabelais had felt the need for a purge of learning. In *Gargantua and Pantagruel*, he tells us that Gargantua's mind is so clogged up with scholastic foolishness that his teacher Ponocrates comes up with a solution for freeing him. His pupil is to be given hellebore, a new drug of forgetfulness, a quick-working medication; the drug produces a powerful desire to sneeze, as a result of which the patient is immediately relieved of all his useless knowledge and forgets the scholastic follies that had been clogging up his mental faculties.[17]

A surfeit of this kind is experienced by exceptional individuals who belong to a learned cultural stratum; but forgetting as annulment becomes a quantitatively different phenomenon when its effects are felt over the reach of a whole culture, permeating its governmental machinery and structure of feeling.

This development has been brought about in two phases. The first was the great archivalisation which was an essential ingredient in the formation of the modern state. We routinely assume now that no state power can possibly exist without its administrative machinery of documents, files and memoranda; and Habsburg Spain was a spectacular pioneer of the modern state in this sense. The overwhelming mass of documentation generated by the Spanish administration in the sixteenth and seventeenth centuries, installed in the great state archive in Simancas, was the first and possibly the most voluminous of such storehouses in Europe. At a later date the administrative core of the British Empire was built around knowledge-producing institutions like the British Museum, the Royal Geographical Survey, the India Survey, the Royal Society and the Royal Asiatic Society, all of which institutions together formed what was thought of as an imperial archive, a fantasy of knowledge collected in the service of state and empire.[18]

The idea of an imperial archive foreshadowed a later historical development, namely the spread at immense speed throughout the globe of new information technologies in the two decades between the mid-1970s and the mid-1990s. Of course, large segments of the world's population – in the American inner cities, in French banlieues, in African shanty towns, in deprived rural areas of India – remain cut off from these innovations. But the dominant groups and territories across the globe had become interlinked by the end of the millennium in a new technological system that had begun to form only in the 1970s. Taken together, the great archivalisation and the new information technologies, the one centralising, the other diffusive, have brought about such a cultural surfeit of information that the concept of discarding may come to occupy as central a role in the twenty-first century as the concept of production did in the nineteenth.

To say that something has been stored, in an archive or computer, is in effect to say that, though it is in principle always retrievable, we can afford to forget it. We now live in a society that has access to too much information and in the foreseeable future the problem can only get worse. Genuine skill in knowing how to manage one's life may come to reside less in knowing how to gather information and more in knowing how to discard it.

This need to discard is felt most acutely, of course, in the natural sciences. As long ago as 1963 it was calculated that 75 per cent of all citations in the area of physics were taken from writings which were less than ten years old. Every scientist needs to learn how to forget in this way if their research activity is not to be crippled by chronic overinformation at the very outset. Indeed, Kuhn's concept of the scientific paradigm is an idea about forgetting. There are at least three different forms of forgetting in play in Kuhn's scheme. First of all, there is the explicit and systematic attempt to overthrow scientific memory in the course of scientific revolutions. Then there is the ordinary forgetting that is constitutive of learning within normal science, which itself takes at least two forms: on the one hand, the selective explicit uptake of information; on the other hand, the tacit and embodied knowledge which grounds practice in normal science, which intrinsically involves forgetting its sources. This is why Kuhn observed that almost always those who achieve fundamental scientific discoveries leading to a new paradigm have either been very young or very new to the field whose paradigm they change: in other words, their scientific imagination has been unburdened by too much scientific memory.

Even if the historical disciplines are not subject to such a drastic process of inbuilt obsolescence, they too have been marked by a paradigm shift and a corresponding cultural forgetting. Fifty years ago historians would often attempt large-scale narratives mapping the course of historical change over long periods, and history was taken to mean politics, the constitution, diplomacy and warfare. Now the flowering of microhistory involves the intensive study of small communities and single events on the model of Emmanuel Le Roy Ladurie's *Montaillou*, and Carlo Ginzburg's *The Cheese and the Worms*, and historians seize upon every aspect of human behaviour and experience, from childhood to old age, from dress to table manners, from smells to laughter, from shopping to barbed wire. The old narratives and the old core stories slowly become effaced. No doubt there are a number of reasons for this change, but one at least may be the wish to circumvent the problems of informational overload which flow from a sheer excess of knowledge.

None of these three types of forgetting – prescribed forgetting, forgetting in the interests of shaping a new identity, and forgetting as annulment – represents a failure. All of them are successful, in the sense that they conduce to the establishment and enhancement of social bonds. Other types of forgetting, however, are forced upon human beings against their will or interest.

A fourth type of forgetting may be called *repressive erasure*. This appears in its most brutal form, of course, in the history of totalitarian regimes, where, as in Milan Kundera's often-quoted words, 'the struggle of man against power is the struggle of memory against forgetting'.[19] But it long predates totalitarianism. As the condemnation of memory (*damnatio memoriae*) it was inscribed in Roman criminal and constitutional law as a punishment applied to rulers and other powerful persons who at their death or after a revolution were declared to be 'enemies of the state': images of them were destroyed, statues of them were razed to the ground, and their names were removed from inscriptions, with the explicit purpose of casting all memory of them into oblivion.[20] But, paradoxically, the explicit purpose of casting the memory of a person into oblivion has the effect of drawing attention to them, and so of causing them to be remembered. The requirement to forget ends in reinforcing memory. *Damnatio memoriae* has the effect not of *destroying* memory but of *dishonouring* it. The French Revolution sought in a similar way to eliminate all remnants of the *ancien régime*: monarchical titles and titles of nobility were abolished; the polite forms of address 'Monsieur', 'Madame' and 'Mademoiselle' were eliminated; the polite distinction between the two forms of the second person, 'vous' (formal) and 'tu' (informal) was supposed to be forgotten; and the names of the historical provinces of France – Burgundy, Provence and so on – were consigned to oblivion.[21]

Repressive erasure can be employed to deny the fact of a historical rupture as well as to bring about a historical break. It was the strategy adopted in English parliamentary debates and pamphlet controversies in the seventeenth century, by Milton, Lilburne, Filmer, Harrington and Hobbes, when they alleged that a set of precedents, principles and maxims were to be found in an ancient constitution, which was asserted to be in some way immune from the king's prerogative action. The plausibility of such claims ran up against one massive obstacle. The Norman Conquest was the one great apparent break in the continuity of English history. The thought that William I might have brought about a systematic importation of new law was incompatible with this belief in an ancient constitution. To acknowledge that there had indeed been a conquest was to admit that the English constitution bore the indelible mark of sovereignty. For if William had truly been king by right of conquest, then the laws and liberties of England forever afterwards depended on that fact. And so, as J.G.A. Pocock has brilliantly shown in *The Ancient Constitution and the Feudal Law*,[22] all the parliamentarians, lawyers and antiquarians joined together in a harmonious chorus, constantly asserting that the establishment of the Normans in England did not constitute a conquest, that William, despite his epithet, was not a conqueror, and that his victory at Hastings brought him no title to change the ancient constitution of England.

This is how the English have come to think of themselves as having been a colonising people but not as having been a colonised people.

Repressive erasure need not always take malign forms, then; it can be encrypted covertly and without apparent violence. Consider, as a further instance, the way in which the spatial disposition of the modern art gallery presents the visitor with nothing less than an iconographic programme and a master historical narrative; by walking through the museum the visitor will be prompted to internalise the values and beliefs written into the architectural script. Entering the Great Hall of the Metropolitan in New York, for example, the visitor stands at the intersection of the museum's principal axes. To the left is the collection of Greek and Roman art; to the right is the Egyptian collection; directly ahead, at the summit of the grand staircase that continues the axis of the entranceway, is the collection of European paintings beginning with the High Renaissance. An entire iconographic programme establishes the overriding importance of the Western tradition and the implicit injunction to remember it. But the collection of Oriental and other types of non-Western art, as well as the medieval collection, are invisible from the Great Hall. They are included, yet they are also half edited out. In exhibiting a master narrative, the museum's spatial script is overt in its acts of celebratory remembrance, covert in its acts of editing out and erasure. Here too the struggle of humanity against power is the struggle of memory against forgetting.[23]

Or yet again: what was the gesture of the Futurists towards past art and museum cities if not a fantasy of repressive erasure? In their manifesto the Futurists declared the wish to free Italy from its infinite number of museums, which covered the country like an infinite number of cemeteries. This museumophobia was no isolated attack but part of an overall assault on all institutions which transmitted traditional knowledge and values, academies and libraries included. These the Futurists saw as not just preserving the past but embodying a cult of the past. It was the fascination exerted over the imagination of artists at the opening of the twentieth century by technological developments which explains the Futurists' call for an elimination of the past. But only in part; we need to take into account another, more complex element. The Futurists wanted the bourgeoisie not only to propel forward a wholesale process of technological revolution but also to identify themselves culturally with that process. But the bourgeoisie's position, as the Futurists saw it, was contradictory. On the one hand, the bourgeoisie urged ever forward the transformation of the everyday life-world; on the other hand, they refused to commit themselves entirely to the destruction of pre-industrial cultures which this entailed. Because of this contradictory behaviour of the bourgeoisie, the Futurists saw a bifurcation opening up between everyday life and culture. Their sense of this bifurcation was at the core of their museumophobia. To the aestheticisation of the past, which found its core institution in the museum, they opposed the aestheticisation of the everyday – aeroplanes, cars, telephones, railways, weapons of mass destruction.[24]

A further type of repressive erasure is found in certain conventions regarding the consumption of food. At first sight, to say this appears to be counter-intuitive. After all, some of our earliest memories, even those of which we cannot be conscious, are memories of food, and, for that reason alone, we would expect food to be powerfully connected with remembering rather than with forgetting, a circumstance which Proust, among others, has elaborated at length. And it is certainly the case that the biblical writers insist emphatically on the mutuality of eating and remembering,[25] that eating plays a crucial role in Christian liturgy, and that Trobriand Islanders locate memory in the stomach. There is even a strong reason for connecting the deprivation of food with powerful memories. The memories which the hunger for food provokes opens up the possibility that there may be many oral histories of hunger that remain to be recaptured; and Heinrich Böll has devoted many memorable passages to the memories of hunger in some of his short stories which are set during the Second World War and its immediate aftermath, as in 'That Time We Were in Odessa', in 'The Taste of Bread' and in 'When the War was Over'.[26]

It is an undeniable fact, nonetheless, that food has been powerfully linked to forgetting. There is the historically significant case where the elimination of the social significance of eating together entails a particular forgetting of family and community life.[27] Then again, there are even what may be viewed as paths towards the liberation from a family or social setting where the forgetting of the food of one's family or culture is a crucial component in a wider process of discarding.[28] There are attempts to edit out the Turkish influences on Greek cuisine which might be viewed as an example of what could be called hegemonic forgetting.[29] More interesting, perhaps, are the cases, reported by Nancy Munn, where in Melanesia the role of food consists for the most part not in remembering the dead but in forgetting them; mortuary rites in Gawa serve the function of a 'temporary memorialisation', but 'when the mourning is over, the chief mourners will return to the activities of daily life and forget . . . the dead'.[30] Nancy Munn, therefore, interprets food exchanges between affines and matriclans in the context of mortuary feasts as a way of *closing* paths of exchange, of *finishing* social relationships that have been put in play during the dead person's lifetime.[31] Much of Debbora Battaglia's research confirms that of Nancy Munn; she shows how mortuary feasting, which goes on over several months, provides what she calls 'phased closure' which deconstructs earlier social relationships in order to provide space for new relationships. Mortuary feasting, she says, 'ossifies, petrifies, and blocks further development by that memory *in the public domain*'.[32] In her work in Amazonia, Beth Conklin adopts a similar approach. She interprets mortuary cannibalism among the Wari as a time for a last remembering of the dead person, before the cutting, roasting and consuming will sunder social bonds with the dead and 'disassemble . . . physical objectification of social identity and social relations'.[33]

A form of repressive erasure is found in Aboriginal societies where the memories of named human ancestors quickly pass into oblivion. Genealogical recall in Aboriginal societies is usually shallow, where a 'shallow' genealogy refers to one with few (for example, only two or three) generation levels above that of the living witness.[34] For Aboriginal people the grandparents' generation is not only dead but barely remembered. Piddington has suggested a convincing explanation for this.[35] In a society which lacks hereditary transmission of wealth and status, dead grandparents cease to be of any sociological significance; and in general, egalitarian peoples who have no property will have no reason to work to produce and remember socially agreed recitations of marked begetters and child-bearers who have long been dead.

If this is the cause for the shallow genealogies characteristic of Aboriginal societies – and the explanation advanced by Piddington seems to be convincing – the mechanism by which this operates depends upon two major tacit prohibitions. The first is the prohibition on the naming of dead people.[36] Ostensibly, this ban works to keep the spirits of the dead at a distance from the living, so ensuring that they will not be provoked to visit the living in response to the invocation of their names. It is believed, for example, that anyone adopting the personal name of a deceased person will not live long: and when a dead man or woman is referred to, it is not by their particular name, but by the general term *muuruukan* 'dead person'. If it is necessary to name a deceased person during the period of mourning, this is allowable only if done in whispers. Not only is there a prohibition upon mentioning the name of the deceased person, but even the names of all their nearest relatives are not to be used during the period of mourning. It is thought to be an insult to the deceased to call them by their own names, and transgressions against this rule frequently lead to fighting and bloodshed.

The second major prohibition requires that if a deceased person had been called after an animal or place or thing, that animal or place or thing must not be mentioned during the period of mourning by any member of the deceased person's tribe, except under another name, because it recalls the memory of the dead.[37] Following each death, it was Tasmanian practice to prohibit the use of the name of the dead person, and then to provide an entirely new label for the totem entity after which the deceased person had been called. In every Tasmanian tribe there was an established custom, upon the death of any individual, of abstaining ever afterwards from mentioning the name of the deceased. It is evident that the enforcement of these two rules of prohibition had the effect of extinguishing the short-term memory of others for the deceased person.

A further type of forgetting, *structural amnesia*, was identified by John Barnes in his study of genealogies.[38] By this he meant that a person tends to remember only those links in his or her pedigree that are socially important. Thus in the genealogies of the strongly patrilineal British peerage, as in those of the Nuer and Tallensi, the ascending male lines are far more memorable than the associated female lines; the names of ancestors who do not give their names to units within the lineage structure tend to be forgotten. Among the Lamba, on the other hand, the matrilineal line of descent is more important than the patrilineal; accordingly, the ascending female lines could be traced for three to five generations, whereas the ascending male lines could be traced back for only one or two generations. The same general principle of structural amnesia is exemplified by the history of cooking, in the sense that the availability of printing systematically affects what recipes are transmitted and what are forgotten.[39] The number of recipes that can be held in written form is unlimited, whereas the number that can be held in the oral memory is limited. Both the standardisation and the elaborateness of modern cuisine depend, therefore, on the production of cookery books and the literacy of cooks. The attraction of regional cooking, on the other hand, is tied to what grandmother did, and the methods of country cuisine are acquired by observation rather than by reading. In these circumstances recipes are systematically forgotten.

Yet another type of forgetting flows from the *planned obsolescence* built into the capitalist system of consumption. Given the limits to the turnover time of material goods, capitalists have turned their attention from the production of goods to the production of services. Most goods, not by accident known as consumer durables – knives and forks, automobiles and washing machines – have a substantial lifetime. Services – going to a rock concert or movie – have a far shorter lifetime. With this shift to the provision of services the turnover time of capital is accelerated. The evolution of a product from its first design and development to its eventual obsolescence – a time span referred to in marketing as the 'product life cycle' – becomes shorter. Long-term planning becomes less important, the facility to exploit market fashions more crucial. Time control focuses more on consumer desire than on work discipline. Under the control of industrial working time, people were needed who aspired to the condition of well-oiled machines. Now they are needed to aspire to the condition of omnivorous children.

Consumer objects obey the pressures of increasing velocity. It has been said that the past is a foreign country but now the present is becoming one too. Alexander Kluge has spoken of the attack of the present on the rest of time, since the more the present of consumer capitalism prevails over past and future, the less stability or identity it provides for contemporary subjects – which is one reason, of course, why there is such incessant talk of identity. Distinction in a culture of mass consumption is demonstrated by acquiring an item which has just come onto the market before others acquire the same item; small time differences in the act of consumption exhibit social distinctions just as they demonstrate fine shades of physical prowess in sport. In so far as individuals designate themselves as members of a group, what counts is the difference of the group as a whole from what it was a year or a month before. Children no longer need to work as auxiliary factory hands; the child's labour now is to produce the consumption of music while the music industry produces the demand for it. This is, as it were, a new form of music while we work. In this way the child acquires a training in the meaning of obsolescence: a fascination with the new which, as Andreas Huyssen has well said, includes the foreknowledge of its own obsolescence in its very moment of appearance.[40] Since the ever-increasing acceleration of innovation for the purpose of consumption produces ever larger quantities of soon-to-be-obsolete objects, it necessarily follows that it must generate ever-more acts of discarding. Vital to this production of obsolescence, forgetting is an essential ingredient in the operation of the market.

There is a seventh type of forgetting in which, though an element of political expediency may play a significant role, this is not the primary or defining characteristic. This type of forgetting is certainly not solely, and may in large part be not at all, a matter of overt activity on the part of a state apparatus. It is manifest in a widespread pattern of behaviour in civil society, and it is covert, unmarked and unacknowledged. Its most salient feature is a *humiliated silence*. Perhaps it is paradoxical to speak of such a condition as evidence for a form of forgetting, because occasions of humiliation are so difficult to forget; it is often easier to forget physical pain than to forget humiliation. Yet few things are more eloquent than a massive silence. And in the collusive silence brought on by a particular kind of collective shame there is detectable both a desire to forget and sometimes the actual effect of forgetting.

Consider for instance the destruction of German cities by bombing in the Second World War. This left some 130 cities and towns in ruins; about 600,000 civilians killed; 3.5 million homes destroyed; and 7.5 million homeless at the end of the war. Members of the occupying powers report seeing millions of homeless and utterly lethargic people wandering about amidst the ruins. From the war years there survive a few accounts in which German citizens wrote of their stunned bewilderment on seeing for the first time the appearance of their ravaged cities. Yet throughout the more than fifty years following the war the horrors of the air bombardment and its long-term repercussions have not been brought to public attention either in historical investigations or in literary accounts. German historians have not produced an exploratory, still less an exhaustive, study of the subject. With the sole exception of Nossack, and some passages on the aerial bombardment in the writings of Heinrich Böll, no German writer was prepared to write or capable of writing about the progress and repercussions of the gigantic campaign of destruction. A colossal collective experience was followed by half a century of silence. How is this to be explained? Sebald retells a story which strongly hints at some of the emotions involved.[41] A German teacher told him in the 1990s that as a boy in the immediate post-war years he often saw photographs, brought out from under the counter of a second-hand bookshop, of the corpses lying in the street after the Hamburg firestorm, and that he observed them being examined, surreptitiously, in a way usually reserved for pornography. We are faced here with the silence of humiliation and shame. The conspicuous paucity of observation and comment on the subject of the bombing and its long-term effects amounts, in other words, to the tacit imposition of a taboo. Confronted with a taboo, people can fall silent out of terror or panic or because they can find no appropriate words. We cannot, of course, infer the fact of forgetting from the fact of silence. Nevertheless, some acts of silence may be an *attempt* to bury things beyond expression and the reach of memory; yet such silencings, while they are a type of repression, can at the same time be a form of survival, and the desire to forget may be an essential ingredient in that process of survival.

It might even be that this desire to forget was most effectively at work in the determination and hectic pace with which the reconstruction of German cities was undertaken after 1945. The ruins which the Germans saw all around them were not just a devastation of their habitat, a mountain of material ruins; at another level they were also ever-present signs of all the destruction which the war had left behind in the consciousness of the German people. We should perhaps view the reconstruction of their cities as something over and beyond the achievement of an economic miracle. It meant the literal covering over, the physical effacement, of all these visible signs of emotional destruction. In this sense, the German people after 1945 can be seen to have been engaged not only in replacing one destroyed material fabric with a new one, but in the wholesale process of covering up their most recent past, the signs of their wounds; their economic miracle, in other words, was a form of forgetting, an effacement of grievous memory traces. The thud and hammer of building accompanied a humiliated silence.

But if any single thing in this historical context demonstrates the power of forgetting as shamed humiliation it is the post-history of the remarkable war diary *A Woman in Berlin*, which for many years remained anonymous because the author had taken a Russian lover at the end of the war. A diary covering the period from 20 April to 22 June 1945, it was written in a Berlin basement while the author sought shelter from air raids, artillery fire, looters and eventually rape. It covers the bombardment, the street-fighting, Hitler's suicide on 30 April, the surrender of the last pockets of resistance on 2 May, and the occupation of the city by the Russian conquerors. It was published in

English translation in 1953, and translated into Norwegian, Italian, Danish, Japanese, Spanish, French and Finnish; but it was a further five years before the German original found a publisher, and then only in Switzerland. The German readership reacted to the book with neglect, silence or hostility, for it broke the taboo of post-war amnesia. German women were supposed not to talk about the rapes, or about sexual collaboration for the sake of survival in the post-war period, as if this dishonoured German men who were supposed to have somehow defended them. Only in the late 1980s did a younger generation of German women encourage their mothers and grandmothers to speak of their wartime experiences, and only half a century after it was written did the work become an international phenomenon.

Or consider the Great War and modern memory. The colossal loss of human life gave rise to an orgy of monumentalisation; memorials to commemorate the fallen went up all over Europe. But were these sites of memory the places where mourning was taking place, as the title of Jay Winter's book on the subject implies?[42] The International Labour Organisation estimated in 1923 that about 10 million soldiers from the German, Austro-Hungarian, French and English armies walked the streets of their countries. These were some 10 million mutilated men: half or totally blinded, or with gross facial disfigurements, or with a hand or arm or leg missing, hobbling around the streets like ghosts. They were badly cared for. The war wounded went financially unrewarded for their pains in millions of households who rarely received the material assistance they needed from the political states on whose behalf they had ostensibly fought. The war dead were annually remembered at memorial sites, and, until 1939, in a ritually observed two minute of silence, people stopped wherever they were in the street, stood still and reflected on the loss. But 10 million mutilated survivors still haunted the streets of Europe. They were dismembered – not remembered – men; many were subject to chronic depression, frequently succumbed to alcoholism, begged in the street in order to be able to eat, and a considerable number of them ended their days in suicide. All sorts of institutional provisions were put in place to keep those mutilated soldiers out of public sight. Every year, the war dead were ceremonially remembered and the words 'lest we forget' ritually intoned; but these words, uttered in a pitch of ecclesiastical solemnity, referred to those who were now safely dead. The words did not refer to the survivors. The sight of them was discomforting, even shameful. They were like ghosts haunting the conscience of Europe. The living did not want to remember them; they wanted to forget them.

The different types of forgetting I have just passed in review have different agents as well as different functions and values. The agents of repressive erasure and prescriptive forgetting are states, governments or ruling parties, and, in the case of the art museum, the gallery's curators as bearers of Western culture or a national or regional inflection of it. The agents of the formation of new identity and structural amnesia are more varied; they may be individuals, couples, families or kin groups. The agents of annulment, as a reaction to information overload, are both individuals and groups of various sizes (for example, families and large corporations) and societies and cultures as a whole. The agents of planned obsolescence are the members of an entire system of economic production. The agent of humiliated silence is not necessarily but most commonly civil society.

NOTES

1 J. Lewis Herman, *Trauma and Recovery* (New York, 1992), p. 175.
2 *Ibid.*, p. 1.
3 W. James, *Principles of Psychology* (Cambridge, 1983), p. 640.
4 F. Nietzsche, *On the Advantage and Disadvantage of History for Life* (tr. P. Preuss, Indianapolis and Cambridge, 1980).
5 See M.S. Roth, 'Remembering Forgetting: *maladies de la mémoire* in Nineteenth-Century France', *Representations*, 26 (1989), pp. 49–68.
6 P. Janet, *Névroses et idées fixes* (Paris, 1884), p. 421.
7 *Ibid.*, p. 404.
8 C. Meier, 'Erinnern – Verdrängen – Vergessen', *Merkur*, 50 (1996), pp. 937–52.
9 E. Renan, *Qu'est-ce qu'une nation?* (Paris, 1882).
10 J. Fisch, *Krieg und Frieden im Friedensvertrag: Eine universalgeschichtliche Studie uber Grundlagen und Formelemente des Friedensschlusses* (Stuttgart, 1979).
11 P. Aguilar, 'Agents of Memory: Spanish Civil War Veterans and Disabled Soldiers', in J. Winter and E. Sivan, eds., *War and Remembrance in the Twentieth Century* (Cambridge, 1999), pp. 84–103.
12 T. Judt, 'The Past is Another Country: Myth and Memory in Postwar Europe', *Daedalus*, 121 (1992), pp. 83–118.
13 J. Carsten, 'The Politics of Forgetting: Migration, Kinship and Memory on the Periphery of the Southeast Asian State', *Journal of the Royal Anthropological Institute*, n.s. 1 (1996), pp. 317–35.
14 R. Koselleck, *Futures Past: On the Semantics of Historical Time* (Cambridge, MA, 1985).
15 E.S. Casey, *Remembering: A Phenomenological Study* (Bloomington, 1987).
16 F. Nietzche, *The Use and Abuse of History* (tr. P. Preuss, New York Library of Liberal Arts, 1957).
17 F. Rabelais, *Gargantua and Pantagruel*, in J. Boulenger, ed., *Oeuvres complètes* (Paris, 1951), pp. 90–1.
18 T. Richards, *The Imperial Archive: Knowledge and the Fantasy of Empire* (London, 1993). For an extended consideration of current questions of archivalisation see V. Mayer-Schönberger, *Delete: The Virtue of Forgetting in the Digital Age* (Princeton, NJ, 2009).
19 M. Kundera, *The Book of Laughter and Forgetting* (tr. M.H. Hein, London, 1980), p. 3.

20 Meier, 'Erinnern – Verdrängen – Vergessen', pp. 937–52.
21 P. Bertrand, *L'Oubli: révolution ou mort de l'histoire* (Paris, 1975).
22 J.G.A. Pocock, *The Ancient Constitution and the Feudal Law* (Cambridge, 1957).
23 C. Duncan and A. Wallach, 'The Universal Survey Museum', *Art History*, 3 (1980), pp. 442–69.
24 W. Grasskamp, *Museumsgründer und Museumsstürmer* (Munich, 1981).
25 G. Feely-Harnik, 'The Lord's Table: The Meaning of Food', in *Early Judaism and Christianity* (Washington, DC, 1994), p. xv.
26 *The Stories of Heinrich Böll* (tr. L. Vennewitz, London, 1986).
27 S. Mintz, *Sweetness and Power: The Place of Sugar in Modern History* (New York, 1985), p. 201.
28 D.E. Sutton, *Remembrance of Repasts: An Anthropology of Food and Memory* (Oxford, 2001), p. 169.
29 *Ibid.*, p. 168.
30 N. Munn, *The Fame of Gawa: A Symbolic Study of Value Transformation in a Massim (Papua New Guinea) Society* (Cambridge, 1986), p. 170.
31 *Ibid.*, p. 171.
32 D. Battaglia, *On the Bones of Serpents* (Chicago, 1990), p. 194.
33 B. Conklin, 'Thus Are Our Bodies, Thus Was Our Custom: Mortuary Cannibalism in Amazonian Society', *American Ethnologist*, 22 (1995), p. 86.
34 B. Sansom, 'The Brief Reach of History and the Limitations of Recall in Traditional Aboriginal Societies and Cultures', *Oceania*, 76 (2006), pp. 150–72.
35 R. Piddington, 'Irregular Marriages in Australia', *Oceania*, 40 (1970), p. 337.
36 J. Dawson, *Australian Aborigines: The Languages and Customs of Several Tribes of Aborigines in the Western District of Victoria, Australia* (Melbourne, 1881).
37 J. Milligan, *Vocabulary of the Dialects of the Aboriginal Tribes of Tasmania* (Hobart, 1890), pp. 11–12.
38 J.A. Barnes, 'The Collection of Genealogies', *Rhodes-Livingstone Journal*, 5 (1947), pp. 48–55.
39 J. Goody, *The Domestication of the Savage Mind* (Cambridge, 1977).
40 A. Huyssen, *Twilight Memories: Marking Time in a Culture of Amnesia*, (New York and London, Routledge, 1995).
41 W.G. Sebald, *On the Natural History of Destruction* (Toronto, 2003).
42 J. Winter, *Sites of Memory, Sites of Mourning: The Great War in European Cultural History* (Cambridge, 1995).

3   Silences

Among the many stories circulating about Wittgenstein, one concerns a train journey he shared with the Italian economist Sraffa. It appears that Wittgenstein was for some time engaged in perplexed reflection, and that he eventually broke his silence to say: 'You see, it isn't possible to say anything without words.' To which Sraffa responded with a shrug.

Sraffa's silence is the more resonant because of our inclination to fear silence. That fear is by no means a cultural universal; in this respect East and West are poles apart. In Asian cultures silence is valued and lengthy silences are gladly tolerated by those who sit or stand together in close proximity. In his study of the modern Japanese novel, Masao Miyoshi remarks that in Japanese society 'reticence, not eloquence, is rewarded' and that 'in art it is not articulation but the subtle art of silence that is valued'; this 'passion for silence', as he calls it, can be found in narrative techniques such as the inclination to set a scene 'by suggestion and evocation' rather than description.[1]

Throughout the Western world, on the other hand, as Ogden and Richards have written, it is agreed 'that it is a matter of common courtesy to say something even when there is hardly anything to say'.[2] Taciturnity is often interpreted as signifying at the very least unfriendliness, and another person's silence, far from being reassuring, is felt to be alarming or possibly even dangerous. Whenever in Western cultures a conversation is interrupted by a lengthy pause, the suspicion arises that the participants have nothing to say, or that they may have something in mind which they do not wish to communicate, or that the subject of the conversation has touched upon a disagreeable or embarrassing topic. It is then felt to be a social responsibility to say almost anything to reanimate the conversation. The flow of words may issue in accounts of irrelevant happenings or statements of the obvious. No matter: they bind the hearer to the speaker by a bond of social sentiment. The breaking of silence is like the breaking of bread; the exchange of words is like the exchange of food. This exchange of words establishes ties which Malinowski calls *phatic communion*.[3]

Apart from phatic communion, the devaluation of silence arises in part from the pivotal role of rhetoric in the public life of Western culture. In debating civic issues the eloquence of Pericles' Athens and Cicero's Rome bequeathed models of excellence to future centuries. Ceremonial occasions called for set speeches of praise or blame, for attack or defence, where public rhetoric flourished. The procedure of law courts placed a premium on eloquent pleading in reaching judicial decisions. The architecture of Christian churches provided pulpits where weekly sermons were delivered. The art of public lectures was cultivated in the centres of advanced learning. Conventions were called to draw up constitutions and nominate candidates for public office through processes of discussion and debate. Contending political parties argued issues before voters in election campaigns.

The pivotal role of public rhetoric in Western culture has its reverse side, in the equation of silence with subordination. Two kinds of literary excavation in particular have alerted us to this circumstance. One is the preoccupation with problems of silence and discourse in women's studies, a preoccupation motivated by the desire of feminists to explain why women have for so long been subordinate actors in history. The other is Bakhtin's study of the carnivalesque, which treats it, through Rabelais' prose, as the ritual location of uninhibited speech, the only place where discourse free of domination – without servility, false pretences, etiquettes of circumlocution – could be heard, where normal power relations which operate chronically to silence subordinate groups are temporarily breached by an explosion of speech.[4] All the movements of oppressed peoples in the second part of the twentieth century concur with the thrust of these preoccupations. All of them consider silence as a manifestation of oppression and emancipatory politics as a reclamation of the right to speech. For previously silenced groups the call to become less inaudible, to acquire a voice, has been endlessly repeated: for the Jews of central Europe, for citizens victimised by government censorship, for participants in land disputes between Aborigines and whites, for the victims of domestic violence, for complainants in rape cases.

The acoustic ecology of the last two centuries has contributed more than anything else to the disappearance of silence. If noise pollution was more blatant and violent in the nineteenth century, it became more dispersed and invasive in the twentieth. Henry Mayhew wrote vividly, in *London Labour and the London Poor*, of the constant hubbub to which the urban poor were subjected in immensely loud, steam-powered factories; for exceptionally long periods of the day they were forced to work in enclosed spaces against the background of a hellish din.[5] By the following century millions of people, and not only those employed in factories, lived in a constantly noisy environment. Overcrowded airports are cacophonous; aeroplanes break up the silence of the night; musak invades restaurants, shops, hotels, elevators; car radios or cassette players provide constant auditory input; with the ubiquitous mobile phone a person is never entirely alone; even people sitting in train carriages have music plugged directly into their ears as do people walking in city streets; and with so many people living in cities there is virtually nowhere to escape the last reverberations of human sounds.

The two minutes' silence introduced after the First World War owed its resonance to the established expectation of urban noise.[6] At no previous period of history could such an effect have been so potent. By 1919 silence was something that many inhabitants of urban Britain had barely known. They had become accustomed to the continuous background noise of a modern society: the sound of people talking and moving in densely populated areas, and the sounds of traffic. By 1919 it would have become difficult to conceive what a city might be like without deliberate noise. Against the shock of the Great War the two minutes' silence provided a new imagining. It meant that all over the railway system, in sheds and yards, in passenger trains, engines stopped wherever they happened to be; that the engine crews stood bare-headed at their footplates; that passengers sat silent in their compartments; that all over the industrial north the machinery of textile mills stopped for two minutes; that throughout the Midlands engineering firms interrupted their work; that telephone exchanges ceased putting through calls. On the day of the first two minutes' silence the *Daily Express* evoked the dramatic effect. 'Nobody can imagine', it wrote, 'what a silent London – still for two minutes – is like. No traffic, no business, no talking – nothing but a brief but sacred space of time.'

So far I have been speaking about silence in the singular. But this is misleading. Silence is not a unitary phenomenon; there are, rather, a plurality of silences.

If we scan the meanings ascribed by great writers to silence we can accumulate an array of the significances attributed to it, ranging from the benevolent to the malevolent. Plutarch spoke of silence as something 'profound and awesome' and said that 'we learn silence from the gods, speech from men'. Thoreau believed that 'silence is the universal refuge, the sequel to all dull discourses and all foolish acts, a balm to our every chagrin, as welcome after satiety as after disappointment'. Hazlitt wrote that 'silence . . . is one great art of conversation'. Heine thought 'silence . . . is the essential condition of happiness'. But George Bernard Shaw believed that taciturnity is 'the most perfect expression of scorn'. Pascal spoke of silence as the greatest persecution. G.K. Chesterton believed silence to be 'the unbearable repartee'. André Maurois wrote that 'men fear silence as they fear solitude, because both give them a glimpse of the terror of life's nothingness'. Thomas Mann concluded that 'speech is civilisation itself. The word, even the most contradictory word, preserves contact – it is silence which isolates.'

La Rochefoucauld distinguished the silence of eloquence, the silence of mockery, and the silence of respect. Bakhtin even suggested that irony is 'a special kind of substitute for silence'; by which he would seem to mean that it is an ultimate reservation in the form of speech.[7]

Linguistic evidence corroborates the fact that there are different kinds of silence. Nouns in various languages, for instance, discriminate between different kinds of silences. German writers can draw upon distinctions among such related terms as *Schweigen* 'silence', including being silenced or silencing oneself, *Stille* 'stillness' and *Sprachlosigkeit* 'speechlessness'. Hebrew provides distinctions between *sheket* 'silence', *dumiyah* 'stillness' and *sh'tikah* 'quietness'. Adjectives describing different modes of silence cover an even wider range of implications. We might speak of threatening, menacing, forbidding, suspicious, brooding, injured, eerie, thoughtful, respectful and worshipful silences. When speaking of people who are felt to exhibit silent behaviour we could refer to them as taciturn, reserved, reticent, retiring or secretive. Silence can express astonishment, discomfiture, embarrassment, caution, resignation, apathy, fatigue, timidity and uncertainty. There is the silence of trust and the silence of suspicion; the silence of peace and the silence of devastation; the silence in the face of the awesome and the silence before the unspeakable. A pause in conversation, a question unanswered, a refusal to greet someone, the avoidance of a topic of conversation: all may be viewed as different forms of silence. Even compulsive articulacy may be an unconscious and heavily camouflaged attempt to conceal a troubling silence from both speaker and addressee.

Then again, we might distinguish the relationship between silence and speech depending on whether we judge that relationship to be enabling or disabling. On the one hand, there are silences that help to shape speech; on the other hand, there are silences that disrupt the sense or flow of speech. The silences of the diplomat, the priest and the spy belong to the first category. The silences of the prisoner, the aphasic and the hysteric belong to the second category.[8]

Silences often play a crucial role in heightening the pragmatics of beginnings and endings. We might term these fore-silences and after-silences.[9] Fore-silences are acts of anticipatory alertness; one readies oneself to hear, in a state of expectancy, as at a concert or before a film or theatrical performance. After-silences are acts which terminate utterances; as when relatives of terminally ill patients frequently do not use words to say the final goodbye to their loved ones. In both cases silence is a sign of intensity.

The ambiguities of silence have been attentively explored by what we might call the professional listeners to silences. Musicians are adept at hearing pauses and silences. They have produced a form of notation which is superior to spoken language at encoding small silences, where a silence is called a 'rest' if it is a precisely measured stoppage (a half-beat, beat or bar) but a 'pause' if it goes on for an imprecise amount of time; and conductors sometimes direct orchestras to listen to silences. Concertgoers, through some unwritten social contract, generally avoid producing noises during a symphonic movement, yet as soon as the music pauses between movements the break will be filled by the noise of people all over the auditorium who at that moment feel that they must cough. Some writers have been particularly attentive listeners. Much of the tension within and between the characters of Oedipus and Teiresias in Sophocles' *Oedipus Tyrannus* hinges on the issue of what is to be said and what is not to be said; in Samuel Beckett's *Waiting for Godot* silence is a pervasive atmosphere; Harold Pinter distinguished explicitly between the work done by pauses, which punctuate or pace a theme, and by silences, which serve to shift from one theme to another; and the writing of Virginia Woolf concentrates stylistically on the spaces between events, words and thoughts.[10] Much information about the 'rules of silence' can be found in the conduct-books which were produced in such profusion in early modern Europe.[11] So we find Erasmus advising that 'when seated with his elders a boy should never speak unless the occasion demands it or someone invites him to do so . . . Silence is becoming in women but even more so in boys'; William Caxton's *Book of Curtesye*, apparently intended for upper-class youths, tells them to be 'hushed in chamber, silent in hall'; and Du Bosc insisted upon the need for 'discretion, silence and modesty' in gentlewomen, advising them to follow the Virgin Mary as a model, since 'Holy Scripture makes no mention that ever she spoke more than four or five times in all her life.'

Oral historians too must possess the gift of secret hearing.[12] They must be able to listen to pauses and hesitations if they are to understand what is being told to them. The precious element yielded by oral history, which no other sources possess in equal measure, is access to the speaker's subjectivity: they tell us what people wanted to do, what they believed they were doing, and what they now think they did. Access to this kind of knowledge can sometimes be blocked, masked as it were, by punctuation. Punctuation indicates pauses distributed according to grammatical rules, where each mark has a conventional place, meaning and length. These marks rarely coincide with the rhythms, pauses and hesitations of the speaking subject. But pauses of irregular length and position accentuate the emotional content of speech, and the precise length and position of the pause or hesitation play a crucial role in understanding the meaning of speech. In addition to the listening skills of oral historians, the microanalyses of conversation in ethnomethodology and conversation analysis, following the work of Garfinkel, Jefferson, Schegloff and others, suggest an alternative method of marking and attending to pauses and silences.

Given the potential ambiguity of silences, one wonders whether it might be possible to discover some form of orientation among them, whether it is possible to carve out a pathway, as it were, through the morass of their possible meanings. I suggest that it might be possible to do so, and to this end I propose that we distinguish intentional silences, on the one hand, and imposed silences, on the other. The same contrast could be made by distinguishing *silence* from *silencing*. The distinction between the two hinges upon the question of agency.

Some of the most obvious as well as the most interesting forms of intentional silence are found in the practice of alternative sign languages. These are developed by speaker-hearers for use during periods when speech is not permitted for ritual reasons or when speech is made difficult by circumstances. The sign systems of the Cistercian monastic orders, of Australian Aborigines and of Native North Americans all fall into this category.

Alternative sign languages should be distinguished from primary sign languages, from gestures and from limited professional gesture systems. They are unlike primary sign languages, for example those used by the deaf, which serve as the principal means of communication for a group of signers rather than as an alternative to spoken language. They are unlike gestures, in the sense that all their movements comprise an overt, recognised linguistic structure, as in the case of a spoken language, whereas gestures, though conventional, are not explicitly formulated as a complex linguistic system. And they are unlike limited professional gesture systems, which have meaning only for specialised groups and not for others and are employed only in limited communication, and, most importantly of all, comprise a relatively small number of signs. There are in fact a vast array of restricted professional codes which are used to overcome obstacles to spoken language. The obstacles may be of various kinds. It might be a question of distance, as for auctioneers, sports referees and truck drivers. It might be a matter of noise level, as for sawmill operators, airport mechanics and stock exchange traders. It might be because secrecy is required, as with head waiters and criminals. Or it might be because silence is required, as for orchestra conductors and broadcasters.

Alternative sign languages differ fundamentally also from both writing systems and spoken language. They differ from all true writing systems – for instance early Sumerian, Egyptian and Chinese – because they contain no phonetic constituent and no attempt to translate phonetic elements into manual symbols, whereas all writing systems soon added some phonetic endeavours, however rudimentary, to the visual delineation of things and acts. They differ also from spoken language, in the sense that speech consists overwhelmingly of elements entirely without inherent resemblance of symbol to signification, whereas the sign language elements overwhelmingly do show some connection or resemblance between gesture sign and meaning.

The bodily movements in alternative sign languages are restricted to the upper extremities: either to single or to paired hand-and-arm movements. The signs mostly to some degree mimic the thing, motion or quality denoted. Kroeber correctly alerts us to the fact that, although many investigations of alternative sign languages speak of signs as pantomimic, pantomime is not a strictly accurate term because it refers to imitation performed with the whole body, whereas alternative sign languages would be better called cheiromimic.[13]

In terms of the size of sign lexicons and the degree of semantic openness, Cistercian sign language occupies a position somewhere between restricted professional gestural systems on the one hand, and Aboriginal and Native American on the other. In his *Cistercian Sign Language*, an historical and descriptive essay, Robert Barakat provides some 330 illustrated signs.[14] He draws attention to the fact that certain places and times are set aside for silence. The places most frequently mentioned are the chapel, the cloister, the dormitory, the oratory, the refectory, the stairs and the scriptorium. Unbroken silence was also to be kept from 8 p.m. until sunrise and from noon until 3 p.m., as well as at other times, including certain work periods and reading hours. Although Cistercian sign language lacks many of the grammatical elements necessary for expressing nuances of thought, it functions very effectively within the setting of monastic life. It gives us a precise sense of the monastic diet; there are signs for apple, cherry, grape, peach, plum, cabbage, carrot, corn, beans, beetroot, potato, cereal, bread and fish. And unsurprisingly many signs refer specifically to features of monastic life. There are signs for offices and officers who make up the government of the monastery (abbot, prior, sub-prior, president, cantor, deacon, chapter), signs to designate the stages through which the monks must pass before becoming fully fledged members of the monastery (postulant, novice, religious or lay brother) and signs for objects of liturgical significance (alb, lavabo towel, linen, chalice, cruet, thurible). Compound signs containing four or more elements present problems, however, because of the rather large and unwieldy number of elements that have to be combined. To formulate signs for biblical characters and events, in particular, requires not only a familiarity with the Bible but ingenuity and imagination. This is where serious difficulties begin. Cain is signed number + one + little + secular + kill + brother; Judas is signed secular + take + three + 0 + white + money + kill + cross + God; and Sodom, more difficult still, is signed bad + secular + courtyard + burn + time + lady + change + true + salt.

The sign language of Australian Aborigines is more impressive for the size of its lexicons and the complexity of the signed sequences employed.[15] Adam Kendon reports that he has collected some 1,500 signs used by the Warlpiri, and LaMont West observes that in the entire history of published travellers' reports and ethnographic studies some 1,980 lexical items have been recorded.[16] Aboriginal sign languages have attained their highest level of development in the North Central Desert area, from the MacDonell Ranges northwards as far as the edge of the Arnhem Land escarpment and the rivers that drain the Fitzmaurice region – up to Newcastle Creek – and westwards to the edges of the area traditionally occupied by the Warlpiri. It is among the latter and the Warumungu that alternative sign languages are most richly elaborated.

Most probably sign languages will flourish where there is frequent contact between people who speak different languages, and where hunting societies need a silent mode of communication to coordinate their activities without scaring away the game. But the high development of alternative sign languages among the Warlpiri and Warumungu suggests that the primary circumstance promoting the elaboration of sign languages is to be found elsewhere. This is located in the existence of extended speech taboos. The two main circumstances in which speech taboos occur in Aboriginal society are in association with mourning and in association with male initiation. In mourning, in many places close relatives of the deceased, particularly female relatives, are required to observe speech bans which may, for example among the Warumungu, extend for widows for as long as two years. In male initiation ceremonies, the novices are often subject to speech bans which in some societies, for instance among the Lardiil, may last for as long as six months. These two sets of circumstances are linked. Speech bans for mourners and for male novices can be understood in the connection of both with death. In Aboriginal society the initiation ceremony for males is viewed as a process in which the boy dies and the man is born; the liminal period is treated as a kind of semi-death during which restrictions are placed on communication, since persons who are dead are unable to speak.

Perhaps the most elaborate and most widespread alternative sign language has been found among the Plains peoples of North America. The largest published collection of their signs is that of Garrick Mallery, whose work contains around 3,000 lexical entries, while the sign corpus obtained by LaMont West for his unpublished dissertation numbered around 3,500. In his 'Introduction to the Study of Sign Language among the North American Indians as Illustrating the Gesture Speech of Mankind', published in 1880 and still in some respects unsurpassed, Garrick Mallery observed that in no other thoroughly explored part of the world had there been found spread over so large a space so small a number of individuals divided by so many linguistic and dialectal boundaries as in North America.[17] Distances of over 1,000 miles intervene between the most widely separated points in both east–west and north–south directions. Plains sign language belongs to the tribes between the Missouri and the Rocky Mountains and from Fraser River, British Columbia, south to the Rio Grande; and by the mid-twentieth century Plains sign language had spread well into the woodland fringe of the northwest, north and northeast – that is to say, British Columbia, Alberta, Saskatchewan and Manitoba – where it was almost completely unknown in the nineteenth century. Throughout this region it was particularly the peoples of the western Plains – Kiowa, Apache, Crow, Cheyenne, Arapaho, Shoshone, Comanche, Blackfoot, Sioux – who used Plains sign language most richly. By means of it they could easily express spatial relationships, physical activities, enumeration and comparison; animal names and descriptions of their characteristics and movements are abundantly represented, as are place names; and many changes in cultural history are reflected in the sign lexicon, such as the military conflict which marked the end of Plains culture, represented by many terms referring to military matters, such as infantry, cavalry and cannon. Plains sign language was convenient inter-tribally and intra-tribally. Inter-tribally: because, with the horse, tribes engaged in buffalo hunting extended their territories, so that many groups, speaking several quite different languages, came into contact with each other for the first time, and trade became a principal agent for the diffusion of sign language throughout the Plains during the nineteenth century. And intra-tribally: in hunting, in story telling and in arranging alliances for attacks on enemies.

Among those who have practised intentional silences is found not only the use of alternative sign language but pre-eminently, of course, the practice of silent worship. Deep emotional agitation, a kind of more or less powerful religious ravishment, sometimes precipitates silence, which is, as it were, the language of the unutterable. We find the phenomenon of silent worship in a number of circumstances, or rather, to be more precise, we should say that there is a variety of silences in worship, since Mensching has proposed a set of fine discriminations in this area.[18] He has distinguished a preparatory silence, a contemplative silence, a worshipful silence, an expectant silence and a monastic-ascetic silence.

Rudolf Otto has proposed a valuable distinction between three phases of silence.[19] There is, first of all, the silence of waiting, the waiting upon God's coming. This is a form of detachment from all outward distractions, an intense inward concentration. Among Quakers this is a particularly marked experience. The presence of something divine may have been felt without a word having been spoken, and the worshippers may part, as they met, without any audible thanksgiving. Then, second, there is what could be called sacramental silence. This is the culminating point in the act of worship, the moment when God is experienced by the congregation as a numinous presence. All the preceding parts of the service have been a period of preparation for this moment. It is found in the forms of worship in ancient Israel and in the Roman Catholic Mass at the moment of transubstantiation. Here, at the climax of the Mass, only silence seems appropriate in the presence of the holy. At this holiest moment of the Mass, liturgical prayer and music subside into a stillness that signifies no mere momentary pause or interlude but is, rather, an absolute cessation of sound. The silence lasts long enough, it is so palpable, that we are able to hear the silence itself. Then, finally, there is the silence of achieved unity, of fellowship. This is an experience of inward oneness, a union of many individuals. Two forms of worship which appear otherwise to occupy opposite poles of religious development share an inner kinship in this respect: the Quaker meeting and the Roman Catholic Mass.

Then again the founders of world religions and others who have played a major role in the history of religions have experienced extended periods of silence. Buddha departed from his father's palace to spend time in the forests and wastelands of northern India. Muhammad retreated to Mount Hira' in the Arabian desert. Jesus of Nazareth undertook a forty-day solitary fast in the Sinai desert. John the Baptist, the prophet who proclaimed the advent of the Messiah, lived for a time in the desert. St Paul, according to his own account, did not begin to preach the gospel immediately after his conversion, but withdrew into the desert of Arabia to undertake a period of preparation. St Anthony lived in solitude for some twenty years. St Catherine of Siena spent three years in seclusion in her little room in the Via Benincasa, during which time she underwent a series of mystical experiences before entering upon an active life of teaching and preaching.

In addition to the withdrawal of individuals into solitude, whole eremitic movements have withdrawn into silence. For some three hundred years, between the third and sixth centuries AD, Christians flocked to the Egyptian and Syrian deserts. That movement was so vast and so dedicated that it provoked the poisonous disdain of Gibbon centuries later. 'There is no phase in the moral history of mankind', he wrote,

of a deeper or more painful interest than this ascetic epidemic. A hideous, distorted and emaciated maniac, without knowledge, without patriotism, without natural affection, spending his life in a long routine of useless and atrocious self-torture and quailing before the ghastly phantoms of his delirious brain, had become the ideal of the nations which had known the writings of Plato and Cicero, and the lives of Socrates and Cato.[20]

It is possible to judge the phenomenon differently. If Christians retreated, in such vast numbers, between the third and sixth centuries, to develop an intense spirituality based on rigorous asceticism and silence, that was because they were engaged in an oppositional practice, as a form of *imitatio Christi* in a post-martyr age. It was oppositional in two senses. Partly, it was because, after the Emperor Constantine embraced Christianity, the church began to become an accepted part of Roman society and Christians came to feel themselves at home in the world; many Christians retreated to the desert to find a purer, more austere, less compromised form of Christianity. Partly, it was because rhetoric, that is to say the art of public speaking, was a central duty for the citizen and a key focus of a Roman education; for Christians, prolonged silence became a marked activity, a kind of great refusal.

Many Christian hermits sought first external silence, fleeing the pressures of the social world, and then internal silence, seeking peace of heart and mind. Their quest took one of two forms: either eremitic, that is to say solitary; or cenobitic, that is to say based in communities. Pachomius, from his monastery of Tabenna near the Nile, was reported to have 7,000 men and women living in various congregations under his rule; Serapion ruled over 10,000 hermits at Arsinoe; the monastery of Tabennisi, near Dendara, had 7,000 men and women living in different styles – some communal, others solitary – under its supervision; there were reported to be some 5,000 monks living on Mount Nitria, to the west of the mouth of the Nile. So vast was the hermetic movement that a traveller through Egypt and Palestine about AD 394 reported that the numbers of dwellers in the desert were almost equal in size to the population of the towns.[21]

Prolonged silences are not limited, of course, to the hermitic movements between the third and sixth centuries AD. Almost all serious writers on the subject of contemplative prayer, in particular the monastic orders, the Benedictines, Carthusians, Carmelites and Cistercians, want us to understand that prayer, which is so foreign to every tendency of modern secular thought, can only be practised in a context that involves a great deal of silence. Monastic silence was freed from the drain on attention and energy which occurs during conversation at meals, small talk, and the innumerable trivialities which dilute the focus of everyday life. Traditional Christian monastic life is built around the two silent enclosures of the church and the cloister. Gardens, where we witness the silent power of growth, have been central to many religious traditions, as places of contemplation and silence: in Zen gardens, in European monastic gardens, in Persian and Moorish water gardens where it was possible to enjoy the exquisite pleasure of overhearing near-silences: crickets singing, the language of cicadas, little bees that leave the hive, the rustling running through the trees in summer. Indeed, the word 'paradise' comes from a Persian word for garden. Cistercian monks in the twelfth century sought out desirable places, remote from civilisation, in which to build their monasteries. In England they found, if not literal wildernesses, then at least figurative wildernesses: most famously at Tintern, in the Wye valley, or Fountains in the Yorkshire dales, and Rievaulx in the North Yorkshire moors. In France also, many monastic settlements were situated in remote areas: on islands off the coast, like Lerins where Honoratus founded a monastery in the fifth century; or on headlands, for example the abbey of St Gilas, where, much later, Abelard lived.

No monastic order has carried silence to such extremes as have the Trappists.[22] They spend seven hours of the day in church, and, apart from the singing of the offices, they are kneeling or standing in silent meditation; the rest of the day passes in mental prayer, in reading and in field labour. There is a special dispensation from the rule of silence for Trappist monks who deal with the abbey livestock when they are addressing their dumb charges. But apart from this, and with the exception of certain officers, for example the abbot and the guest-master, the rule of silence is absolute. A special deaf-and-dumb language for cases of necessity has been codified; and the entire lifetime of a lay brother who does not participate in the singing of the offices may pass without the utterance of a word beyond the confessional or his spiritual conversations with the abbot.

At the dawn of the modern period we then witness two opposite practices of religious silence. Even though opposite, they share a common background. In the Middle Ages, historians tell us, the sense that established the richest contact with the world was hearing. The primacy of hearing was theologically guaranteed. One listened to the Scriptures. One listened to the words of the Mass. The ear alone, Luther said, is the Christian organ. There followed two forms of extreme withdrawal from this position. One was that of the Quakers, the other that of the Jesuits. The Quakers withdrew from hearing into communal silence. The Jesuits withdrew from hearing into a form of silence moulded by interior sight, the training of the image-forming capacity. The Quaker retreat led to a spontaneous silence, the Jesuit retreat to a rigorous silence.

Anything that smacked of customary formalism was strictly excluded from Quaker worship. Sometimes the participants might sit in silence for as long as two or three hours before someone felt called upon to speak; on other occasions an entire meeting might take place in complete silence. Although any member of a meeting, male or female, was eligible to speak in prayer, praise or exhortation, most people spoke seldom, if at all. There were good and valued Friends who never found themselves moved to speak a word in public. No one was required to speak. In this respect Quaker worship is unlike other forms of Protestant devotional life, which, with its emphasis on preaching, can sometimes be a 'noisy' form of worship. Quaker worship, by contrast, is one of the most spiritual forms of divine service ever practised.

Silence, for the Quakers, as the cessation of outward speaking, was a metaphor for the suppression of all that attracted people to natural, fleshly concerns, the refusal to yield to the lusts of the carnal mind. Joys, pleasures, profits, the delights of the flesh: all these, the Quakers believed, were but vanities, antithetical to the suppression of the earthly self and to the subjection to God's will that alone are necessary for the attainment of a proper spiritual state. 'Cease from those discourses that draw the mind from an inward, deep sense of the invisible, immutable power of the Lord God Almighty', advised Charles Marshall; 'It's better to speak little than to utter a multitude of vain words', wrote Edward Burrough; and Thomas Symonds inveighed against all 'wicked singing and idle jesting, and foolish laughter'.[23] The silence of the Quakers was not an end in itself, then, but a means to attaining the defining spiritual experience of early Quakerism, which was the direct personal experience of the spirit of God within oneself. Silence was understood to precede speaking, to be the ground of speaking, and to be the consequence of speaking.

At the opposite pole from Quaker silence, in terms of its rigorous structure, stands Loyola's *Spiritual Exercises*.[24] Dating from 1548, the exercises were intended to be completed by the practitioner in about thirty days. Accordingly, they are divided into four weeks, corresponding to the four parts into which the exercises are divided. First comes the consideration and contemplation of sins; then the life of Christ up to and including Palm Sunday; then the Passion of Christ; and finally, the Resurrection and Ascension. Within these weeks, Loyola directs that an hour must be spent every day on particular exercises or contemplations, all of which are specified in detail. It will be seen that in Loyola's silences, unlike Quaker silences, everything is divided, subdivided and classified, into weeks, points and exercises.

The material of the *Spiritual Exercises* is made up of interior images. It marks a phase in the art of memory that has been so beautifully described by Frances Yates. Practitioners are called upon to live out the 'scenes' from the life of Christ as if in a psychodrama. The narrative of the New Testament must be imprinted on the mind's eye. These visual anecdotes or envisaged scenes are conjured up in painstaking detail. Practitioners must envisage how Our Lady, almost nine months pregnant, and seated on a donkey, with Joseph and taking with them an ox, set out from Nazareth for Bethlehem to pay the tribute which Caesar had imposed on all those lands; they must look in the mind's eye at the place or grotto of the Nativity, see how big or small it was, how low or high, and what was in it; they must contemplate how the child Jesus was obedient to his parents at Nazareth; they must see with the eyes of imagination the synagogues, towns and villages where Christ preached; they must see how Christ went from the River Jordan into the desert; how Christ appeared to his disciples on the waves of the sea; how with his eleven disciples he came down from Mount Sion, where he had supper; how he left eight of his disciples in a place in the valley and three others in a part of the garden; how his sweat became like drops of blood; how he awakened his disciples; how Judas gave him the kiss of peace; how Christ was arrested as a criminal and taken to the house of Annas; how he was taken from the house of Pilate to be nailed to the cross; and practitioners must envisage, finally, the period of time that elapsed between the raising up on the cross and Christ's death; and from the taking down from the cross to the laying in the sepulchre.

In addition to silences *within* ritual there are also silences *about* ritual. Pausanias' *Guide to Greece*, a text on which he worked for at least fourteen years between the late fifties and the late seventies of the second century AD, is a telling instance of this.[25] Pausanias' silences are not implicit, but intentional. On no fewer than thirteen occasions he interrupts his narration to declare that he is in possession of certain details of cult interest which he is nonetheless not at liberty to impart. In Book I, after he has mentioned the ancient dispute between the Athenians and the Argives about the supremacy of the cult of Deiope and the disputed genealogy of Triptolemus, he declares that he cannot continue with the description of the Eleusinian sanctuary because of a vision in a dream. Again in Book I, after he has named the altar and the field of Triptolemus, he interrupts his description to state once more that a dream prevented him from describing the things that are to be found in the enclosure which is sacred to Demeter, because just as those who were uninitiated were forbidden to see these things, so it would not be permissible for them to hear of them. In Book II, he describes Corinth, and tells of how, along the road that leads from the agora to the Lechaeum gate, one comes across a bronze Hermes sitting next to a ram; but he declares his intention not to pass on what is said of Hermes and the ram, even though he knows it. In these cases Pausanias' silence is specifically marked by reference to a prohibition. Either he is unable to make revelations to the 'uninitiated' or he refers to the information which he withholds as something which it is not permissible to reveal to everyone.

The greater part of Pausanias' reticences appear to refer to mystery cults. Many cult experiences may have contained an initiation rite which was an essential preliminary step before a person was accepted into the group of those who could have knowledge of secret rituals, and it is at least permissible to speculate that, in addition to the initiation, there may have been a rule of silence which prevented the divulging of such secrets to those who had not been initiated. In each case, it is possible to trace a close link between Pausanias' explicit silences and a prohibition which was tied to the sacred character of the subject about which he is writing. Always there appears to have been a recurrent link with a type of archaic society founded upon an agricultural economy, in which drought and famine were lived through as divine punishments, and in which, as a result, there were highly motivated fertility rituals.

In the arts the most effective means of representing the numinous is found in the experience of the sublime. Here again we encounter the phenomenon of silence. We can sense this silent awe in the face of the sublime when we contemplate the erection of gigantic blocks of rock, whether they are unworked or are hewn, and whether they consist of single monoliths or of giant rings of stone as at Stonehenge. For, as Mircea Eliade has written, nothing is 'more direct and autonomous in the completeness of its strength, nothing more noble, or more awe-inspiring, than a majestic rock or a boldly-standing block of granite'.[26] In stone we intuit a tangible resistance, something that transcends our humanity, something which, in its strength, its motionlessness, its size, is not human. In its grandeur we are faced with a force that belongs to some world other than the profane one of which we are part. The motive behind such erections as Stonehenge, therefore, may have been to store up what was felt to be the numinous power which is found in the solid presence of stone. Again, those who were responsible for the construction of the pyramids and obelisks of ancient Egypt must surely have experienced this same sense of awe in the face of stone as an experience which precipitated a sense of the sublime. And although Chinese architecture does not achieve the impression of awe which we associate with the imposing altitudes of Gothic cathedrals, it does accomplish a silent amplitude in its enclosed spaces and courtyards, as exemplified, for instance, in the imperial tombs of the Ming emperors at Nanking and Peking.[27] Again, the waters, clouds and mountains depicted in Chinese landscape paintings exude a profound calm. It is a special Chinese art to paint empty space, so much so, in fact, that we are tempted to say that almost nothing is painted in these landscapes, for it is as if the void itself had become the subject.

The charm which depictions of seas, mountains and landscapes exert upon the Western imagination dates from a more recent period. It is only since the end of the eighteenth century that this particular sensitivity of the soul has been evident, although an early prototype can be found in the landscape paintings of Claude, with their placid lakes occupying the middle distance and their calm Arcadian serenity. We find in Addison's *Spectator* essays on the 'Pleasures of the Imagination' the first explicit statement of the theory of the 'natural sublime'; Addison claims that we are flung into a pleasing astonishment when we encounter unbounded views, that we 'feel delightful stillness and amazement in the soul at the apprehension of them' and that such objects convince us that there does indeed exist an Almighty Being. Such vistas convince us as much as a metaphysical demonstration would, Addison notes, because by the greatness of the material object the idea is produced in our mind of a Being circumscribed neither by time nor by space. Later, in Burke's *Philosophical Enquiry into the Origin of Our Ideas of the Sublime and Beautiful*, there is a section entitled simply 'Privation', where, asserting that 'all general privations are great, because they are all terrible', Burke cites, apart from vacuity and darkness, solitude and silence;[28] and in a journal entry of 1851 Henry David Thoreau speaks of seeing evening descend over a river and describes how he experiences there 'a quiet beauty in the landscape at that hour', a 'greater stillness, the serenity of the air'.[29] In Frederic Edwin Church's painting *Twilight in the Wilderness*, the light in the upper part of the picture is transmuted in the picture's lower half into what Barbara Novak has called a light of 'silent unstirring energy';[30] and in Thomas Cole's great painting *View from Mount Holyoke, Northampton, Massachusetts, after a Thunderstorm*, which is usually referred to simply as *The Oxbow*, and was executed in 1836, there is a tranquil sublimity. In the flatlands, Cole depicts a serene space whose placidity is reinforced by the presence of a slow-moving ferry and a view of mountains in the distance.[31] In his 'Essay on American Scenery' Cole speaks of rocks, wood and water as evoking a 'spirit of repose', and of the 'silent energy of nature', where it is above all the presence of water which leads us to perceive 'the expression of tranquillity and peace'.[32]

Paradoxical though it may sound to say so, music also offers a rich terrain for the examination of silences. This is suggested, obliquely, by the Japanese novelist Junichiro Tanizaki in his book *In Praise of Shadows*, where in the course of writing about Japanese culture, which is so alien to the Western way of perceiving things, and which cherishes dim half-light and candlelight, he brings into close alignment the experience of shadows and the experience of silence.[33] He writes that whenever he sees the alcove of a tastefully built Japanese room, he marvels at the Japanese comprehension of the secrets of shadows and the sensitive use of shadow and light. The Japanese will some-times encounter an empty space marked off with plain wood and plain walls, so that the light drawn into it forms dim shadows within emptiness, and when they gaze into the darkness, although they know perfectly well that it is mere shadow, they are overcome with the feeling that in this small corner of the atmosphere there reigns, he says, 'complete and utter silence', and 'here in the darkness immutable tranquillity holds sway'. The 'mysterious Orient' of which Westerners speak probably refers, he concludes, 'to the uncanny silence of these dark places'.[34]

Susan Tomes, a pianist and writer on music, has picked up Tanizaki's clue and developed the thought with particular subtlety.[35] Silence, she suggests, is the material which runs through the pauses and gaps in the musical notes. It is heard in every tiny musical rest. It could even be said that silence is the essence of rhythm, because rhythm is the organised interaction between sound and silence. Silence is the realm into which any individual note inevitably dies away.

The pianist's need to play silences as well as notes means, Tomes writes, that music is a lot more precise than banking. In banking you need to be extremely precise now and then, but a lot of work done by bankers is not directly to do with figures. In music, on the other hand, you have to be accurate all the time: accurate about the notes, and *accurate about the silences and pauses*, sometimes infinitesimal, between the notes.[36] That is why Tomes suggests that, when we are speaking of pianists, a comparison more appropri-ate than that with the banker is that with the craftsman. In his book on *The

Craftsman, Richard Sennett writes about the long period of training which alone enables a craftsman to master his materials patiently through the exercise of great discipline, so that he is able to achieve an intense focus which is not accessible to those who have not undergone a long training in the exercise of a craft.[37]

Elsewhere, Tomes suggests that the accomplishment of a skilled rhetorician is in some ways comparable to that of a skilled musician in the management of silences and pauses. We are fortunate in being able to listen to an exemplification of this in the speeches of President Obama.[38] The intonation of his speeches gives great pleasure. It displays a mastery of the art of phrasing, of cadence, and an intelligent use of breathing and pauses; and it is because of this that his speech rhythms are so gripping. His words remain in the minds of his hearers more effortlessly than is the case with many politicians because he occupies a zone, as it were, between speech and singing.

If not in *producing* silences, then at least in *listening* to them, in decoding them, psychoanalysts are virtuosi. In their search for hidden clues they are detectives of absences: the hearers of subjects dropped, of overtures rejected. Behind silences psychoanalysts might sometimes detect a massive amount of unprocessed sorrow. Freud perceived the unheard or disguised loquacity within verbal silences, as well as the silences that are masked by loquacity. In his account of the 'Dora' case, he wrote that 'he who has eyes to see and ears to hear was convinced that mortals can conceal no secrets. He whose lips are silent, chatters with his fingertips; betrayal oozes through every pore.'[39]

As a defiance of the therapeutic process, silence can offer resistance along a spectrum of possibilities ranging from muteness to a deeply depressive state. Masud Khan proposes that we should in fact distinguish muteness from silence.[40] Muteness, he argues, has a destructive, aggressive, belligerent tone to it, whereas silence is a more benign or at least a more neutral state. An attitude of passivity, inertia and silence could be registered by the psychoanalyst as varying from, at its most negative, muted rage, sullen anger and helpless dependency to, at its most positive, pleasant well-being. Some silences, which were not in any marked way directed against the analyst in a hostile or vicious or vindictive way, demonstrate that the analysand is mired in a deadly depressive state. Sometimes, when the latter is the case, and the analyst suggests to the analysand that he is testing him, provoking him, attacking him with his silences, the analysand may become sullen, his body-tone may flop and he may appear more or less lifeless on the couch.

There are other types of silence in the psychoanalytic session, however, which, far from expressing a force of resistance, are best described as what Christopher Bollas has called 'generative silences'.[41] He specifies that such generative silences may occur when the analysand is experiencing what he calls the 'unthought known', by which he means to refer to a form of knowledge that has not yet been mentally realised, that has not become known in the form of fantasy or dreams, and which yet may so permeate a person's being, may be such a fundamentally guiding and imposing force, that it is articulated through dominant, through perhaps latent, assumptions about modes of human relationships, modes that the analysand simply is in thrall to and takes for granted. There may exist a wish that some day what at the moment is beyond knowing will eventually become known and so become available for psychic redistribution, for example, into an element of memory. When this process of transfer is taking place, the transfer may be registered, Bollas observes, through a 'particular kind of deep silence on the patient's part',[42] and through a struggle within the patient to push forward an internal experience so that it can be thought.

Bollas describes a generative silence of this kind when one particular patient, who ordinarily gesticulated a great deal, moving his hands about frequently, would let his hands flop at his sides or would fold them over his chest. Perhaps he would turn his head to the side and look out of the window, where he might observe a tree. When the patient emerged from such states he would often say how pleasant it was to look out of the window, or he might comment on objects in the room, telling the analyst which painting he liked, for example. These relaxed silences were usually brief, lasting only a few minutes.

Silence is often a necessary condition for the processing of the analysand's internal world. It is an evocative mental process that occurs when the mind is receptive and at rest. Masud Khan has written about this condition; he speaks of this state of rest as 'lying fallow',[43] an accomplishment which is a form of tranquillity and which is essential to the self-analytic function of the analysand. The analyst needs to know that the analysand should be left alone at these times. Winnicott has referred to these moments in the psychoanalytic session as the 'uninterpretative act of the analyst', which is necessary to the development of the analysand's internal development.[44] The analyst here performs much the same function as the mother did with her infant who could not speak but whose moods, gestures and needs were utterances of some kind that needed maternal perception and reception.[45] Or again, one might suggest that the silence of the analysand on those occasions is something like the silence of the small child some ten or twenty minutes before falling asleep. During this special transition period from wakeful life lived in relation to important objects, to unconsciousness and dreams, children will lie in a tranquil state in their beds with their eyes open, imagining features of their life. Sometimes they will be going over events of the day, and there will be a consistent interplay between, on the one hand, gazing at some external object and, on the other hand, contemplating internal objects. A child may look at a toy, may imagine himself for a few minutes to be a space pilot, or may look at a toy rocket and notice that it is damaged. All these wandering reflections may take only a few seconds and over the course of, let us say, twenty minutes the child may muse on many things. This valuable time before sleep is a vital experience for children, and it may last from early infancy through adolescence. In this condition the mind will be musing silently, and the musing will be an aimless lingering among perceptual capacities such as imagining, hearing, touching and remembering. It is in such states that, for the analysand, the more active elements from what Bollas calls the 'unthought known' will arrive in consciousness.

Susan Sontag has remarked upon another positive value which is to be found in silence.[46] Everyone has experienced how, when they are punctuated by long silences, words come to weigh more, how they become, as it were, palpable. And everyone has also experienced how, when one talks less, one begins to feel more fully one's physical presence in a given space. Silence, as Sontag has well put it, undermines 'bad speech', by which she means to say that it undermines dissociated speech: speech, that is to say, that is not organically informed by the sensuous presence, the particularity, of the speaker, and by the individual occasion for using language. When speech has become in this way unanchored from the body, its quality deteriorates. It becomes false, inane, trivial, trite. Silence can inhibit or counteract this tendency towards a deterioration in the quality of speech, because silence gives speech a form of balance, a kind of ballast. One of the most valuable effects of silence is to stop in its tracks the spurious speed of speech as it runs along on automatic pilot into the inauthentic.

Tactful silences, finally, acknowledge *what ought not to be said* in non-cultic contexts and so what helps to avoid offensiveness. The Book of Proverbs in the Old Testament is rich in advice about such silences. There are many counsels of caution which advise against the unfortunate consequences of hasty and unconsidered statements. So it is said that 'Wise men lay up knowledge: but the mouth of the foolish is near destruction',[47] or again 'In the multitude of words there wanteth not sin: but he that refraineth his lips is wise',[48] or yet again 'He that keepeth his mouth keepeth his life, but he that openeth his lips shall have destruction.'[49] Dissimulation, or what was called 'prudent silence', was a primary concern of writers on 'reasons of state' and the art of discretion in the early modern period.[50] This is the conduct recommended by Shakespeare's Polonius, to 'give every man thy ear, and few thy voice'; it is the dissimulation of princes described by the Spanish writer Baltasar Gracián in a famous courtesy book, *El discreto*; and it appears again when Castiglione associates restraint with nobility and prolixity with salesmen and tradesmen. Satow's *Diplomatic Practice* advises diplomats to listen more than they talk, and cautions them against showing off that they are privy to secrets.[51] Recommendations regarding appropriate behaviour are always couched in generalities. Even if tactful persons know how to behave in situations which require particular sensitivity, their knowledge about how to do so is not derived from general principles, since an essential feature of tact is its inexplicitness and inexpressibility.

Turning now to imposed silences, or silencing, we find that the most blatant and brutal form of imposed silence consists in the exercise, or the threat, of physical coercion against the person, a coercion which effectively silences them.[52] Jesus and Socrates are, of course, the most famous examples, although the final effort to silence them seems in both cases to have been as signal a failure as their adherents might have hoped for. The Roman Emperor Trajan laid down the principle that to be a Christian was an offence punishable by death; the Emperor Domitian ordered that the historian Hermogenes be crucified on the grounds that his writing libelled the emperor; and the Holy Roman Emperor Frederick, who reigned between 1220 and 1235, promulgated a decree requiring that all heretics in his dominions in Germany and Italy be outlawed, that those who refused to recant be burned, that those who recanted be imprisoned, and that if they relapsed they be executed. Giordano Bruno, who constructed a religious philosophy based partly on Epicurus, was burned in Rome in 1600; between 1660 and 1756 some 870 prisoners were confined to the Bastille for violations of censorship laws; Strauss was rewarded for his *Life of Jesus*, which entirely rejected belief in the supernatural, with the deprivation of his professorship at Tubingen; and Renan, who also rejected belief in the supernatural, lost his chair at the Collège de France as a penalty for his *Life of Jesus*.

Haunted by shame and fear lest their experience become public, victims of rape frequently remain silent about the crime inflicted upon them.[53] Maya Angelou has narrated a dramatic account of one such fate: raped as an eight-year-old by an adult friend of the family, she was persuaded to reveal his name; within hours of sentencing, the man was murdered; and then, believing that she had caused his death, she sequestered herself in virtual muteness from which she only fully emerged many years later.[54] In writing her autobiography, Harriet Jacobs broke a profound cultural silence about white male sexual coercion of slave women and the collusion of their white mistresses in the sexual exploitation of their enslaved sisters.[55] Again, the unwritten rule of *omerta*, the wall of silent complicity presented to the outside world in general and to criminal investigations in particular, is applied by the Mafia with particular force to the world of women.[56] It is true that, faced with the terrible loss of a murdered husband or son, women occasionally decide to collaborate with the authorities. But they pay a high price for this; those who break the tacit law of silence risk their lives and the lives of the people they love, and find themselves alone, isolated by their neighbours and by the people of the neighbourhood.

Short of direct, personal physical coercion, book burnings have been a favoured form for seeking to impose silence.[57] Protagoras, one of the greatest of the Sophists, had copies of his work *On the Gods* burned when he sought in that text to demonstrate that we cannot know the gods by reason. In Acts 19:19, St Paul endorsed book burning as an act of faith. The Emperor Augustus codified a law which legitimated public book burnings. A decree of Pope Gregory IX in 1239 ordered that all copies of the Talmud be burned; wagonloads of Talmud manuscripts were seized and burned by order of King Louis IX of France in 1242, and similar spoliation spread from Rome through northern Italy in 1533 and again in Poland in 1757. If you were a resident of Geneva and wrote books disagreeing with Calvin's theology you would have to throw all available copies of your writings into the fire with your own hands. The books of Hobbes were burned in the reign of Charles II. Rousseau's *Emile* was publicly burned in Paris and his *Social Contract* was burned in Geneva. Roquain lists 368 titles of books condemned to the fire between 1715 and 1798. The choice of these books showed particularly refined judgement: they include the thoughts of Pascal, Voltaire, Diderot, D'Holbach, Montaigne and Beaumarchais.

After book burning, censorship sought to impose silence.[58] When printing destroyed the church's monopoly over texts, an Index of the Inquisition of Rome published the first list of prohibited books and authors in 1545. Admittedly, the strategy sometimes backfired. The fame of Montaigne, Copernicus, Galileo, Kepler, Bayle, Swift, Voltaire and Montesquieu was secured by the Index. Indeed, the publication of the Index was so ambiguous in its effect that the church found it necessary to outlaw lay possession of copies of the 'Index Liborum Haereticorum' (a catalogue of the proscribed titles prepared annually) because booksellers found it such an invaluable guide in locating the titles which would be in greatest demand on the illegal market in the coming year. But at least the Inquisition virtually destroyed the book trade in Spain and Portugal, and even in an open city like Venice, dealing in illicit texts became a capital crime. Within a year of its publication in 1751, volume 1 of the *Encyclopédie* was ordered to be suppressed and the printing of volume 2 was prohibited by a decree of the king's council. Dissimulation, double entendre and satiric irreverence are so closely identified with French literary style that we tend to forget that they have their genesis in persecution.

Persecution has indeed in some cases refined the art of writing. The twentieth century saw many attempts to silence oppositional voices by censorship. Although the Korean War of 1950–3 was as brutal as the Vietnam War and its casualties almost as high, events such as the massacre of hundreds of civilians perpetrated by American troops were made public in newspapers only many years later.[59] The film *Octobre à Paris*, directed by Jacques Panijel in 1962, which deals with those who had survived the French massacre of Algerians in the repression of October 1961, was banned for the following ten years. The suspension of regular TV and radio programmes was applied in Poland in December 1981. Despite perestroika, in 1989 the centrally controlled Soviet press remained silent about several world events of international importance, including the fatwah against Salman Rushdie and the massacre by the Chinese government of student opposition in Tiananmen Square. The government of the United Kingdom maintained long-term censorship of the BBC coverage of hostilities in Northern Ireland, and imposed censorship of both print and electronic media during the invasion of the Falkland Islands in 1982.[60]

A distinctive method of silencing by censorship, practised in ancient Rome and superbly analysed by Charles Hedrick, was the institution known as *damnatio memoriae*.[61] It requires a prohibition of respectful observance at funerals, the eradication of visual representations of the person, and a ban on the use of the name. Roman authors of all periods describe the *damnatio memoriae* as an attempt to eradicate memory. The Theodosian Code refers to the *damnatio memoriae* as an 'interdict of silence'. From the time of Constantine onwards unsuccessful pretenders to the imperial throne were routinely described as 'tyrants' in public documents and their names were not mentioned, even though anyone who chanced upon an allusion to them would know who was meant; Augustus in his *Res Gestae* refers to some of his enemies without using their names, as when he claims to have raised an army to free the republic from what he calls the 'tyranny of a faction', where Cassius and Brutus are not mentioned by name, but are nonetheless clearly implied in the reference to 'those who assassinated my relative'; and Tacitus tells us that historians were not permitted to use certain names, such as Cremutius Cordus, Arulenus Rusticus and Herennius Senecio. The institution of *damnatio memoriae* entailed a paradox. Tacitus noticed this, and drew attention to it repeatedly. The paradox operates in the following manner. To attempt to forget something consciously, by not referring to it, requires that one think of the thing, and to think of the thing is the opposite of forgetting it. If one must continually remember not to mention a person, then one is not forgetting that person. When we are told to remember to forget, we are in effect being told to remember what is supposedly forgotten. *Damnatio memoriae* produced significant silences, particularly powerful and resonant signs. It works to preserve rather than to annihilate; it does not so much *destroy* memories as *dishonour* them. Tacitus was correct, therefore, to insist not only that memory will persist in the face of political repression, but that political repression will actually strengthen the persistence of memory.

More painful and profound than the significant silences of *damnatio memoriae* are traumatised silences: more painful and profound because a crucial feature of traumatic experience is the element of delay. It retards us. It takes time, sometimes a considerable amount of time, to digest. In *The Burden of Our Time*, written in 1951, Hannah Arendt wrote that understanding genocide was the burden bequeathed to the twentieth century.[62] Her argument began to be acknowledged only much later; before monuments of memory were built to the Shoah, a long period of silence had to be lived through. Kenzaburo Oe, in his notes on the city of Hiroshima written in 1965, says that even twenty years after the bomb fell many of those he interviewed were unable to speak of what happened on that day.[63] On the basis of her interviews with children of Holocaust survivors, Nadine Fresco has described with great sensitivity the silence that had swallowed up their past.[64] Even if their parents might be able to share their experiences with other survivors, a mutually protective collusion of silence separated parents and children. Sometimes the silence assumed the misleading form of a verbose carapace, all the more implacable because it concealed what had occurred behind a screen of words, always the same words, a tale repeated over and over again, constructed out of selective anecdotes from the period of the war. Or the world of silence might be interrupted occasionally by clues to a drama, all the more tantalising because the child was forbidden to hear an explicit account of the drama which might have aided them to reach a better understanding of it. But parents explained nothing and children asked nothing. Children feared to ask for answers to the question which they dared not ask their parents. Parents transmitted to their children only the wound, but refused them the memory. Children grew up in the ambience of the unspeakable.

Closely related to traumatised silences are others, sometimes difficult to discriminate from them, in the sense that they originate in deeply shocking and painful experiences. We might term these narrative silences, since they signify the refusal or inability to tell certain narratives. Camus was alert to the existence of such silences. Shortly after the end of the Second World War, in his essay 'Neither Victims nor Executioners', he wrote that 'the years we have gone through have killed something in us. And that something is simply the old confidence man had in himself, which led him to believe that he could always elicit human reactions from another man if he spoke to him in the language of a common humanity.'[65] The consequence, he argued, was that 'a vast conspiracy of silence has spread all about us, a conspiracy accepted by those who are frightened and who rationalise their fears in order to hide them from themselves'. Both in *The Plague* (1947) and in *The Fall* (1956) he returned to the theme of silence in allegorical form. In *The Plague* he writes of those who refused to tell the story of the plague; 'Calmly they denied', he wrote, 'in the teeth of evidence, that we had ever known a crazy world in which men were killed off like flies . . . they denied that we had ever been that hag-ridden populace a part of which was daily fed into a furnace and went up in oily fumes.'[66] Again in *The Fall* he turned to the wish to minimise the Holocaust by the suppression of information and by silence.

Contrasting with the twelve years of Nazi power in Germany, a time span of many decades moulded the character of recollection and oblivion in the Soviet Union. It had been dangerous to remember since at least the 1920s. Misery was literally driven underground. Millions of manila files were preserved in the miles of underground corridors beneath military buildings, where the public had no access to them and little knowledge of their existence and extent; and the secret police often concealed mass graves by planting trees over them. For half a century, until the fall of Communism, many families had been deprived of even the minimal comfort of telling their stories, instead keeping their bereavements to themselves, some hiding their pain even from their children, for fear of the damage that might be unleashed by an unwary revelation. Those who had fallen victim to the first wave of repression in the 1920s – members of the so-called 'exploiter classes', former aristocrats and White officers, later the Social Democrats and the social revolutionaries, and later still the Trotskyites – were, as a rule, unable to emerge from the Gulag system before the 1950s. Among Stalin's former prisoners that threat of re-arrest was palpable enough to reinforce silence for several decades after 1956. Nobody could be sure whether Khrushchev's thaw would last; there was an apprehension, well founded as it turned out, that it might be brief and followed by further repression.

Under Stalin even the telling of anecdotes had been a possible justification for arrest. One informant recalls that in Stalin's time people did not cry; within me, she says, there had always been some sort of internal prohibition against crying which comes from that time. When we travelled in a crowded tram, another reported, I knew I had to remain silent and sensed that everybody felt the same way. Even in the home it was perilous to talk about relations who had been arrested because, it was said, 'the walls have ears'. People destroyed incriminating letters and photographs and hid them from their children. The oral historian Irina Sherbakova reports that with her informants in the 1970s, she constantly used to find that they became instantly silent when they saw her tape recorder.[67] In the Kuban, Daria Khubova, who was undertaking interviews for Memorial (an organisation in the then Soviet Union, with branches in many cities, established for the purpose of coordinating oral history interviews which would excavate the repressed history of the Stalinist era), found that many people would refuse to be interviewed, saying 'No, I'm not going to speak. In case things change, I'm not going to say anything.'[68] When approached by oral history interviewers, it often transpired that people had not had any opportunity to speak openly about their experiences for more than fifty years.

Although Memorial is an organisation on a scale infinitely larger than any oral history society in the West – an organisation with perhaps 5,000 members in Moscow, 5,000 in Leningrad and 15,000 in Lvov in western Ukraine – great secrecy remained in the early 1990s about whether there were copies of their material in one person's house, and duplicates somewhere else. For decades people lived in an acoustics of paranoia and a society of whisperers. One informant, recalling her childhood in the 1920s, said that if her parents needed to talk about something important, they would always go outside the house and speak to one another in whispers. Another reports that after three years spent living on the run, she and her sister had grown accustomed to not talking; we had learned, she said, to whisper rather than talk. A husband, terrified of his neighbours in the next room, reminded his wife: 'whisper or we shall be arrested'. Time and again, Anna Akhmatova and Nadezhda Mandelstam speak of Russians whispering. In any event, there is an interesting contrast in the perception of Stalin's crimes and the perception of Hitler's crimes. The victorious powers at Nuremberg could photograph and film the thousands of bodies found at Bergen-Belsen. But we have only a handful of rare archival photographs of the Gulags, and there are no photographs of the kulakisation. Terror in the Communist world was organised in strict secrecy. In a media-saturated society, where the photographed or televised image is seen as the witness of truth, this disparity conduced for a long time to the relative silence about Stalin's terror by comparison with that exercised by the Nazis.

If those born after the war were to rely on the testimony of writers, they would scarcely have been able to form any idea of the extent, nature and consequences of the devastation inflicted on Germany. The legacy of unparalleled humiliation felt by millions never found written expression. Those directly affected by the experience neither shared it with each other nor passed it on to the next generation. No German writer, with the exception of Nossack, put precise facts down on paper about the progress and repercussions of this gigantic, long-term campaign of destruction. Of all the literary works written at the end of the 1940s, probably only Heinrich Böll's *Der Engel Schwieg* ('The Angel was Silent') conveys some sense of the depths of horror visited upon anyone who looked at the landscape of ruins; and significantly, this text was published only half a century later, in 1992. Even German historians had not, fifty years later, produced a comprehensive study of the subject. The question of whether the bombing campaign could be strategically or morally justified was never the subject of open debate in Germany. Memory was silenced by experiences so far exceeding the tolerable.[69]

Spain after the Civil War also suffered from an unmentionable history, even if of a less devastating kind.[70] Throughout the period of Franco's dictatorship, the vanquished who remained in Spain, their families, widows, orphans and the disabled, were denied the relief of expressing their grief publicly. Many autobiographical accounts of growing up in Republican families speak of the almost unbroken silence about the past. The ideals which had animated the Republican forces were taboo. Almost nothing of the revolutionary achievements of the Civil War period were imparted to those who came to adulthood in the post-war period, who found it virtually impossible to discover what had happened, even from parents and grandparents. As in Russia, the vanquished remained silent in order to protect their families, particularly their children, for fear that, outside the relative safety of the home, they might speak of what they had heard of their parents' experiences in the war, or of their criticism of the dictatorship.

History, indeed, is drenched in such narrative silences.[71] No mention was ever made in eastern Europe after the Second World War of the sufferings of national, ethnic or religious minorities, whether at the hands of Russians, Germans or the local population. In a short history of the Communist Party, Trotsky's role as commander of the Red Army vanishes, his election as president of the Supreme Soviet in September 1917 disappears, and Lenin's praise of him in October 1917 is obliterated. The massacre of over a million Armenians in Turkey was followed by over sixty years of complete silence on the part of the Turks; in the highly learned *Cambridge History of Islam*, which dedicated 170 pages to Turkey and the Ottoman Empire, no mention is made of the Armenian massacres in the section written by Turkish historians. European historical writing remains largely silent about Russian history before the time of Peter the Great, that is to say before the moment at which Russia was 'Europeanised'. Much attention is paid in Spanish history textbooks to the conquest of Mexico and Peru, but no mention is made of the extermination of the Native South Americans. In Indian school histories little is said of the Arabs and Turks, or of the Persians and Afghans, all of whom were constant predators upon the subcontinent; while Indianisation in Cambodia, Java and Sumatra is always represented as a spontaneous adoption of the Indian way of life, rather than, as it was in reality, the exertion of Indian influence by means of force. Although black African historians justifiably record the crimes committed against their ancestors by European occupiers, they hesitate, most probably out of shame, to write about the crimes committed by the Arabs who castrated thousands of their men and deprived them of their progeny.

The refusal or inability to reconstruct certain narratives often leaves its mark in what might be called terminological silences. Indeed, it might be possible to undertake a systematic exploration of the restriction upon what may be talked about and of those things that are consigned to the sphere of the 'not-said'. For if keywords provide a rich access to a culture's structure of feeling, the itinerary of its silences may also offer a fertile, if more intractable access to its preoccupations. For the power to silence others resides not simply in the power to prevent them from talking; it lies also in the power to shape and control the talking that they do, to restrict the things they may talk about and, more specifically, the ways in which they are permitted to express their thoughts. As Shoshana Felman has said, this type of silence is 'not a simple absence of an act of speech, but a positive avoidance – an erasure – of one's hearing, the positive *assertion* of a deafness, in the refusal not merely to know but to *acknowledge* ... what is being heard or witnessed'.[72]

In Russia, for example, the denial of the fact of mass death during the Stalin period meant that the word 'starvation' was banned in 1932; and the ability to conceive of the narrative of an individual life as that of a moral life had become so attenuated by the 1930s that the word 'conscience' had gone out of public use; it was no longer current in newspapers, books or schools, since its function had been taken over first by 'class feeling' and later by 'the good of the state'. As in this case, silence about one unmentionable word leads to its replacement by another word. The English seem to have remained for a long time embarrassed by the political upheaval of the mid-seventeenth century, preferring to refer to it as a 'civil war' rather than a 'revolution'; indeed, the present writer remembers the pleasant alienation effect he experienced on discovering as a student that he could attend a course of lectures given by an eminent historian on 'the coming of the English revolution'. Again, in Jane Austen's *Mansfield Park* Thomas Bertram's overseas possessions provide his wealth, occasion his absences from England and establish his status at home; but Fanny Price reminds her cousin that after asking Sir Thomas Bertram about the slave trade, 'there was such a dead silence'[73] as to suggest that one world could not be connected with the other, since there was no common language for both. Yet again, 'in the United States', according to the historian Richard W. Van Alstyne in *The Rising American Empire*, 'it is almost heresy to describe the nation as an empire'.[74] Again, the documents produced by the British imperial government in India were contingent on reasons of state, intended primarily for administrative use: that is to say, for the information of the government and for the determination of its policy; they made sense only in terms of a code of pacification.[75] Refusing to ascribe conscious will and design to the subaltern group, they assimilated peasant revolts to natural phenomena: these were said to break out like thunderstorms, to heave like earthquakes, to spread like wildfires, to infect like epidemics.

Sartre's *Réflexions sur la question juive*, published in 1946, launches a polemic against anti-Semites, yet he neglects to mention, even in one word, the Holocaust.[76] Or yet again, we might consider the case of France, when from November 1954 until March 1962, French troops fought in Algeria to keep Algeria a part of France; when there were permanently 500,000 young conscript soldiers from France in Algeria; when the war cost 35,000 French soldiers their lives; and when the end of the war saw the departure for France of one million French people who thought life in Algeria would be impossible for them under the new regime. French society never felt that the Algerian war was a fully legitimate one. After all, were the methods of French soldiers in Algeria so very different from those of German soldiers during the occupation of 1940–4? Because of the feeling of shame which never left it, the Algerian war disappeared from French collective memory. More still: in France the conflict was never officially acknowledged to be a war at all. It was an unnamed war, referred to, if it had to be referred to at all, as an 'operation to maintain public order'.[77] A generation later, the publication of the multi-volume work *Lieux de mémoire*, edited by Pierre Nora, enables us to gauge the extent of this massive ellipsis. Forty-four distinguished French historians contributed to this collective enterprise, but, although there is a chapter on Vichy, not a single chapter is devoted to Algeria. Algeria is not a 'place of memory'.

Or yet again: an almost mute generation of parents was silent about the German past. In 1983, the philosopher Hermann Lübbe delivered a widely discussed speech in the Berlin Reichstag, in which he argued that, after the downfall of the Third Reich, the transformation of the German population into the citizenry of the new Republic took place in an atmosphere of what he called 'a certain silence', and with a 'silence treatment' being allocated to the brown-shirted elements in people's life stories. This silence, he argued, 'was the sociopsychologically and politically necessary medium of transformation': necessary because, although the new state could be constituted in opposition to Nazi ideology, it could not possibly have been firmly grounded in opposition to the majority of the German people.[78] Even in the 1980s when the children of that generation came to be interviewed about the immediate post-war years, some claimed that immediately after the end of the Second World War the word 'Hitler' did not exist; others claimed that nothing was learned about the concentration camps at school; and others, who were by then in their sixties and seventies, still could not bring themselves to utter the term 'concentration camps' or the word 'exterminated', opting instead to speak of 'work camps'. In the 1950s and 1960s, whenever Germans referred to the Nazi period, they acknowledged the existence of the Third Reich only elliptically, by referring to it as 'damals' ('then').

Then, finally, there is the silence of the dying.[79] The mere sight of the dying shakes the defences which people try to construct like a barrier to protect themselves from having to face the fact of their own inevitable death. The embarrassment that is so often experienced in the presence of those who are dying causes those who have to witness that slow process to become hesitant and uncertain about what they might appropriately say to the dying person. So the dying come to form a population of the deserted even while they are still alive. A silence spreads around the dying as the living withdraw from them. Never before in the history of humanity have those who are dying been removed so hygienically from the scenes of everyday life. Never before have the dying lived in conditions of such solitude. Many old people's homes are deserts of loneliness.

There is a type of depression which is frequently found among those who are dying, one which, like so many states of depression, is a silent condition.[80] In this state the dying person is unlikely to be stirred any longer by news or problems from the outside world. Most probably they will be exhausted and no longer feel talkative. They may now want the television to be shut off. They will often be grateful if those who still bother to visit them simply sit quietly with them. In this state of preparatory grief, when the dying person is losing everything he or she loves, there is little need any more for words. It is now better if relatives or nurses who sit with the dying person comfort them with a touch of the hand, a stroking of the hair, or just simply by the sharing which the act of sitting silently together gives. The dying patient will be reassured now, not by futile words, but by the holding of a hand or by a look. The dying person may wish to sit in silence, a silence which means far more than words. You could even say that this is the therapy of silence. And then, finally, within the everyday continuing setting in which there are heard the sounds of the nursing staff preoccupied with their occupations, there is the sound, a sound like no other, of the newly dead.

The distinction between intentional silences and imposed silences is a contrast between ideal types. It follows that in any particular case we may encounter mixed or hybrid forms. This is particularly so in the case of intentional silences. Australian Aboriginal sign language is intentional; but since the primary circumstance promoting the elaboration of such sign language is found in the existence of extended speech taboos, the language contains an impositional component. The silence of upper-class girls in Burundi when they meet members of other families is intentional, since careless talk might give away what, for considerations of strategy and bargaining, they do not wish to disclose; but the fact that they receive elaborate training in the art of evasiveness implies an element of subjection on their part. Pausanias' silences in his *Guide to Greece* are intentional; but once again they contain an impositional component in the sense that he declares himself not at liberty to impart certain details of cult interest. Nevertheless, and with this general proviso having been made, the overall distinction between silence on the one hand and silencing on the other obtains.

NOTES

1 M. Miyoshi, *Accomplices of Silence: The Modern Japanese Novel* (Berkeley, 1974), p. xv.
2 C.K. Ogden and I.A. Richards, *The Meaning of Meaning* (London, 1923), p. 11.
3 B. Malinowski, 'Phatic Communion', in J. Laver and S. Hutcheson, eds., *Communication in Face to Face Interaction* (Harmondsworth, 1972), pp. 150–1.
4 M.M. Bakhtin, *Rabelais and his World* (Cambridge, MA, 1968).
5 H. Mayhew, *London Labour and the London Poor*, 4 vols (London, 1967).
6 A. Gregory, *The Silence of Memory: Armistice Day 1919–1946* (Oxford, 1994).
7 A number of these quotations are to be found in R. Flesch, ed., *The Book of Unusual Quotations* (New York, 1957), p. 350.
8 For an extended discussion of enabling and disabling silences, see P. Valesio, *Ascoltare il silenzio: la retorica come teoria* (Bologna, 1986).
9 I borrow the terms 'fore-silences' and 'after-silences' from B.P. Dauenhauer, *Silence* (Bloomington, 1985).
10 See, for an extended consideration of this, P. Laurence, *The Reading of Silence: Virginia Woolf and the English Tradition* (Stanford, CA, 1991).
11 P. Burke, 'Notes for a Social History of Silence in Early Modern Europe', in *The Art of Conversation* (Cambridge, 1993), pp. 123–41.
12 See in particular A. Portelli, 'The Peculiarities of Oral History', *History Workshop*, xii (1981), pp. 96–107; L. Passerini, 'Memories Between Silence and Oblivion', in K. Hodgkin and S. Radstone, eds., *Contested Pasts: The Politics of Memory* (London and New York, 2003), pp. 238–54.
13 A.L. Kroeber, 'Sign Language Inquiry', in A.J. Umiker-Sebeok and T.A. Sebeok, eds., *Aboriginal Sign Language of the Americas and Australia. Vol. 1* (New York and London, 1978), p. 196.
14 R. Barakat, *Cistercian Sign Language* (Kalamazoo, MI, 1975).
15 A. Kendon, *Sign Languages of Aboriginal Australia* (Cambridge, 1988).
16 L. West, 'The Sign Language: An Analysis', 2 vols, PhD thesis, Ann Arbor, 1960.
17 G. Mallery, 'Introduction to the Study of Sign Language among the North American Indians as Illustrating the Gesture Speech of Mankind', in Umiker-Sebeok and Sebeok, *Aboriginal Sign Language*, pp. 1–76.
18 G. Mensching, *Vergleichende Religionswissenschaft*, 2nd edn (Heidelberg, 1949).
19 R. Otto, *The Idea of the Holy* (London, 1936).
20 Quoted in H. Waddell, tr., *The Sayings of the Desert Fathers* (London, 1936).
21 On eremitic movements, see D.J. Chitty, *The Desert a City* (Oxford, 1966); A. Louth, *The Wilderness of God* (London, 1991); P. France, *Hermits* (London, 1996).
22 P. Leigh Fermor, *A Time to Keep Silence* (London, 1957).
23 Cited in R. Bauman, *Let Your Words Be Few* (Cambridge, 1983), pp. 21, 22, 23.
24 St Ignatius Loyola, *Spiritual Exercises* (tr. C. Seager, London, 1860).
25 D. Foccardi, 'Religious Silence and Reticence in Pausanias', in M.G. Ciani, ed., *Regions of Silence: Studies in the Difficulty of Communication* (Amsterdam, 1987), pp. 67–113.
26 M. Eliade, *Patterns in Comparative Religion* (London, 1958), p. 216.
27 Otto, *The Idea of the Holy*, p. 69.
28 E. Burke, *A Philosophical Enquiry into the Origin of Our Ideas of the Sublime and Beautiful* (Harmondsworth, 1998), p. 113.

29 Quoted in E.S. Casey, *Representing Place: Landscape Painting and Maps* (Minneapolis and London, 2002), p. 20.

30 B. Novak, *Nature and Culture: American Landscape and Painting, 1825–1875* (Oxford, 1980), p. 43.

31 See Casey, *Representing Place*, pp. 60–73 for an extensive discussion of *The Oxbow*.

32 T. Cole, 'Essay on American Scenery', repr. in J. McCoubrey, ed., *American Art, 1700–1960* (Englewood Cliffs, NJ, 1965).

33 J. Tanizaki, *In Praise of Shadows* (tr. T.J. Harper and E. Seidensticker, London, 2001), pp. 32–3.

34 *Ibid.*, p. 33.

35 S. Tomes, *Out of Silence: A Pianist's Yearbook* (Woodbridge, 2010), pp. 115–16.

36 *Ibid.*, p. 26.

37 R. Sennett, *The Craftsman* (London, 2009).

38 Tomes, *Out of Silence*, pp. 228–9.

39 Quoted in P. Gay, *Freud, Jews, and Other Germans: Masters of Modernist Culture* (New York, 1978), pp. 55–6.

40 M.M.R. Khan, 'On Lying Fallow', in *Hidden Selves: Between Theory and Practice in Psychoanalysis* (London, 1983).

41 C. Bollas, *The Shadow of the Object: Psychoanalysis of the Unthought Known* (London, 1987), p. 267.

42 *Ibid.*, p. 263.

43 Khan, 'On Lying Fallow'.

44 D.W. Winnicott, 'Playing: A Theoretical Statement', in *Playing and Reality* (London, 1971).

45 Bollas, *The Shadow of the Object*, p. 235.

46 S. Sontag, 'The Aesthetics of Silence', in *Styles of Radical Will* (New York, 1966).

47 Proverbs 10:10.

48 Proverbs 10:14.

49 Proverbs 18:19.

50 Burke, 'Notes for a Social History of Silence', pp. 123–41.

51 I. Richards, ed., *Satow's Diplomatic Practice* (Oxford, 2009).

52 On physical coercion against the person as silencing, see J.B. Bury, *History of Freedom of Thought* (London, 1913).

53 S. Brownmiller, *Against Our Will: Men, Women and Rape* (New York, 1975).

54 A.V. Ettin, *Speaking Silences: Stillness and Voice in Modern Thought and Jewish Tradition* (Charlottesville, VA, 1994), p. 99.

55 See H.L. Gates, Jr., 'Introduction', in Gates, ed., *The Classic Slave Narratives* (New York, 1987); J.F. Yellin, 'Written by Herself: Harriet Jacobs' Slave Narrative', *American Literature*, 53.3 (1981), pp. 479–86.

56 L. Passerini, 'Introduction', in Passerini, ed., *International Yearbook of Oral History and Life Studies. Vol. 1: Memory and Totalitarianism* (Oxford, 1992), pp. 1–20.

57 On book burnings, see Bury, *History of Freedom of Thought*.

58 S.C. Jansen, *Censorship: The Knot that Binds Power to Knowledge* (London, 1991).

59 Passerini, 'Memories Between Silence and Oblivion', pp. 238–54.

60 A. Jaworski, *Power and Silence* (London, 1993).

61 C.W. Hedrick, *History and Silence: Rehabilitation and Purge in Late Antiquity* (Austin, TX, 2000).

62 H. Arendt, *The Burden of Our Time* (New York, 1951).

63 K. Oe, *Hiroshima Notes* (New York and London, 1997).

64 N. Fresco, 'Remembering the Unknown', *International Review of Psychoanalysis*, 11 (1984), pp. 417–27.

65 Cited by S. Felman and D. Laub, eds., *Testimony: Crises of Witnessing in Literature, Psychoanalysis and History* (London, 1992), p. 117.

66 A. Camus, *The Plague* (tr. S. Gilbert, New York, 1972), pp. 276–7.

67 I. Sherbakova, 'The Gulag in Memory', in L. Passerini, ed., *Memory and Totalitarianism* (Oxford, 1992), pp. 103–16.

68 D. Khubova, A. Ivankiev and T. Sharova, 'After Glasnost: Oral History in the Soviet Union', in Passerini, *Memory and Totalitarianism*, pp. 89–102.

69 On German silence after 1945, see W.G. Sebald, *On the Natural History of Destruction* (Toronto, 2003).

70 M. Richards, *A Time of Silence: Civil War and the Culture of Repression in Franco's Spain 1936–1945* (Cambridge, 1998).

71 For a global survey of narrative silences in historical accounts, and the source for much of this paragraph, see M. Ferro, *The Use and Abuse of History: Or How the Past is Taught to Children* (London and New York, 1984).

72 Felman and Laub, *Testimony*, p. 183.

73 J. Austen, *Mansfield Park* (ed. T. Tanner, Hammondsworth, 1966), p. 213.

74 R.W. Van Alstyne, *The Rising American Empire* (New York, 1974), p. 6.

75 R. Guha, 'The Prose of Counter-Insurgency', in R. Guha and G. Chakravorty Spivak, eds., *Selected Subaltern Studies* (New York and Oxford, 1988), pp. 45–88.

76 J-P. Sartre, *Réflexions sur la question juive* (Paris, 1946).

77 A. Prost, 'The Algerian War in French Collective Memory', in J. Winter and S. Sivan, eds., *War and Remembrance in the Twentieth Century* (Cambridge, 1999).

78 H. Lübbe, 'Der Nationalsozialismus im politischen Bewusstsein der Gegenwart', in M. Broszat *et al.*, eds., *Deutschlands Weg in die Diktatur: Internationale Konferenz sur nationalsozialistischen Machtübernahme im Reichtagsgebäude zu Berlin* (Berlin, 1983).

79 N. Elias, *The Loneliness of the Dying* (Oxford, 1985).

80 E. Kübler-Ross, *On Death and Dying* (London, 1973).

4   Spatial orientation

The body's orientation is patterned by four dyads, and these are cultural universals. All four dyads – above/below, right/left, front/behind, inside/ outside – are omnipresent and can never be wholly forgotten by us. The body's morphology is transferred and transformed onto topographical structurings of symbolic classification, and these classifications are decoded and can be read back, because they have their matrix in a set of oppositions located in the human body. Human spatial memory is so powerful because it has this bodily self-aware frame of reference; the primary set of relationships within the network of places is the relationship between these topographic features and the person.

With respect to each of the categorical oppositions just passed in review – above/below, right/left, front/behind, inside/outside – it is possible to generate a wide variety of culturally diverse symbolic classifications *which are in all cases precipitated by* and *refer back to* the physical differentiation universally given by the morphology of the human body. In every case it is possible to represent the binary classifications so produced in a two-column schema, listing the oppositions in what is analysed as a dual symbolic classification. This is a mnemonic device, bringing together in a coherent fashion a series of oppositions.

All these oppositions are not, of course, as coherent a total arrangement of oppositions as they have sometimes been thought to be. There is a powerful temptation to map one binary opposition onto another, as, for example, when the opposition man/woman is misleadingly mapped onto the binary opposition culture/nature. This misleading mapping appears in European culture when verticality has been valorised. European culture has tended to conflate differentiations marked out upon a scale of verticality with the perception of differences between different types or categories as such. It has been assumed that, since 'above' is valorised by contrast to 'below', what is 'different' has been considered to be different in the sense of being 'above' or 'below' that from which it is different. The conflation of variations along a vertical dimension with variations along a dimension of differences in type or category has led to deep and long-lasting misperceptions with regard to the facts or person so categorised.

Yet, paradoxically, what is a *defect* when viewed from the perspective of categorical mapping turns out to be an *advantage* when viewed from the perspective of those categorical mappings considered as systems of mnemonic devices. It is a mistake to suppose that one set of binary oppositions can simply be mapped onto another set of oppositions. But these false 'mappings', these 'over-mappings', as it were, have had a cultural 'surplus-value' when the oppositions operate as mnemonic systems. From the vantage point of anyone who remembers with the aid of this cascade of categories, misleading 'over-mappings' actually *reinforce* the cultural value of the oppositions *as mnemonic devices.*

The mnemonic scheme works so effectively because the system of places with which it operates is constituted differently from the coordinate system employed in geometrical space. For there is a salient feature which all four dyads have in common. As Edward Casey has observed, it is impossible to specify, with respect to any of them, a straightforwardly singular location, whereas the specification of singular locations is a feature intrinsic to geometrical space.[1] That is to say, I am unable to state, of any of the binary terms contained in the dyads, either that they are to be found situated in my body, or that they are to be found in the world surrounding my body. What is 'above' exceeds my body, since it might include, for instance, the ceiling of the room I am in; but I can grasp this phenomenon of something being 'above' only because my head is intuitively felt to be above the rest of my body, so that 'above' always includes my body. What is to the 'right' of me may be, for example, the perceived character of part of the room where I am presently located; but it is also part of my own body, my right side. And the area 'behind' me is back there in some zone of the unseen; but it is also my own back. The locus of these dyads is both *in my body* and *in the world surrounding my body.* It follows that the orientations which these dyads yield – and so the power of the mnemonic systems they generate – are not points or positions in geometrical space; rather, they are relationships of my lived body towards things, relationships which are constituted through the interplay between my acting body and the world of places upon which my body acts.

The point that these dyads are located both in our bodies and in the world surrounding our bodies returns us to Kant's essay of 1768 on the 'ultimate ground of the differentiation of regions in space', where he sought to demonstrate, at least with respect to the first three dyads, that this ultimate ground, the source of spatial orientation, is located in the body. Things in the world of places would not be endowed with the quality of directionality if they were considered merely as occupying positions relative to each other, because without the body's role in the interconnection between bodies and life-spaces

material entities would simply not be oriented: they would lack the directionality of above and below, right and left, front and behind – or, we might add,
inside and outside. To perceive things as oriented in regions and places
presumes the pregiven fact that our bodies are always already constituted
with directionality. The true basis of orientation and directionality in space,
therefore, is our own oriented body. Only because we experience our bodies
as always already composed of asymmetrical counterparts are we able to
constitute and remember the life-spaces in which we are emplaced as oriented
in certain directions. It is from and with our directed bodies that we are able to
constitute the directedness that makes regions and places configured in
distinctive, and therefore memorable, ways.

This crucial fact is relevant to the ancient insight that memory is dependent
on topography. The so-called 'art of memory' was located within the great
system of rhetoric that dominated classical culture, was reborn in the Middle
Ages, flourished during the Renaissance, and only entered upon its demise
during the period from the invention of printing to the turn of the eighteenth
century.[2] Cicero gave a succinct statement of its operative principle. 'Persons
desiring to train this faculty of memory', he writes, 'must select places and
form mental images of the things they wish to remember and store those images
in the places, so that the order of the places will preserve the order of the
things.'[3] Accordingly, this 'art of memory' was described as a 'method of loci'.
A locus is definable as a place easily grasped by the memory, such as a house,
arch, corner, column or intercolumnar space. The loci or places in question can
be actually perceived or they can be simply imagined. The real or imagined
place or set of places functions as a grid on which the images of the items to be
remembered are placed in a certain order; and the items are then remembered
by mentally revisiting the grid of places and traversing them step by step,
always in a particular sequence. The premise of the whole system is that the
order of the places will preserve the order of the things that have to be
remembered. The art of memory relies essentially on a stable system of places.

But why speak of memory and the *body's* topography? The term is in itself
ambiguous, and intentionally so. For it might be taken to mean that the
culturally specific topography into which we are inserted and which we daily
or occasionally negotiate is imprinted on our memories, frequently more
indelibly than we might imagine or even wish to acknowledge. Or it might
be taken to mean that the structure of the human body itself has its own
specific morphology, its own distinctive topography, and that our acts of
remembering are ineluctably bound up with this culturally universal circumstance. In speaking of the body's topography I mean to underline both of these
possible senses of the phrase. Topography, the disposition of places around
us, exists as a mnemonic *for* the body, and it exists as a mnemonic also *by
virtue of the fact* of the body's own topography.

The two meanings interlock. And they do so in an important sense; for I wish to highlight a mnemonic function of places which the 'art-of-memory' tradition, though it understood itself as a 'method of loci', failed to theorise or reflect sufficiently upon. The art of memory was considered by its practitioners as a *cognitive* achievement and a cognitive performance. But I wish to focus on humanity's enormous *libidinal*, or affective, investment in topography. The art-of-memory tradition failed to theorise this particular feature because it thought of its method as an intellectual or cognitive or heuristic device, a stratagem consciously adopted, as the occasion required, as a mnemonic aid. In so doing the art-of-memory tradition neglected the *affective investment in life-spaces* and the repercussions of that affectivity for cultural memory.

Bodily orientation is exhibited, as I have said, by culturally universal systems of orientational metaphors: above/below, right/left, front/behind, inside/outside. In his article 'On the First Ground of the Distinction of Regions in Space' Kant argued that, however much we may abstract concepts from the sensuous world – the concept of orientation, for instance – images still adhere to those concepts; that we would be unable to assign any meaning to our concepts if there were not already some intuition underlying them; and that all orientation begins with what he called a sensuously *felt* distinction: for example, the palpable feeling we have, by virtue of our human morphology, of the distinction between the right hand and the left hand.[4] It is only by starting from the basis of this and other sensuously felt distinctions, he inferred, that we are eventually able to ascend to the concept of orientation as such. It is the human body, therefore, that provides us with the primary, the sensorily intuited system of reference, to which all our spatial distinctions between regions around our bodies are indirectly transferred. It is from the set of intuitions given by the specific structure of our body that we derive the fundamental spatial orientations organised into the binary oppositions of above and below, right and left, front and behind, inside and outside. The systems of orientational metaphors with which we constitute our world are grounded in the ontologically given oppositions out of which our bodies are constituted.

The valorisations we attach to the opposition between above and below are grounded in the fact that the shape of the human body is determined in virtually all its details by our upright posture.[5] Even on those occasions when other primates are able to stand and walk upright, they always stand stooped because their legs remain bent at the hip and knee joints. The human upright posture is distinguished by the fact that the vertebral column takes on the architectural function of a column, firmly supporting the head much as the column of a building supports its roof; and by the fact that the lines connecting the centres of hip, knee and ankle joints are all located in the same frontal plane, the centre of the hip joint being vertically above the centre of the knee and ankle joints. These two features constitute the distinctive verticality of the human posture, a verticality whose importance for us is the more marked once we set it in a temporal perspective. For within the individual's lifetime progress towards the upright posture is a slow acquisition; even when the physiological conditions on which it depends, such as the maturation of fibres, are accomplished, it still takes a number of years. And throughout human life the upright posture remains a task to be accomplished, the end of an endlessly repeated intentional effort. Our heart beats from its foetal beginning until death without our active intervention, and our lungs neither require nor allow voluntary interference with the process of breathing outside fairly narrow limits. But whenever we get up we must oppose the force of gravity, as becomes evident from the fact that the resistance we must over-come in doing so progressively diminishes as we rise. Neither the heart nor the lungs offer us an image, an incarnation, of the concepts of responsibility and autonomy, and hence one necessary condition for being able to have the concept of responsibility and autonomy. Only the act of standing does this.

Falling, we could even say, is a necessary condition of standing; for it is only by and through falling that we learn the upright posture. Though the fear of falling may not be as primal as the fear of being forgotten, it is still one of our first fears. That of course is why clowns make use of falling as a reliable trick to provoke children's cathartic laughter. Edgar Allan Poe, who evokes the terror of falling on the first page of 'The Pit and the Pendulum', writes elsewhere that we get an inkling of our ultimate end when we faint; 'the danger of the annihilation' of our entire being in death, he says, may be indicated with 'distinctness, by a swoon'.[6] Even less physically extreme experiences indicate how important the maintenance of verticality is for us. If, for instance, we observe a depressed person we see the verticality of the human posture in an impeded state: the head is bent, the shoulders lowered, the arms fallen to the sides, and movements take place with short, slow steps, not with a stride but with a trudge. When we speak of our regrets or remorse or resentment – all states in which our hidden past is experienced still as an oppression on us and within us – we speak of them as something which weighs us down. Anyone who has lost the capacity to stand and remain standing, even if only temporarily, depends for self-preservation on the help of others. We cannot live horizontally. The dynamics of crawling are alien to the human condition: which is why, when we want to give vent to an overwhelming sense of repulsion or mistrust vis-à-vis someone, we may speak of them as a 'snake in the grass' or even as 'reptilian'; and why to speak figuratively of someone as 'crawling' is a calculated insult. On the other hand, the etymological root of standing – *sta* – is one of the most pervasive linguistic elements in Greek, Latin, French, Spanish, English and German, with its derivative idioms of 'standing for', 'standing by' and 'making a stand'; and that etymological root remains recognisable in a proliferation of abstract nouns, all of which refer to something that, like human verticality itself, is in a state of always threatened equilibrium: as, for instance, state, status, estate, standard, statute, institution, constitution, substance, establish, understand.

As upright beings, our bodies give us the first model for the asymmetry of above and below in the life-spaces in which we are emplaced, the physiological basis for the construction of binary symbolic classifications. That is why some places are located up above: as with Plato's celestial spheres and the Christian heaven which are situated above in what Binswanger calls the 'ethereal world',[7] or as the Homeric gods dwell high on Olympus, or as Moses receives the Ten Commandments on Mount Sinai. That is why other holy mountains – Golgotha, Garizim and Haraberazaiti – figure largely in the world religions. And that is why sacred architecture is distinguished by its greater verticality, as with the pyramids, Mayan temples and Gothic churches.

Palladio, who devotes a chapter to 'The Heights of Rooms' in *The Four Books of Architecture*,[8] remarks that when people stand in rooms they are especially sensitive to the height of the rooms, which symbolise and amplify their own upright posture. It is not surprising, then, that in older monuments, the roof or ceiling was often reserved for the representation of the powers presiding over the building: as with the gods in the pediment of a Greek temple, or the figure of the Pantocrator on the dome of a Byzantine church, or the allegory of the prince's virtue, wisdom and generosity on the ceiling of Renaissance and Baroque palaces. When, in the nineteenth century, the history of art was representable as a narrative in museum collections, and taken to be further representative of humanity's highest achievements, whoever claimed state power claimed the highest part of the museum's ceremonial space: the ceiling.[9] Successive regimes displayed their supersession of the regime preceding them by inscribing their signature on the museum's ceilings: as when, under the first French Republic, all marks of royalty were removed, to be replaced by republican symbols such as ears of wheat and rosettes; or when, with the Restoration, the Bourbons employed painters who obligingly changed the head of Napoleon into that of Jupiter; or again when, under Napoleon III, Napoleons once more proliferated on the ceilings. It is on museum ceilings that we discover the most elevatedly stylish graffiti.

For thousands of years, in the organisation of pages of books, different value has been assigned to the top and bottom, to the arrangement of fields of inscribed, textual and graphic information. Even while the lines of Hebrew are written from right to left, and those of Chinese from top to bottom, in both cases top is still 'elevated' over bottom. Systems of literacy, transferring a systematic assignment of value from the morphology of the human body, use a field of inscriptions to record information which configures and vivifies that field with values and polarities thought of as belonging to the field more or less intrinsically. Again, in valorising the above/below asymmetry, traditional Christian and Chinese culture are at one. The author of *The Human Comedy* appreciated the author of *The Divine Comedy*: Balzac said of Dante that he explained in a very lucid way the 'constant revelation of our destiny' in the 'passion for rising' that is shared by all persons, drawing the dominant images of his iconography from the corporeal fact of rising and falling.[10] With equal conviction, traditional Chinese culture endowed the composition of the human body out of an above and a below with cosmological significance, the head being thought to represent the sky, the feet to represent the earth which they touch: which is why for a long time it was prohibited for Chinese sovereigns to display their court dancers doing a handstand, since to perform this is precisely to turn the world upside down.[11]

In a handstand, since the body's upright posture is reversed, the navel is upside down. That may seem a frivolous remark, but it is not. For in a number of early belief systems the navel of the human body is projected onto an imaginary geography: as in Palestine, where Mount Gerizim was known as 'the navel of the earth'; or in Mesopotamia, where it was believed that the Holy One created the world like an embryo, which, just like an embryo, then spreads from the navel outwards; or as in the Islamic belief that the first site created by God, who subsequently extended the earth from this point, was the Ka'ba, which, as the navel of the earth, was held to be the place that procured nourishment for the entire earth and that formed the mediating link between the upper world and the lower world.[12] Many other places within the geographical imaginary, being regarded as deficient and degraded, are located down below in the 'tomb world', as with Hades and the world of shadows, or as with the circles of Dante's Inferno. The myth of Orpheus descending into hell to bring back his recently dead wife Eurydice has its analogue in Polynesian, North American and Central Asian myths, where a hero is said to descend into hell to recover the soul of his dead wife.[13] In Roman mythology the world, the *mundus*, was believed to be the point of communication between three spheres along a vertical axis, and the Roman temple was thought to represent the zone of intersection between the higher divine world, the terrestrial world and the subterranean infernal world.[14] Rarely, if ever, has the depletion of conviction, within Christian iconography, been more palpably represented, as Julia Kristeva has eloquently shown, than in Holbein's painting of *The Body of the Dead Christ in the Tomb* of 1522.[15] That depletion is effected primarily through a shrinkage of the vertical dimension. The tombstone is depicted as weighing down on the upper portion of the painting, which is a mere twelve inches high – the relation of height to width is 1:7 – so as to intensify the feeling of a corpse that will never rise again; the portrayal is of such abjection that it provoked Dostoyevsky's Prince Myshkin, in *The Idiot*, to exclaim, when he saw a reproduction of it in Rogozhin's house, that 'some people may lose faith by looking at that picture'.

Like our verticality, our bilaterality is given in the body's topography and then transferred by analogy to construct binary symbolic classifications in the life-spaces within which we are emplaced. The ontological status of the right/ left distinction along the lateral plane becomes evident from a couple of thought experiments. Suppose that you have arrived blindfold in an unfamiliar room and remain blindfolded there. Given your sensory deprivation, how are you going to find your bearings within this space? In fact, you would be able to gain and retain a sense of orientation only by reference to one constant: that is to say, through the continuing sense of the difference between the right and left sides of your body. It is only because you would be able to refer continually to the contrast between your two sides that you would be able to know, with respect to the room in which you were situated, which way you were turning at any particular time; and it is only because you could reliably continue to count on this system of reference given by your right and left sides that you would have the capacity to become steadily oriented within the room.

Another thought experiment reinforces the essential importance of the body's bilaterality. For suppose now that you are trying to read a map. If you want to find your way around in space by reference to a map, you must first find a way of orienting the map in relation to your body, and it will become apparent that there is only one way in which you can achieve this: that is by establishing a particular relationship between this paper representation and the right and left hands that hold it. You will first need to locate the north point of the map in relation to your right and left hands. Once you have done so, you will be able to orient yourself in relation to the entire scheme of representation by automatically associating east with your right hand and west with your left hand. Only by establishing a systematic relationship between the topography represented on the map and the bilateral topography of your body will the concept of north take on a meaning relative to the other directions of south, east and west, and only by this means will you be able to infer reliably from this known direction on which side of the horizon you can expect the sun to rise.

It was Kant who suggested these two examples in order to demonstrate that our capacity to discern the distinction between different regions in space and to know the location of different places relative to each other such that it becomes for us everyday, tacit knowledge – becomes unreflective, taken for granted and reliable – is possible for us only because we are inserted into the place world in a particular, fundamental and unavoidable way, as bilateral bodies.[16] This means that the corporeal structuring already operative in the bilateral morphology of our bodies is a necessary condition for our capacity to perceive an ordering of regions and a specific arrangement of the places located in them. In saying this Kant is not simply claiming that our ordinary knowledge of the position of places would be of no use to us without the pregiven fact of our bilaterality. He is making the stronger claim that the most everyday knowledge of the arrangement of places could not come into existence, could not be constituted, unless we were able to orient the things structured, and the system of their reciprocal relationships, by implicitly referring them to the right and left sides of our bodies.[17] In other words, our bilaterality is essentially, not just contingently, related to our orientation in space. Nor do we need to resort to the two particular thought experiments with which Kant has provided us to take the full measure of our bilaterality. Everyday observation shows us that lateral space provides the matrix of human skills, both elementary and sophisticated. The use of the carpenter's saw, the weaver's shuttle, the potter's wheel, the mason's trowel, the painter's brush, the violinist's musical instrument, all operate within lateral space; spinning and sewing, stirring and ironing, sowing and welding, indeed most human crafts, the use of computers included, require dextrous manipulations of hand and arm in lateral space.

The symbolic asymmetry between right and left was remarked by Hertz, who observed that the widespread pre-eminence of the right hand is obligatory and guaranteed by sanctions, while prohibitions weigh upon the left hand: the right hands are joined in marriage, the right hand takes the oath, the right hand is extended in greeting.[18] Massive evidence points to this symbolic pre-eminence. The symbolism of right and left is richly developed in Islam, where the Koran assigns the elect to the right hand of the Lord and the damned to the left, and where one must neither eat nor drink with the left hand, but one spits to the left and holds the genitals with the left hand.[19] The ancient Greeks concur over this asymmetry: in Homer, the right hand is used to pour libations and to give a solemn pledge, and omens on the right are auspicious, while those on the left are inauspicious; and even a detailed knowledge of different biological species, in many of which no marked distinction between right and left is observable, did nothing to diminish Aristotle's belief that the right side is the stronger and more honourable and that the differentiation between right and left was a mark of humanity's superiority to animals.[20] Belief in the pre-eminence of the right hand is widespread in Africa too. Since, for the Nuer, the right arm designates what is strong and virile, masculinity, the paternal kin and lineage, it is mandatory, during discussions regarding bridewealth, which take place in the byre of the bride's home on her wedding day, for the bridegroom's people to sit on the byre and for the bride's people to sit on the left side;[21] the Masai suppose that a man visiting a sick woman, when hearing the call of the bird Ol-tilo to his left, knows that the woman is very ill, but if he hears the call on his right, knows that she feels better; and the Bushmen believe that there exists a kind of devil who has made everything with the left hand. The same asymmetry reappears in North American sign language, where right designates 'me' and left designates 'not me', 'others'; and where death, destruction or burial are designated by carrying the right hand to the left and placing it below the left hand.

The evidence is massive, but not universal. The cultural encoding of physiology in traditional Chinese civilisation disproves the claim, first advanced by Hertz, that symbolic pre-eminence is attributed universally to the right hand. Although right and left are components in a system of bipartite classification, left being Yang and belonging to the male, right being Yin and belonging to the female, the structure of the world governing both physiology and cosmography obeys the principle of rotation, a cylic alternation, which, far from prescribing a fixed predominance or absolute opposition, imposes instead a delicate choice between right and left within a complexly inflected system of symbolic representations.[22] When, for instance, fresh fish is to be served at table, the symbolic weight which is always attached to bilaterality varies according to the season. If it is summer, the belly of the fish must be turned to the left; if winter, to the right. Since winter is the reign of Yin, and since Yin corresponds to below, the belly, being the underneath and best-nourished part of the fish, is Yin, so that in winter the fish is placed with the belly to the right because one has to eat with the right hand and one begins by eating the good parts; the most succulent morsel must therefore be placed to the right. The principle of rotation requires that in summer, when Yang reigns, everything changes round. The Chinese principle of symbolic alternation does not contradict, but rather reinforces, the more fundamental claim, advanced by Kant, that bilaterality *as such* is a condition for the topographic arrangement, and so by implication the symbolic significance, attributed to different regions in space.

The most distinctive feature of the front/behind dyad, as with the above/below dyad, and as contrasted with the right/left opposition, is its obvious physiological asymmetry.[23] Our face, feet and chest are the most visually differentiated parts of our body and all point forward, whereas the backside of our body is comparatively undifferentiated. We look, touch and create objects in front of ourselves. We move in the direction of our vision. When we listen to someone who speaks, we face them. The distinction between front and back separates the world that we are able to view and manipulate from the world that we cannot easily view and manipulate. Although when I hear something I am attuned to all that goes on 'around' me, sight is the most definitive sense when dealing with places in front of me; as Aristotle pointed out, sight, most of all the senses, makes us know and brings to light many differences between things. To be bodily 'directed towards' something is to be actively engaged in, or at least to be open to, what lies in front of me. When we speak of someone 'confronting' a predicament, we think of them, figuratively, as facing towards it, and when we want to express our difficulty in dealing with some great obstacle we sometimes say that we simply cannot face it. We speak of getting ahead, and of getting ahead of others; the phrase 'ahead of' indicates meta-phorically a positive direction on any scale to which it might be applied.

I cannot see towards the back. Seeing towards the back is in fact a functional impossibility; for even if I were to turn my head around, considered functionally, I would still be oriented forwards. Because the area behind me is mostly out of sight, it has about it a quality of hiddenness, both real and figurative. This hiddenness refers to the back side of my own body, which I am unable to scrutinise except partially and fleetingly by using a mirror; and it refers also to whatever is behind my body, whether this is a hidden person or an object, as something which is not present to my perception in so far as it does not fall within my field of vision. What is behind me, in either of these senses, is on the side of me from which I feel most vulnerable. So I speak of being gossiped about 'behind my back', of being 'stabbed in the back' and of being 'held back'. This peculiar vulnerability is not only a matter of suscepti-bility to external forces which might be hostile or in some way detrimental to me. My I is implicated in the bodily asymmetry. For what is behind me, even if it is part of me, is felt to escape the control of my self. What is *behind* me is behind *me*. It is not accidental that in some branches of psychoanalysis the analyst is positioned behind the analysand.

Once again, a whole range of symbolic classifications flows from and refers back to this physiological differentiation.[24] In the eschatological myth in the *Republic*, Plato represents the souls of persons as divided by their judges into two groups: the just, who travel to the right and upwards, carry tokens of their judgement on their fronts; while the unjust, who travel to the left and downwards, bear their tokens on their backs. In Aristotle, front, together with right and above, is said to be one of the archai, the starting-points or principles, of the three types of change found in all living beings, namely locomotion, growth and sensation; and front, with right and above, is not only defined by certain functions, but held to be more honourable than its opposite. Again, in traditional Chinese culture, it is prescribed that the chief should receive his vassals standing with his back to the north and his face to the south, so that he receives the full rays of the sun and thus assimilates the Yang, the luminous principle; while the vassals prostrate themselves facing north, towards the Yin. It follows that the front of the body and the chest is Yang; and that, inversely, Yin is equivalent to behind, and the back.[25] In modern Western culture the valorisation of the front/behind opposition is expressed in a new concept of revolution. Traditionally, the term 'revolution' signified a continuous rotation in a cyclical motion; it was applied in this way in astronomy to refer to celestial movements, and to political upheavals which we now consider revolutions, like the English and American, and which at the time were thought of as rebellions to restore ancient liberties. Subsequently the concept of revolution came to denote not a rotatory or cyclical motion, but a forward movement: a break with the past, an assertion of the innovative potential of the present, and a vision of the future as an open horizon. When, between roughly 1790 and 1830, the concept of revolution was transformed, a whole array of terms – history, modernity, progress, emancipation – conceptualised this changed world-view in which, once more valorising the difference between front and back, humankind as a whole was figured as facing towards the future and turning its back on the past.[26]

By comparison with the above/below, the right/left and the front/back dyads, the binary opposition formed by the opposition between the inside and the outside of the human body is markedly elusive. This arises largely from the hiddenness of the inside of the human body. Technological advances have extended our capacity to know the inside of our bodies, so that we can look at our lungs and see damage to our bone structure with X-rays, read blood pressure through a sphygmomanometer, and look at the folds of our colon through a colonoscope. But although medical technologies now yield a visualisable knowledge of our viscera, I would not be able to recognise my own viscera even if I were to be shown them in technologically visualisable form. Though I know where my legs and arms and hands are, and have little difficulty in locating sensations on the surface of my body, even unpleasant visceral sensations, such as bloatedness or cramps, have indistinct borders, and my kidneys, my bone marrow and my spleen are almost entirely insensitive.

There is therefore a sense in which my internal bodily functions work within me automatically. The circulation of my blood and the beating of my heart depend upon me, in the sense that they can be affected by my chosen diet, only to a relatively small extent; my multiple hormonal balances are continually re-establishing themselves, again with the same proviso, largely without my help; and my digestion is only to a small extent dependent upon my will, for I have little feeling of controlling my digestive processes. This is why, with respect to the inside of my body, although I may feel a responsibility to exercise certain forms of self-restraint, Ricoeur can say that at a certain level of my existence 'I no longer appear to myself as a *task*, as a project.'[27]

Nevertheless, although the inside of my body is hidden from me, the visible and palpable boundaries of my body, expressed as a distinction between an inside and an outside, provide the matrix for my sense of a separation between the inside and the outside of external objects, so that, here again, the morphology of the body is transferable to the topography within which bodies are emplaced. This awareness can be observed with particular vividness in the experiences of infancy. Since, in the physical experiences of infancy, the processes of ingesting and of spitting out are primary, they come to provide the self with a model for more highly developed forms of mental discrimination; ingesting and spitting out, as Wollheim has argued, are the physical prototypes in the life-history of any person for that person's most undeveloped forms of moral judgement.[28] And the fact that we are conscious of having an inside as well as an outside makes it possible for us to understand and represent to ourselves figuratively some conditions of emotional illness experienced in adulthood, such as depression, as part of a life-history in which we have 'internalised' past objects of affection; for, figuratively speaking, we internalise particular persons, and the loss, or the threatened loss, of such internalised persons is what is frequently happening in episodes of depression. This is why, in his great paper on 'Mourning and Melancholia', Freud, when speaking of those occasions when we have to confront the real or imagined loss of a person important to us, says that our 'ego identifies with and takes inside itself that object', and that the continuance of this internalisation is in part a 'means of preserving the lost object, or a way of mediating and mastering loss', which is the loss of personal memories to which we are deeply attached.[29]

So far, I have been looking at the dualism of outside and inside in the structure of the human body while entirely ignoring one obvious distinguishing feature, namely, the fact that the human body is always a gendered body. Once attention is trained upon the body of a woman, in the context of considering the cultural importance of the dyadic morphology of outside and inside, that dyad assumes ever greater significance. Woman envelops. Woman envelops as a mother, since the woman's body is a place for the prenatal child. And woman envelops as a heterosexual lover, since the lover's body is a place for the man's penis, accepting it, receiving it, retaining it and metamorphosing its form. Woman is doubly enveloping, as a vessel for the foetus and the lover.

Luce Irigaray draws particular attention to the lips, both facial and genital, since they connect inside and outside at a threshold of the body; here, what is within the body palpably meets what is outside the body. Neither wholly inside nor wholly outside, facial lips never stop moving and opening.

There is an irony in the gender-specific features of woman's enveloping capacities. The masculine is drawn to the feminine as a particularly desirable place. As Luce Irigaray puts it, precisely as an inviting and sheltering double sheath, women's bodies become for men 'the first and unique place', that which is at his disposition, without his offering to women a place of his own.[30] Yet, on the other hand, men have shown throughout vast tracts of human history a disinclination to offer women significant cultural and political emplacement; the woman has been threatened because of what she lacks, a 'proper' place. Might there not be a causal connection between these juxtaposed facts? Might not those who rule in a patriarchal culture be motivated, subliminally at least, by *ressentiment*: could they not have been so driven to deny woman a social-political place of importance because they were so drawn, so much in need, of the places of a woman, and consequently grew so resentful, even if unconsciously, of this need, the subjection to the power of this desire? Goethe's dictum that 'the eternal feminine draws us on' would then find its counterpart in Virginia Woolf's plea that a woman should have 'a room of one's own'.

The morphology of the human body, as structured around the inside/outside dyad, is transferred onto the topography within which persons are emplaced to form a complex method of distinction in places between an outside and an inside, and then read back off again and deciphered by persons so emplaced. To build any structure at all and to dwell in it presupposes the difference between being inside and being outside that building, so that the setting up of boundaries is the primeval architectural act. Some places are inside, in the sense that they are permissible places, with access to them being open and encouraged, as, for instance, with the entrances to public squares; whereas other places are outside, in the sense that they are prohibited places, whether because they are considered holy or because they are viewed as being malevolent. Not all places are divided into the beneficent and the malevolent; yet already in the opposition between beneficent and malevolent places the inside/outside opposition given universally by the structure of bodily morphology is transformed outwards onto the evaluation of places.

The opposition between outside and inside operates with respect to buildings generally. The area outside a building normally has fewer categorical differences mapped into its spaces, and does not, on the whole, exert a particularly high degree of control over a person's movements, since many people will have access there to areas of inhabitation where few controls are imposed over their movements. The area inside a building, on the other hand, generally has more differences mapped into its interior zones, more precisely defined differences read into the relationship between these interior spaces, and a greater degree of definition operates there with regard to what is permitted to occur in these differentiated interior spaces, where precisely that is permitted, and to whom it is permitted.

Those who are admitted to buildings generally belong to one of two categories. They may be inhabitants or workers in the building, in which case they have some investment of power with respect to that building; or they may be visitors to the building, in which case they will be subject to certain interdictions, their movements within the building being controlled, whether they are diners in a restaurant or visitors to a museum or patients in a hospital. The inside/outside distinction further generates interfaces within many public buildings, by means of a shallow area for visitors. The building's permanent inhabitants, during working hours, occupy an area beyond this, usually with its own means of access; the deeper a person inhabits this interior zone, the greater their power will be; the bank manager will occupy an area deeper than that of bank clerks. The regular emplacement of hospital consultants exhibits a metaphysical principle whose highest manifestation is God: the greater the absence, the greater the power. The visitors to the building, on the other hand, generally interact with its permanent users at some special barrier which prevents their enjoying the privilege of any deeper penetration into the building, whether the barrier is the counter of a shop or the bar of a pub.

Within the interiors of private buildings the distinction between an outside and an inside reappears, with the difference that here the affective features of this mapping generally become more emphatic. This was a particularly well-marked feature of European bourgeois dwellings in the nineteenth century, where there were always areas which remained 'outside' within the interior of the private dwelling house; servants and domestic staff generally lived in the upper rooms, and in those areas of the house where servants, owners and visitors intermingled it was presumed that a certain decorum would prevail. Much of the humour surrounding the relationship between Jeeves and Bertie Wooster in the novels of P.G. Wodehouse presupposes this decorum in public areas; what the butler saw is crucial, and Jeeves observes what is taking place in the public areas of upper-class dwellings, and infers what must have taken place in its private areas, with a minute forensic acumen far beyond the capabilities of either its inhabitants or its visitors. Again, this is the point to the social offensiveness, in Kasuo Ishiguro's *The Remains of the Day*, when one of the dinner guests, with wounding cruelty, pointedly asks one of the servants, who is presumed to be ignorant of such matters, about the currently complex world political situation of the 1930s. Within the interiors of bourgeois dwellings in Europe during the nineteenth century and even beyond, the distinction between an inside area and an outside area within the interior of large homes made it possible to express a quality of interiority which was explicitly signalled by heavy curtains isolating the inside from the outside. There is yet a further 'interior' inside the interiority of such upper bourgeois buildings. The censoring of this interiority, the area of Eros, was signalled in the nineteenth century by the existence of hidden or withdrawn areas in the interior of the dwelling, forming a layering of interior spaces which may well have left its mark on what Freud called, explicitly, the 'topography' of the individual psyche.

The inside/outside distinction decipherable in public and private buildings reappears in the opposition between an outside and an inside within larger territorial areas, as for instance in the cities so characteristic of European culture from classical antiquity, through the Middle Ages, and on into the period of the Renaissance. City walls marked a material separation grounded in the exercise of political power; fortified towns held sway over the surrounding countryside, for, although they depended upon them for their livelihood, these small cities both protected and exploited the areas of land immediately outside the city walls. This feature, so characteristic of the antique culture of the Mediterranean, beguiled Heidegger into arguing – misleadingly – that the 'essence' of 'place' depends on the concrete, clearly defined nature of its boundary. In making this claim he appealed explicitly to the example of ancient Greek culture: 'a boundary', he wrote, 'is not that at which something stops, but, as the Greeks recognised, the boundary is that from which something begins its presencing'.[31]

The inside/outside distinction is literally slippery when applied to the human body and figuratively slippery when applied to the topography within which the separation between inside and outside is placed. An excessive insistence upon the distinction between an outside and an inside of places entails the danger of overlooking the complexity of the relationship between the inside and the outside of topographical features, just as the relationship between outside and inside is a particularly complex dyad with respect to the morphology of the human body. It is often possible to experience something as being 'in', in an area which is otherwise outside, as is the case with the front porch of a house. Conversely, we can experience something that is outside as a 'within', as when there is an inner courtyard within the area of a house. At the official entrance to buildings, and even on private porches, we find ourselves to be neither entirely 'inside' nor entirely 'outside', but between outside and inside; even a garden, which is usually outside, can be turned into part of an inside if it is incorporated into that interior space by means of a glassed-in porch. The inside/outside opposition is both permeable and reversible. So it comes about that there are many *transitional* spaces between outside and inside, which, as thresholds, are freighted with emotional and sometimes ritual weight: to cross a threshold without permission, which is sometimes done by hostile or aggressive or uncultivated persons, is grossly offensive.

Windows and doors are such transitional spaces. A window has two orientations. Windows are framed differently outside, for the perspective from the outside, and inside, for the perspective from the inside. Each side of the window, its outside and its inside, bears the distinctive marks of its transitionality. A door brings to a close the space of a room or of a street, while it is also a figure, or a prefiguring, of the reception to be expected in the house or in an adjacent room of a house. The transference of the body's morphology, with its own inside and outside, may often be felt subliminally at doorways, and sometimes the transference from morphological to topographical structure is expressed with particular vividness, as in Anasazi architecture, at the Pueblo

Bonito in Chaco Canyon, New Mexico, where doorways are openings which explicitly represent the human body by being roughly the same size.

Since the distinction between the outside and the inside has such symbolic weight, any fundamental changes in the way in which the relationship between outside and inside is structured, particularly those which affect transitional spaces, must be expected to have great cultural repercussions and therefore implications for the possible transformation of cultural memory. When Frank Lloyd Wright set out to abolish enclosing walls inside buildings, he initiated a whole sequence of repercussions. In reducing walls to surfaces, his intention was that houses should be flooded with light, so that from all of its rooms, now less insulated as containing areas, nature outside the house could be more easily perceived and enjoyed. His new architectural designs marked the inaugurating moment when the sheer materiality of thick, heavy walls inside buildings played an ever less significant architectural role in the design of both public and private buildings; from then onwards a lesser signifying importance was assigned to interior walls. The exterior walls of buildings also increasingly lost the earlier sense of material substantiality which they had previously imparted, under the impact of a form of architectural thinking guided by a model of transparency. The sense of architecturally circumscribed space began to disappear with this effacement of exterior walls. One historian, without referring to architecture, has spoken of the 'burden of history' weighing upon late nineteenth-century Europeans. As the feeling for mass became slowly erased from both interior and exterior walls, solidity melted into immateriality and the weight of a particular kind of historical memory, so dominant in the late nineteenth century in Europe, was lifted.

From the way in which Kant formulates his claims regarding the activity of orientation, it might appear that the body's morphology remains autonomous in relation to its cultural, historical and social circumstances. If Kant's notion of an intuitive and sensuous orientation inherent in the body's constitution is the ground that allows the mapping of cultural meaning and memory on to a place, and that permits place to become symbolic and symbolised, it would appear that this presupposes that the human body is originally pre-cultural, even if the body and its surroundings eventually become, through this process of mapping, culturally co-extensive. One might want to claim, against Kant, that the body is always already culturally and socially incorporated, produced by material practices and by symbolic meanings elaborated in places. In which case, the question arises as to whether this consideration might invalidate Kant's claim regarding the grounds of spatial orientation, in whole or in part, or whether, less drastically, Kant's position might need to be in some way reformulated in the light of this consideration.

If Kant had had the opportunity of reading a number of texts which he obviously could not have read – the texts of Marx, Weber, Simmel, Durkheim, Mauss, Malinowski – he might have formulated his thoughts differently. It is mainly owing to these thinkers that many persons are now disposed to the view that the body-subject, to speak with Merleau-Ponty,[32] is always already culturally and socially incorporated, that the body-subject is produced by the way in which it incorporates culturally available repertoires. As against this now common assumption, Kant formulates his understanding of orientation in such a way as to imply an originally pre-cultural body. Yet if Kant really does mean to imply this, and if we want to reject that implication, this would entail the rejection of Kant's claim that the three dyads, or in my reformulation of his position, the four dyads – above and below, right and left, front and behind, inside and outside– are transcultural, that they are cultural universals. It would mean only that we could claim that these are indeed cultural universals, but that, still as universals, they are also always already culturally and socially inflected. No logical contradiction is entailed in holding these two positions. Rather the reverse: the claim for variability reinforces, rather than undermines, the claim for universality, because if there is variability, that can only be so in relation to what does not vary, what is universal. Otherwise, the term 'variable' would have no meaning.

This circumstance may perhaps be illustrated by an analogy, and indeed one taken from the body itself. We can easily see that a certain anatomical structure is constitutive of the human body, yet the necessary existence of such an *anatomy*, which is distinctive of human morphology, is in no sense impaired or impugned by the further, also correct, observation that blood circulation is essential to human *physiology*. As the claim regarding the body's being always already culturally produced is to physiology, so Kant's claim regarding orientation is to anatomy.

It can sometimes happen that experience of one's body and its surroundings is not one of orientation but of disorientation. Such an experience is invoked by Thomas Mann in *The Magic Mountain* (*Der Zauberberg*), when his protagonist, Hans Castorp, who is a long-staying guest in a sanatorium in the Swiss Alps, gets lost in the snow. Castorp first became perturbed when 'the contours of the peaks dissolved, disappeared, were dissipated in mist, while the vision, led on from one pallidly gleaming slope of snow to another, lost itself in the void'.[33] 'One moment a great space of snow-covered rock would reveal itself, standing out bold and free ... But if one ceased to fix one's gaze upon it, it was gone, in a breath.'[34] Points and lines of demarcation were effaced: 'these upper regions blended with a sky no less misty-white than they, and where the two came together, it was hard to tell. No summit, no ridge was visible, it was a haze and a nothing, toward which Hans Castorp strove.'[35] As the snow began to fall more heavily, 'it was nothingness, white, whirling nothingness, into which he looked when he forced himself to do so'.[36] 'There was no path' and 'while he could see his hand before his face, he could not see the ends of his skis'.[37] His struggle against oncoming sensory confusion was now feverish and abnormal. He came to a hut and, to get his bearings, examined it. He came to the conclusion that

he had approached it from the same direction as before – namely, from the rear; and therefore, what he had accomplished for the past hour – as he reckoned it – had been a sheer waste of time and effort . . . You went in a circle, gave yourself endless trouble under the delusion that you were accomplishing something, and all the time you were simply describing some great silly arc that would turn back to where it had its beginning.[38]

What happens when, as here, experience of one's body and its surroundings is one of disorientation is that one is memorably reminded of how important orientation is in order to be able to remember where one is. Somewhat similarly, a sense of disembodiment is possible through traumatic historical experience – Kosinski has given a remarkable account of one such case in *The Painted Bird* [39]– and this makes surrounding places harder to represent and remember; this absence demonstrates the importance of what is normally present, if taken for granted, in everyday experiences of embodiment; and that shows, once again, how essential our embodiment is for representing and remembering the places that surround us.

However much the life-spaces we inhabit may change, we never lose this ultimate ground of the differentiation of regions in space. Whatever the nature of my perceptive field, my body is the stable centre within that field. My body has what Husserl calls a 'privileged position'[40] because it is always experienced by me as 'here'. I am never 'there'. My body remains 'here' when my body is moving and when things move round me. I can get closer to or further away from other particular places, but I never get closer to or further away from the particular place that is my body. In this sense, wherever I am, I am always 'here'. And from this it follows that the *true stability of place* – and therefore *the guarantee of place's memorability* – is not so much located *in enduring spatial landmarks* as rather situated *in myself.*

A further consequence flows for the way in which memory is dependent on topography. As has been said, the art of memory relies essentially on a stable system of places. But the 'art-of-memory' tradition is in fact grounded, as I have argued, in a prior premise which it fails to theorise or reflect upon: the premise that the order of the body will preserve the order of the places which in turn ensures that things will be remembered. The art of memory relies, most fundamentally, not on a stable system of places, but on a stable system of places in the body.

NOTES

1 On dyads, see E. Casey, *Getting Back into Place* (Bloomington and Indianapolis, 1993), pp. 49–70, 146–7, 180, 186, 313–14.

2 See F.A. Yates, *The Art of Memory* (Chicago, 1966); M. Carruthers, *The Book of Memory: A Study of Memory in Medieval Culture* (Cambridge, 1990); P.H. Hutton, *History as an Art of Memory* (Hanover and London, 1993).

3 Yates, *The Art of Memory*, p. 2, quoting Cicero, *De oratore*, II, lxxxvii, 351–4.

4 I. Kant, 'On the First Ground of the Distinction of Regions in Space', in J. Handyside, ed., *Kant's Inaugural Dissertation and the Early Writings on Space* (Chicago, 1929).

5 E. Straus, 'The Upright Posture', in *Phenomenological Psychology* (New York, 1966).

6 L. Binswanger, 'The Case of Ellen West', in R. May, E. Angel and H. Ellenberger, eds., *Existence* (New York, 1958), pp. 303–12. For Edgar Allan Poe on falling see G. Bachelard, *Air and Dreams: An Essay on the Imagination of Movement* (Eng. tr. Dallas, 1988), pp. 96, 97, 101, 103.

7 Binswanger, 'Case of Ellen West'.

8 A. Palladio, *The Four Books of Architecture* (New York, 1965), Bk 1, chs 22, 23.

9 C. Duncan and A. Wallach, 'The Universal Survey Museum', *Art History*, 3. 4 (1980), pp. 442–69.

10 Bacheland, *Air and Dreams*, pp. 56–7.

11 M. Granet, 'Right and Left in China', in R. Needham, ed., *Right and Left* (Chicago, 1973).

12 A.J. Wensinck, *The Ideas of the Western Semites Concerning the Navel of the Earth* (Amsterdam, 1917); M. Eliade, *Patterns in Comparative Religion* (London and New York, 1958), pp. 375, 377, 378; M. Eliade, *Images and Symbols* (London, 1961), pp. 42–3.

13 Eliade, *Images and Symbols*, pp. 64–5.

14 J. Rykwert, *The Idea of a Town: The Anthropology of Urban Form in Rome, Italy and the Ancient World* (Cambridge, MA, 1976), pp. 37, 59, 117, 121–6, 127, 129.

15 J. Kristeva, 'Holbein's Dead Christ', in M. Feher, ed., *Fragments for a History of the Human Body* (Cambridge, MA, 1989), pp. 238–69.

16 J.A. May, *Kant's Concept of Geography and its Relation to Recent Geographical Thought* (Toronto, 1970).

17 Kant, 'On the First Ground of the Distinction of Regions in Space'.

18 R. Hertz, *Death and the Right Hand* (London, 1960).

19 J. Chelhod, 'A Contribution to the Problem of the Pre-eminence of the Right, Based upon Arabic Evidence', in Needham, *Right and Left*.

20 G. Lloyd, 'Right and Left in Greek Philosophy', in Needham, *Right and Left*.

21 E.E. Evans-Pritchard, 'Nuer Spear Symbolism', in Needham, *Right and Left*.

22 Granet, 'Right and Left in China'.

23 E. Casey, *Getting Back into Place: Toward a Renewed Understanding of the Place-World*, 2nd edn (Indiana, 2009).

24 G. von Bonin, 'Anatomical Asymmetries of the Central Hemispheres', in V.B. Mountcastle, ed., *Interhemispheric Relations and Cerebral Dominance* (Baltimore, MD, 1962).

25 Granet, 'Right and Left in China'.

26 R. Koselleck, 'Neuzeit', in *Futures Past: On the Semantics of Historical Time* (Cambridge, MA, 1985), pp. 231–66.

27 P. Ricoeur, *Freedom and Nature: The Voluntary and the Involuntary* (tr. E. Kohák, Evanston, IL, 1966), p. 418.

28 R. Wollheim, *The Sheep and the Ceremony* (Cambridge, 1979).

29 S. Freud, 'Mourning and Melancholia', in *The Standard Edition of the Complete Psychological Words of Sigmund Freud. Vol. 14* (London, 1917), pp. 243–60.

30 L. Irigaray, 'Place, Interval: A Reading of Aristotle *Physics* IV', in *The Ethics of Sexual* Difference (tr. C. Burke and C. Gill, Ithaca, NY, 1993), p. 54.

31 M. Heidegger, 'Building, Dwelling, Thinking', in *Poetry, Language, Thought* (New York, 1971), p. 154. This essay first appeared in German in 1954.

32 M. Merleau-Ponty, *Phénoménologie de la perception* (Paris, 1945).

33 T. Mann, *The Magic Mountain*, tr. H.T. Lowe-Porter (Harmondsworth, 1960), p. 471.

34 *Ibid.*, p. 472.

35 *Ibid.*, p. 478.

36 *Ibid.*, p. 483.

37 *Ibid.*

38 *Ibid.*, p. 487.

39 J. Kosinski, *The Painted Bird* (New Brunswick, NJ, 1965).

40 E. Husserl, 'Ding und Raum', in U. Claesges, ed., *Husserliana. Vol. 16* (The Hague, 1973). For an account of Husserl's inquiries into spatial orientation, see Claesges, *Edmund Husserls Theorie der Raumkonstitution* (The Hague, 1964).

5   Tradition as conversation and tradition as bodily re-enactment

In his *Sketch for a Theory of Practice* Pierre Bourdieu argues that

if all societies and all total institutions that seek to produce a new man through a process of 'deculturation' and 'reculturation' set such store on the seemingly most insignificant details of *dress*, *bearing*, physical and verbal *manners*, the reason is that, treating the body as a memory, they entrust to it in abbreviated and practical, i.e. mnemonic, form the fundamental principles of the arbitrary content of the culture. The principles em-bodied in this way are placed beyond the grasp of consciousness, and hence cannot be touched by voluntary, deliberate transformation, cannot even be made explicit; nothing seems more ineffable, more incommunicable, more inimitable, and, therefore, more precious, than the values given body, *made* body by the transubstantiation achieved by the hidden persuasion of an implicit pedagogy.[1]

I intend in what follows to look at one way in which the body is treated as a memory, in which it is entrusted in mnemonic form with the fundamental principles of the content of a culture, when the principles embodied in this way are placed beyond the grasp of consciousness.

Mnemonic strategies are necessary in all preliterate societies; such societies need performative utterances on a large scale which both describe and enforce the values and habit patterns of the group. These linguistic statements will include repeated examples of correct moral procedure and rough definitions of standard technical practices; and such statements will need to be cast in a standardised form so that they can be repeated by successive generations. In preliterate societies oral verse is a particularly appropriate instrument of cultural reproduction because, in the absence of written records, its rhythms and formulae are suitable mechanisms of recall. They are suitable, in particular, because they enlist the co-operation of a whole series of motor reflexes throughout the entire human body.

I shall seek to reinforce the strength of this reading in a roundabout way: that is to say, by contrasting it with Gadamer's interpretation of the process of understanding a tradition, in which the role of the human body is evacuated from his account. Gadamer speaks of those who receive a tradition as being the addressees of messages which they hear or to which they listen or which they allow to speak to them. But he is using the terms 'hearing', 'listening' and 'speaking' here purely metaphorically. He would probably wish to claim that the metaphors of hearing, listening and speaking are strong, but I would want to claim that, on the contrary, they are weak. That this is the case is, I want to argue, demonstrated by the fact that those who receive tradition in the oral verse of preliterate societies enter sympathetically and effectively into what they hear not metaphorically, in Gadamer's sense, but literally. They receive a tradition bodily, by re-enacting it – re-enacting it with lips and larynx and limbs, and with the whole apparatus of their unconscious nervous system.

My justification for approaching the process of cultural reproduction via a reading of Gadamer's hermeneutics is that he presents his account of interpretation as one which he claims to be culturally universal. But the effect of my approach will be to counterpose against Gadamer two irreconcilable interpretations of tradition: tradition understood as conversation, as he would interpret it, and tradition understood as bodily re-enactment.

The question which Gadamer seeks to answer is this: what are the conditions which make understanding possible? This is not, he insists, an inquiry about the methods or techniques which we ought to adopt when we set out to understand a text or an artefact or a set of behaviours which may be viewed as analogous to a text. What he is describing is not simply a scientific method or the characteristic of a particular group of sciences. It is a natural capacity of all persons. He wants to envisage in a universal way what always happens when an act of comprehension takes place.[2]

This is a modern problem. It was the Enlightenment that first made it at once possible and necessary to pose such a question. Gadamer's question assumes, with Schleiermacher, that interpretation is now to be seen as the explicit, conscious and self-reflective understanding of tradition under conditions when it has become endangered or problematic.[3] And his question deals with what is common, in the Kantian sense of their conditions of possibility, to all modes of understanding;[4] the problem-shift from the question 'What should we do when we interpret?' to the one 'What does interpretation do?' is the decisive achievement of philosophical hermeneutics in respect of a theory of interpretation: it discloses the functions of the varying cultural practices of exegesis, historical reconstruction, canon-formation and so on as forms of a 'productive' assimilation of tradition.

But if Gadamer's question is unthinkable without the Enlightenment, his answer is directed against the Enlightenment; specifically, against its conception of prejudice. We now take prejudice to mean both precipitation – in the sense of judging something too quickly – and predisposition – in the sense of following custom or authority. This usage has become self-evident for us; but it was not always so; indeed, it was only in the Enlightenment that this concept of prejudice came to have the essentially negative aspect we now take for granted. The German *Vorurteil*, the English *prejudice* and the French *préjugé* all at that time became limited in usage, so that the word came to have then, as it continues to have today, the sense simply of an unfounded judgement.[5]

How are such unfounded judgements to be understood? It is an established fact for the Enlightenment that all unfounded judgements, that is to say all tradition that reason shows to be nonsense, can only be understood historically, by going back to the past's way of looking at things. The *exceptional case* of nonsensical tradition – that is, prejudice – later became the *general rule* for modern historical awareness. Meaning that is generally accessible through reason is now so little believed that the whole of the past, and eventually even the thinking of one's contemporaries, is viewed only 'historically'; all meanings and all values are to be understood as historically specific products and viewed in relation to the specific horizon of a particular age or a particular cultural system. Historicism thus understood is not the *refutation* but the *culmination* of the Enlightenment. The discrediting of all prejudices, first proclaimed by the Enlightenment, becomes in historicism radical and universal.[6]

This is the point at which Gadamer begins his critique. He wants to say that the fundamental prejudice of the Enlightenment, as of historicism, was the prejudice against prejudice itself. He wishes instead to recover a less unequivocally negative sense of the word; a sense in which the primary meaning is of a judgement that is given before all the elements that determine a situation have been finally examined. This places the stress not on what is partial but on what is anterior. The meaning that now comes into focus is that of pre-judgement. Pre-judgements, in this sense, refer not to those parts of our perception or beliefs which need to be eliminated, but rather to essential constituents of all our understanding. As such, it is not so much that pre-judgements *prejudice* our subsequent judgements as that they are *premonitions* of those judgements.

The point of rehabilitating this sense of pre-judgement – 'Vorurteil' – is to prepare the way for the claim that our understanding of anything is from the outset directed by our pre-judgements, by what Gadamer calls the anticipatory movement of our pre-understanding. These very terms themselves, 'pre-understanding' and 'pre-judgement', echo, and are indeed intended to recall, the prefixes of *Being and Time*, where Heidegger lists a series of expressions possessing the prefix 'vor': thus 'Vor-habe', 'Vor-sicht', 'Vor-griff'. All these expressions point, in Gadamer as in Heidegger, to a fundamental characteristic of understanding: to the fact that no one can approach an object of possible knowledge without some previous notion of that kind of object. Always in the act of understanding some pre-understanding is in play.

To reject the Enlightenment concept of prejudice is therefore to abandon far more than a single concept; it is to disown the whole antinomian mentality of the Enlightenment in which all thought is bounded by dualistic concepts: prejudice and reason, tradition and modernity, ancient and modern. In abandoning this system of contrasts Gadamer abandons also the historicist version of the dualism, the opposition between historical research and traditional norms. What he wishes to dispute is the very possibility that there might exist a technique or procedure of understanding which renders traditions impotent by methodically abstracting from them. For if historical research attempts to read texts only 'historically', only as documents of a period or a society in which they originate, it remains an abridgement; those texts retain a dimension which has not entered into such a conception of historical understanding. Beyond their existence as documentation, all transmitted texts contain a *surplus* because the claims and the mental configurations they contain continue to be effective beyond the situation of their origin; continue to be effective, in particular, in shaping the horizon of expectations with which interpreters cannot but be equipped as they approach the objects they seek to understand.

The beginning and end of all wisdom, in other words, is the hermeneutic circle. The circular movement of understanding runs backwards and forwards along the text, interpreting the whole in the light of the parts and the parts in the light of the whole. We can decipher the individual parts of a text only if we anticipate, in however diffuse and incomplete a manner, an understanding of the whole; and conversely, we can correct this preliminary understanding only to the extent that we explicate individual parts of the text.

Gombrich's account of his wartime experiences breaking coded messages intercepted over the radio nicely illustrates the procedure involved. He describes how, when transmissions are often scarcely audible, the trick is to interpret the few fragments of speech sound that are all you have to go on. You have to know what might be said in order to hear what is said. You must select from your already existing knowledge of possibilities certain word combinations and you must try to project those combinations into the noises heard. Even while you keep thinking of possibilities you must keep your projections flexible, you must remain prepared to try out fresh alternatives and to admit the possibility of defeat. This is the most striking experience of all: once your expectation has become firmly set and your conviction settled, you cease to be aware of your own activity, the way your expectations guide your hearing and the noises appear to fall into place and to be transformed into the expected words.[7]

There is a certain inaccuracy in this account. Gombrich's account of code-breaking, I said, illustrates the procedure involved. But – and this is Gadamer's point – it is, strictly speaking, incorrect to think of understanding as a specific *procedure* we adopt. The activity of understanding is not one of a number of possible behavioural strategies which an individual or group might or might not adopt; it is the inescapable mode of being in the world. We could not, as it were, step outside the circular movement of understanding even if we wished to do so or even if we took methodical steps designed to allow us to do so. For it is an unavoidable characteristic of understanding that no one – neither the literary critic nor the historian nor the code-breaker nor the mythical man in the street – can approach his object without some previous notion of that kind of object. What is called the hermeneutic circle when we are speaking of interpreting texts or breaking codes consists only of particular instances or derived forms of this primary pre-structure of all understanding. The circle of understanding therefore exists at a level anterior to any particular procedural rules. The circle of understanding is not a *strategic device* but the *primary process*.

It is from this point that Gadamer rethinks the idea of tradition. To understand a tradition is now seen to be not the freely chosen action of a subject confronting that tradition; rather, all acts of understanding are moments in the life of the tradition itself. An interpreter can only assimilate a tradition by coming to meet it from a horizon of expectations which is already preformed by that tradition; so that we have always already in a certain sense partly understood, diffusely comprehended, the tradition with which we are confronted as something which we seek to understand.

The idea that an encompassing circularity is to be found whenever the process of understanding takes place culminates in the notion of what Gadamer calls 'consciousness exposed to the effect of history' ('wirkungs-geschichliches Bewusstsein'). By this he means that in all understanding the power of effective history is at work whether we are explicitly aware of it or not.[8] For power does not depend on its being *recognised*; it is operative in post- as well as in pre-Enlightenment conditions. The burden of this argument is that 'this quality of being determined by effective history still dominates the modern, historical and scientific consciousness and that beyond any possible knowledge of this domination'.[9]

What does this claim look like when elaborated in detail? How can this idea be given the persuasiveness of the particular?

Gadamer seeks to do this by finding the model for the hermeneutic process in conversation, and by mobilising a whole series of figures of speech in order to secure the power of this analogy. He says that all understanding, whether historicist or otherwise, 'lets itself be addressed by tradition'.[10] He says that we must inhibit the over-hasty assimilation of the past to our own expect-ations of meaning because 'only then will we be able to listen to the past in a way that enables it to make its own meaning heard'.[11] He says that to hear is to be addressed and that this inevitably places the addressee under a certain constraint; anyone who is addressed 'must hear, whether he wants to or not'; he 'can look away but he cannot "hear away"'.[12] Gadamer says that the concept of the classical expresses not only the distant unattainability of a particular historical phenomenon, but also the sense of 'ultimate community and sharing in the world out of which the classic work speaks';[13] so that to describe something as classical is to affirm that 'the duration of the power of a work to speak directly to us is fundamentally unlimited'.[14] He says that reading is a kind of inner speaking or metaphorical listening; that there is 'no sharp differentiation between reading aloud and silent reading'; that 'emphasis, rhythmic ordering and the like are also part of a wholly silent reading'; and that to understand a written text 'always contains an inner speaking as well'.[15] And since all these locutions are intended as more than mere figures of speech he draws the conclusion that 'all writing is a kind of alienated speech'.[16] Because the meaning of all written signs has undergone a self-alienation through being written down, the task of the interpreter is to return what has been transmitted in literary form out of its condition of alienation and into 'the living presence of conversation'.[17] And from all this he concludes that 'it is more than a metaphor, it is a memory of what originally was the case, to describe the work of hermeneutics as a conversation with the text'.[18]

Gadamer's next step is to say that all genuine conversations, and therefore all conversations with a text, have a structure of question and answer. By this he means two things. He means, first of all, that anyone who tries to interpret a text can understand the meaning of that text only when he has understood the question to which the text was meant as an answer. But Gadamer also means, second, that the text – that is, the answer to the question which is to be reconstructed – itself poses a question to the interpreter, and thus brings his assumptions into the open. The reconstructed question, to which the text is supposed to be the answer, passes over into the question 'which the tradition is for us'. The reconstruction of the question to which the text is presumed to be the answer 'takes place within a process of questioning through which we seek the answer to the question that the text asks us'.[19] The structure of question and answer is built in the image and likeness of the hermeneutic circle.

Common sense prompts Gadamer to make a concession at this point. No text, he admits, can speak to us directly as a living interlocutor can; it is 'we, the ones who comprehend', who 'must for our part first enable it to speak'.[20] No text can literally speak to me; it can be said to pose questions to me only by virtue of the mental activity of the persons who ask questions. The stylistic device of speaking about a question which the text poses to the interpreter can have no more value than that of an image or metaphor with the help of which I am able to express the peculiar inescapability of the contents of tradition within which I stand, whether I take up a sympathetic or critical position to that tradition.

Having issued that caveat Gadamer persists with the metaphor. To interpret a text or a text-analogue, he has said, is like engaging in a conversation, and a conversation has the structure of question and answer. Now it is quite evidently the case that not all linguistic exchanges which we might think of as conversations, and not all questions and answers which are to be found in the context of such exchanges, can be appropriately described as having the structure of question and answer. Indeed, the peculiarity of many so-called conversations is precisely that they appear to have this character but in fact do not do so. They therefore have to be eliminated from the account of what might be called Gadamer's ideal conversation situation.

The rhetorical question is not a true question because there can be no genuine questioning when the thing spoken of is never really questioned.[21] The pedagogic question of the kind asked in formal oral examinations is a question without a questioner; the examiner poses questions as if shooting bullets from a revolver and the examinees reply with pistol shots of their own.[22] The therapeutic question of the kind that is frequently asked by a doctor of a patient has a unilateral character; its point is for one partner to discover information about the other without seeking material agreement with the other and without such agreement being necessary.[23] The sophistic question is one in which the questioner plays the role of the pupil and the ensuing discussion is merely an occasion for the sophist's self-assertion in front of an audience; the pupil's questions do not help discover the answer but give the sophist the opportunity to test out a certainty, from a dominant position, on the pupil, since the ground of the sophist's competence in this type of controversy is independent of the questioning process.[24] Historicists' questions seek to establish a methodical abstraction so that the criteria of their own knowledge cannot be called into question by what they seek to understand; effectively historicists seek to give up any attempt to find in the past any truth valid for themselves.[25] Historicists seek to insulate themselves from those to whom they address their questions, just as the rhetorician is insulated from the interlocutor, the examiner from the examinee, the doctor from the patient, and the sophist from the audience. All of these questioners have withdrawn themselves, by the structure of the 'questions' they pose, from any truth claims which the partner in the conversation might wish to advance. All of them hold on to the presuppositions which as so-called questioners they bring with them to the conversation. All of them pretend to an openness which they do not have. But the essence of the genuine question, says Gadamer, is 'the opening up, and keeping open, of possibilities'.[26]

Gadamer finds the model for the genuine conversation in the Socratic dialogue. Hence it is not simply out of piety towards Socrates as a master of conversation that Plato recorded his philosophy in the form of written dialogues; rather, the literary form of the dialogue receives its *raison d'être* from the fact that it 'places language and concepts back within the original movement of the conversation'.[27] In doing this it demonstrates, says

Gadamer, 'the act of conducting a real conversation' because it shows us that 'the art of questioning' resides in the ability 'to go on asking questions'.[28] This ability to persist in questioning, in turn, depends upon one of the greatest insights given to us in Plato's account of Socrates: the perception that, contrary to the general opinion, it is more difficult to ask questions than to answer them.[29] When the partners in the Socratic dialogue are unable to answer Socrates' awkward questions and try to turn the tables by assuming what is, as they suppose, the advantageous role of questioner, it is they who come to grief.

Behind this comic motif in the dialogues there lies the critical distinction between genuine and false discourse. For those addicted to false discourse, for those, that is, who use dialogue only in order to prove themselves right and not to gain insight, it will certainly appear to be easier to ask questions than to answer them. But in fact, of course, the imminent collapse of the interlocutor shows that those who think that they know better cannot even ask the right questions. For in order to be able to ask such questions they must want to know, and in order to want to know they must know that they do not know. All questioning and all desire to know therefore presuppose a knowledge that one does not know; indeed, it is a particular lack of knowledge that leads to a particular question.[30] This is what Gadamer means when he says that to ask a question means to bring something into the open, that the essence of a genuine question is 'the opening up, and keeping open, of possibilities'. And that is why he sees in the Socratic dialogue the model for the art of breaking the power of concepts which have become rigidified. The art of Socratic questioning shows us how we can bring to light what is really meant by the moral and political meanings contained within our received normative concepts; and so how we can shatter the power of normative ideas which have taken on the appearance of self-evident truths.

It is important to be clear about the precise weight of the claim that is being made here. Gadamer's interpretation of the Socratic dialogue, and indeed Gadamer's work as a whole, could be read as providing a *normative* account of tradition, a description of how transmission should take place – much as Oakeshott may be said to have done, for example, when he wants to say that knowledge of a tradition of behaviour should be knowledge of detail, so that what has to be learned is not an abstract idea but a concrete, coherent manner of living in all its intricacies; or as Eliot does, when he says that whenever a new literary work appears it reanimates the whole of a tradition by rearranging it so that this brings about an alteration in the meaning of each component literary text. Read in this way, the rich intellectual history with which Gadamer elaborates his systematic argument in *Truth and Method* is not simply a heavy freight of erudition but rather a series of specific demonstrations of how transmission should take place. Gadamer certainly *is* doing this;

but he is also doing something else; and he took the opportunity of the preface to the second edition of *Truth and Method* to spell this out.[31] His concern, he says, is not with procedures which we ought to adopt, but with what happens to us over and above our choosing any procedure in particular. The reading which Gadamer gives us of the Socratic dialogue is set in the context of his *ontological* claim.

It is clear that the technique of Socratic questioning is a particular social practice. This point is consistent with the account given by Gadamer, although it receives no particular emphasis in his presentation. In pursuing dialectic Socrates is led again and again to consider ethical and political questions. 'Can "excellence" be taught?', he asks; or 'Is it really necessary to have a master to teach one "excellence" in order to acquire it?' Not so, he answers: virtue, excellence, is not a technique and hence something that can be taught, nor is it inscribed within the social rank of each individual. Thus the target of his questioning is invariably the authority socially invested in the leading citizens. The sophists belonged to this group of notables and spoke with the peremptorily slick confidence of those long accustomed to being surrounded by people who play the role of sycophantic amplifiers. Under the challenge of Socrates' questions these leading citizens must respond, they must seek to justify themselves by their answers. But when they try to do this their alleged knowledge is revealed for what it really is – a social pretence. What Socrates is calling into question is the idea of *socially accredited mastership*.

But there is a further sense in which the art of Socratic questioning is a social practice. This sense is, it is important to stress, inconsistent with the account given by Gadamer. We cannot learn this from the early Platonic dialogues; we can infer it, rather, from the *Republic*: specifically, from Books 3 and 10 of the *Republic* where Plato discusses the nature of poetry. Gadamer has written extensively on poetry as well as on the history of philosophy and he can certainly not be accused of hiding his classical erudition. Yet on the subject of Plato's attack on the poets he is strangely reticent. He does indeed say at one point that Plato's attack is intended 'in a deeply ironic sense'.[32] This remark whets the appetite and leaves it unsatisfied. Precisely why and how Plato's attack should be interpreted as 'deeply ironic' is left unexplained. The matter is quietly dropped. Nothing could speak more eloquently than this massive silence.

It is of course well known that Plato wants serious steps to be taken against poets as a group of people who engage in socially undesirable practices. To appreciate the point of this we must set on one side the associations automatically conjured up when we hear the word 'poetry' and remember instead three things. We must note, first of all, that Plato views poetry mainly as a didactic instrument for transmitting a tradition. In describing poetry as though it were a kind of reference library or treatise on ethics and politics he is reporting on its function in an oral culture and reminding us, in effect, that this remained its function in Greek society down to his own day. We must note, second, that in Plato's discussions the relationship of the student or the public to poetry is assumed to be that of listeners, not readers, and the relationship of the poet to his audience is assumed to be that of a reciter or actor, not that of a writer. And we must note, finally, that Plato chose the term 'mimesis' to describe the poetic experience because that term focuses attention on the artist's mastery of certain quite particular psychological mechanisms – his capacity to make an audience identify sympathetically with the content of what he is saying, so that poeticised recitations generate a kind of emotional drama both for the reciter and for the audience.[33]

Gadamer is more forthcoming on the subject of mimesis than on that of Plato and the poets.[34] Mimesis, he says, means recognition. Recognition involves not merely the fact that something which we already know is perceived anew by us. The joy of recognition lies in the fact that more is perceived than what was already known. This 'more' is made perceptible to us because in mimesis the enduring forms of things are, as it were, purified of the accidental aspects in which we normally encounter them. Imitation is not simply a repetition but a bringing into relief. Whoever imitates must leave out and emphasise and exaggerate. This idea of representation, says Gadamer, also entails the fact that, in a certain sense, one perceives oneself in this process: in the sense that one is brought to recognise the interpretations which shape the world of one's beliefs and actions. Recognition is the experience of a heightened intimacy or familiarity with a world of shared meanings. Furthermore, recognition is possible, he says, only because there exists a tradition which is held to be valid and which provides a shared set of understandings; and this common set of understandings was provided in Greek thought by myth. Myth was the culturally shared resource of artistic representation; and it was through the recognition of what was contained in that resource that the Greeks deepened their familiarity with their interpreted world, even in the theatrical experiences of pity and terror. Gadamer concludes that the process of recognition which took place in the ancient Greek theatre was held together by the Greek religious tradition, with its stories of the gods, its legends of heroes, and its ways of relating Greek contemporary experience to their mythic-heroic past.

What is missing in this account of mimesis is any sense that intimacy or familiarity with a shared tradition is more than the inheritance of a common set of ideas, or *cluster of conceptual resources*. If these conceptual resources are to be inherited at all, they must be structured by certain forms. Gadamer's understanding of imitation is, as it were, disembodied because he loses sight of what might be called the *mechanics* of mimesis.

In what, then, does this mechanics of mimesis consist? It consists – and here I acknowledge my considerable debt to the work of Havelock[35] – in three mutually reinforcing levels of patterned behaviour, patterns of organised action the function of which is mnemonic. The first level is metrical. Speech is here produced by a series of bodily reflexes and these are organised into metrical patterns. The statement 'Hector is dead', for instance, is a piece of speech articulated by a set of movements on the part of the lungs, larynx, tongue and teeth which must be combined unconsciously and accurately into a given pattern. I can set up a rhythm merely by repeating the statement. But rhythms which repeat a group of words over and over again will not allow a new statement. The main burden of repetition, which memory needs as its support, must therefore be displaced. It is displaced on to the meaningless metrical pattern which is held in the memory so that any new statements can be so expressed that they fit into the pattern. In this way the possible combinations of spoken words and phrases, and the possible combinations of bodily reflexes performed by the lungs, larynx, tongue and teeth, are subject to a drastic restriction.

This is reinforced by a second level of acoustic patterns. For the reciter the performance on the lyre involving a motion of the hand and fingers generates a corresponding rhythm in another part of the body which acts in parallel with the motion of the vocal organs. This lends his metrical pattern further mnemonic support. His strumming on the lyre, arranged in the form of a melody, generates an acoustic rhythm; and to the extent that the reciter as he arranges his speech sounds and his accompaniment also listens to these acoustic effects, the melody on the strings will reinforce the pattern of his bodily reflexes and so confirm the memory of the pattern which he is following.

This is reinforced in turn by a third level of kinesic patterns. There is another part of the body which can be set in motion parallel to the motion of the vocal organs. This is the legs and feet, and their motions are organised in dancing. This pattern of reflexes moves in a rhythm which parallels that of the spoken words, and so further amplifies the 'acting out' of the recital. Either the audience perform this kinesic repertoire themselves in the course of the recitation, or they watch it being done, so that the mnemonic assistance is mediated to them through the eyes as they watch the dance rhythm. Kinesic, acoustic and metrical behaviours are all structured together as mnemonic devices in an embodied performance.

Mnemonic strategies of this kind are necessary in all preliterate societies. These strategies are suitable because they *overdetermine the mechanisms of remembrance* by enlisting the co-operation of a whole series of motor reflexes throughout the body. Those who receive a tradition in this way are not therefore the addressees of messages which they hear or to which they listen or which they allow to speak to them. The pattern of behaviour in the artist and in the audience is therefore in some important respects analogous. It may be described as an act of emotional identification made possible by the continual repetition of rhythmic acts.

The target of Plato's attack on the poets is this mechanism of identification.[36] The imitative process which he has described in Book 3 of the *Republic* as 'making yourself like somebody else' is later disclosed in Book 10 as 'surrender' of one's self, a 'following-along' while we 'identify' with the emotions of others; indeed, Plato even includes a reference to the fact that these experiences are 'recollections'; the task of poetic education, that is to say, is to memorise and recall. What he wants to reject, then, is the malign educational institution of the poetic performance, a performance based on identification, an identification which he speaks of as the surrender to a spell. The social practice that was the Socratic question was also designed to break the surrender to that spell. The Socratic question was of course directed against the immediately present sophistries of what claimed to be discursive argument. The function of the dialectic question was to force the speaker to repeat a statement already made. This repetition does not reinforce a pattern of thought; it breaks it. The speaker is invited to repeat himself because it is assumed that there was something unsatisfactory about his statement and that therefore he should rephrase it. Many statements, if they concerned matters of cultural tradition, would frequently be poeticised statements of a rhythmic kind. They would be statements which invited the listener to identify with some emotively effective example, to identify with it by repeating it over and over again. But to say 'What did you mean? Say that again' shatters the pleasurable security of the rhythmic formula. It loosens the seductive hold of motor reflexes by requiring that the speaker should try to find different words. The Socratic question asks the interlocutor to examine his experience and rearrange it; to reconsider, analyse and evaluate it, instead of 'imitating' it.

It might be objected that the figure who plays so prominent a part in this historical drama is not a particular individual but a mental construct, not the concrete historical Socrates but an idea of Socrates. This idea of Socrates is an invention of the *philosophes* who cast him in the role of that hero of thought whose teaching marked the point of transition from myth to rationality; and this figure recurs again and again in the nineteenth century, in Schleiermacher and in Hegel, in Kierkegaard and in Nietzsche. Even if Gadamer never explicitly adverts to this motif it is inconceivable that he could be unaware of it; it forms part of the pre-understandings which he brings to his own variation on the theme. But if that is so, does not this same horizon of interpretation also shape and prejudge that contrary view of Socratic method which I have begun to sketch out against Gadamer, the view which sees his teaching, as Havelock does, as undermining the cultural hold of those mimetic devices characteristically found in oral composition? Does this counter-argument not also subsist within the shadow of that same figure, drawing its cogency from the continuing resonance of this retrospective heroisation of Socrates as marking *the* decisive historical transition? In which case, does not the counter-statement which I have just begun to etch out lose its footing in empirically demonstrable social reality, and suffer the effects of a kind of subsidence; does it not begin, in its turn, to crack and erode?

I think not; for I believe that it is possible to rescue a kernel of truth from the exuberantly speculative context I have been sketching out. In order to do this, I shall focus on two particular kinds of evidence which might be drawn upon in support of the foregoing interpretation.

The first of these relates to the character of formulaic utterance. The most promising area in which to approach this question is that of Homeric poetry.[37] As is well known, Parry took the first twenty-five lines of the *Iliad* and of the *Odyssey* and underlined those groups of words which he found repeated elsewhere in Homer; a glance at his charts makes it clear how many formulae there are in those samples. Not simply 'repetitions' or 'stock epithets' or 'epic cliches' or 'stereotyped phrases', for the point of Parry's work was to reach a degree of precision which such terms did not allow. It was necessary to distinguish theoretically between the conventional kind of repetition that marks the formulae, and other, irrelevant kinds: as, for instance, accidental repetition, semantically and pragmatically motivated repetition, and the many kinds of poetically motivated repetition – refrains, parallelism, allusion and so on. By a 'formula', Parry meant a group of words regularly employed under the same metrical conditions to express a particular idea.

Parry was clearly right in connecting the exigencies of strict metre with the completeness and economy of formulaic repertoire that he strikingly demonstrated for Homer. His definition of the formula has, of course, been subject to successive modifications and expansions as it was found too narrow to account for the phenomena that other scholars saw as formulaic. Hainsworth,[38] in particular, has warned that an extension of the term 'formula' to cover almost all Homeric diction would make the judgement that Homer is largely formulaic 'vacuously' true; and he goes a long way towards correcting Parry's original restriction of the formula to words used 'under the same metrical conditions'. Hainsworth scrupulously documents examples of the displacement of formulaic groupings from a familiar location and rhythm by such factors as declension, inversion and separation of the words habitually used. Such a demonstration has been helpful in showing what no one would have seriously disputed; namely, the flexibility of the Homeric formula: fixed formulae, which appear in a constant shape; and flexible formulae, which can be inflected, expanded, and split by other words. The refinement proposed by this descriptive analysis confirms again the influence and power of the oral-formulaic approach initiated by Parry.

Corroborative evidence is provided from another angle by the careful investigations of Detienne into the attitude of Achaean society to the singer and the attitude of the singer towards his craft: corroborative, because referring not to the performer's devices of composition but to his self-interpretation.[39] The Hellenic singer's characteristic boast, as a performer, is that he is able to preserve the truth about heroic deeds without having to be an eye-witness to them. He claims access to the truth simply by virtue of the fact that he hears from the Muses what they saw. As the singer declares at the beginning of the *Catalogue* (*Iliad*, II, 485–586): 'You are gods: you are there and you know everything; / But we know nothing: we just hear the *kleos*'; by which is meant: 'you know everything; / But we singers know nothing: we just hear the *kleos*'. Since the singer begins his performance by asking the Muses to 'tell him' the subject, his composition is being presented to the audience as something that he hears from the custodians of all stages of reality: the Muses are speaking to him as one who has the mandate, the delegated power, of words. Thus the claim to know nothing is a sophisticated conceit.

From its etymology, we know that the Greek word *kleos* was originally an abstract noun simply meaning 'the act of hearing'. From its usage in Homer, we know that this etymology was exploited in order to yield a double-layered meaning. The word came to mean 'fame' or 'reputation' when it was appropriated by the singer as performer to designate that to which his performance referred, the actions of gods and heroes. But in addition to this, *kleos* was the formal word the singer himself used to designate the songs he sang in praise of gods and men, and, by extension, the songs which his audience learned to sing from him; the implication being that the audience continues the *kleos* of the singer's song, which amounts to 'praising' it too. Thus access to an anterior reality and the act of celebrating that reality are presented as oral and aural. Indeed, it is as if the antecedent action exists for the sake of the poetic landmark which recalls it. This conceit marks the extent to which Homer is conscious of the relation between the reality of action and the practice of song which records it. For this poet there are, as it were, two levels of reality – that of the action reported in his song, and that of the performance of this song; and the two levels are woven together verbally through the conceit of the *kleos*.

Having indicated this area of evidence, let me restate my objection to Gadamer's account of the Socratic dialogue. It is unnecessary, I think, to stake the whole weight of criticism on a view of this dialogic procedure which sees it as revolutionary because it marks *the* definitive moment in the transition from myth to rationality. The point, rather, is this: to adopt a procedure of the kind demonstrated in the Socratic method of question and answer undermines conventions of formulaic utterance of the kind I have pointed to; and it undermines them not so much because it rejects or criticises or modifies their content, but rather because it replaces one method of transmission by another method of transmission.

Gadamer removes the art of Socratic questioning from its historical conjuncture. He finds the model for the hermeneutic process in conversation and the model for conversation in the Socratic dialogue. This leads him to view all transmission in the perspective of one specific canonic type. He wants to claim, in effect, that all tradition aspires to the condition of Socratic dialogue. He would of course admit that a very great deal of tradition is quite evidently a wholly inadequate approximation to the pure movement of question and answer; yet it is, nonetheless, from the model of the Socratic dialogue that he believes the performative actions of transmission are best understood. But the claim that the Socratic dialogue is the paradigm for tradition can be maintained only at the price of misrepresentation. It is historically inaccurate because it misrepresents the linguistically revolutionary nature of the Socratic method, a device of interrogation which helped to break the forms of cultural reproduction enshrined in the mimetic activity of pre-Socratic poetry.

Gadamer thus extrapolates from a particular type of social action which effectively broke a specific process of cultural reproduction; he decontextualises a particular linguistic strategy in order to produce a normative account of tradition as a whole. But the problem is not simply one of historical misrepresentation. The problem, rather, is that the procedure which Gadamer adopts in this particular instance is a characteristic one. His whole method of analysis rests on a systematic process of decontextualisation.

This decontextualisation is anchored in the proposition that a man's 'relation to the world' is 'fundamentally linguistic in nature', so that language is 'the universal medium' of the 'mediation between past and present'.[40] The process is further anchored in a view of tradition which sees it as unitary. Only thus can Gadamer claim that 'for the historian' the individual text makes up, together with other sources and testimonies, 'the unity of the total tradition'.[41] The object of interpretation is this 'unity of the total tradition';[42] and this object the historian must try to understand 'in the same sense in which the literary critic understands his text in the unity of its meaning'.[43] Remarks of such a kind are flagrantly inattentive to the socially variable forms in which linguistic exchanges are channelled. This inattentiveness is not a matter of little local difficulties which might be met by inserting a series of qualifications into the argument; on the contrary, it crucially affects the substance of the argument. Or to put the point in the form of an image: the difficulty is not a kind of intellectual adiposity which might be rectified by submitting to a strict diet of anthropological fieldwork, but rather a kind of arthritis which damages the bone structure of the thought.

This is so because Gadamer necessarily has to set about the task of explaining his paradigm by reference to a whole range of linguistic phenomena part of whose intrinsic nature it is to be institutionalised through certain social forms. The reading of a lyric poem which reaches us in printed form; the translation of a text from one language to another; the asking of questions in the context of a philosophical inquiry; the conducting of a telephone conversation; the playing of a game; the attempt to decipher the meanings in a picture – on all these matters Gadamer has subtle and finely observed remarks to make. But what his observations systematically leave out of account is the fact that all of these phenomena occur within particularised contexts; that they are institutionalised in varied ways not as a matter of chance but necessarily; that the ways in which they are thus institutionalised exert varying degrees of social constraint on those engaged in these activities; and that these varying degrees of constraint in important ways affect what can be transmitted and the extent to which we can criticise it.

It is evident that the structural and institutional conditions for the social recollection of the past are mediated not only through dialogue, whether literally or metaphorically understood, but through particular types of linguistic communications whose very structure consigns potentially awkward questions to oblivion. There are, for instance, conversational exchanges which obey tacit rules of propriety as to what are permissible utterances in context, and there are sequences of ritual utterances which obey even more strict ceremonial rules regarding such matters as intonation, range of vocabulary, syntax and possible responses to previous utterances.[44] Linguistic communications of this type – and the formulaic devices of oral poetry may be taken as further instances of the type – are best understood as strategies of social persistence. To study them is to study mechanisms of cultural reproduction. But Gadamer has little to say about such linguistic exchanges.

This is not an accidental fault. If the linguistic performances of the type referred to are inaccessible to Gadamer, this is because of his complicity with inherited hermeneutic theory and practice. If Romantic hermeneutics is the *bête noire* of *Truth and Method*, that is because its author is more completely trapped than he wishes to admit in the prejudices of certain received ideas from which his self-understanding – and misunderstanding – demands that he distinguish himself. Gadamer focuses on the written text; in doing so he repeats the method of his predecessors. Throughout its history, the emphasis of hermeneutics has arisen from and returned to philology; that is to say, to the kind of relation with tradition which is grounded in the transmission of texts, or, at the very least, of documents and monuments to which authority is ascribed because they are held to have a status comparable to texts. It is no accident that Schleiermacher, while founding a general theory of interpretation, was the exegete of the New Testament and the translator of Plato; that Dilthey, while producing a critique of historical reason, located the specificity of interpretation (*Auslegung*), as contrasted with the direct understanding of the other (*Verstehen*), in the phenomenon of fixation by writing and, more generally, inscription; or that Gadamer, in his turn, while addressing the problem of the universality of understanding, should prove himself such an erudite exegete of Plato and Aristotle, Schleiermacher and Dilthey.

For in so doing Gadamer, like his predecessors, decontextualises the practice of distancing which is implied by fixation in writing. Writing is not simply a matter of the material fixation of discourse; this fixation is the condition of a more basic phenomenon, that of the relative autonomy of the text. This autonomy, as Ricoeur has stressed, relates both to the social conditions of the production of the text, and to the social conditions of the production of its audience.[45] The peculiar characteristic of the literary work, to which traditional hermeneutics ascribed the authority of model, lies in its capacity to transcend its social condition of reproduction and reception; and thus to open itself to a potentially unlimited series of socially situated readings. The literary work, because it is inscribed, decontextualises itself; it provides, in its mode of transmission, a deconstruction of itself of a kind necessarily absent from non-textual transmission. A hermeneutics with its eyes trained on the literary text replicates this act of deconstruction. Its method, in Gadamer no less than in Schleiermacher, requires that the traces of its social origins be repressed and forgotten. But these traces are detectable, nonetheless, in its figures of speech. Thus the term 'context', which is etymologically derivative from, and hence subordinate to, 'text', indicates where authority in transmission has been customarily assigned; while Gadamerian metaphorology, which returns with an insistence as stubborn as it is subtle to the acts of listening, hearing, speaking and addressing, is generated by the ostrich-like denial of the particular conditions of production and reception applicable only to writing.

This metaphorical network does not simply obscure, it is designed to obscure, the social conditions of writing's creation and acceptance. Hence the problem in Gadamer – a problem which his argument by analogy strategically denies – is not simply one of a particular historical misrepresentation regarding the practice of Socratic dialogue; nor again is it simply that the method of analysis adopted by him rests on a systematic process of decontextualisation; it resides, in addition, in the fact that such a practice of decontextualisation is necessarily entailed in the traditional hermeneutic focus on writing, a focus shared by Gadamer despite his disclaimers. All these factors are involved and reinforce one another.

We need to distinguish, therefore, between three distinct levels of his analysis. There is, first of all, the ontological level, which is concerned with statements regarding what exists. There is, second, the phenomenological level, which is concerned with statements regarding the world as it appears to us. But there is a third level: this concerns statements about the social forms and constraints on behaviour which are both patterned and historically variable. The problem with Gadamer's analysis is that he wants to argue directly from the phenomenological to the ontological; he wants to ground his claim regarding the primary process by adducing a vast range of subtly observed illustrations from the world as it appears, but illustrations which are consistently decontextualised, so that he systematically loses sight of the ways in which communicational acts are affected by or affect different social formations. From this arises the false ontologisation which is contained in Gadamer's implicit social theory from the point at which he takes the conversation as the model for the hermeneutic process.

To say this is not simply to make a tritely negative point. It is to suggest three points of a more positive nature.

First, Gadamer is right to see tradition as a transaction. In doing this he breaks with the antinomian thinking which has guided so much European thought since the Enlightenment. In the Enlightenment, in Romanticism and again in classical social theory, discourse moved around a binary frame of reference, in which a series of oppositions was generated in order to identify the organising principles of modernity. In each case abstract nouns were used in order to set up a firm contrast between two types of mentality, or two types of social structure; and in each case the first of these pairs of concepts, those referring to the prior condition, played the role of a foil, a residual category. It was necessarily residual because the point of the exercise was to establish a frame of reference for characterising the mentality, or social structure, of the present; the aim was always to set up an idea of the past which could be used, schematically, as a comparative point of reference for understanding that present.[46] In consequence, the term 'tradition' came to be used as an abstract noun to characterise a whole mentality or a principle of social life, rather than in its traditional verbal form – *tradition*, literally, 'handing on'.

This entailed an abbreviated understanding of transmission. For tradition is the presence in us of a past, a presence which causes us to respond to a play of forces. A tradition can act upon people only because they still carry history, as a living thing, in themselves. This history is immanent in our present; we are inheritors and have access to self-awareness in actively receiving this heritage; a heritage which we are unable to receive without also reanimating it. This inheritance is, in a certain sense, inscribed in us; and yet the language so inscribed has latent in it an unavoidable element of amnesia. In all language there is a forgetting; the meanings retained, yet also in a sense 'lost', in the hold of words are constantly being reanimated, awoken from their semantic slumbers. This transaction, in the very act of restituting a presence to what was past, produces something new. In this sense we may speak of tradition as an act of creative recovery.

The second point is that Gadamer's model can be, as it were, turned on its head; that despite himself he has provided – implicitly – an account of how tradition does not operate. Whereas Gadamer claims that the act of understanding, and therefore the act of handing on a tradition, essentially turns upon the 'opening and keeping open' of questions, it might be argued, on the contrary, that the opposite is the case. Anyone who is interested in the handing on of traditional understandings will want to focus his attention on the way in which some kinds of dialogue are occluded. The study of cultural reproduction, on this view, is not so much the study of dialogues in which questions are asked, but rather the study of occluded questions. This type of inquiry would not seek to show the way in which questions are 'opened up and kept open', but rather how the social structuring of communications is so organised as to foreclose and keep closed the very possibility of asking questions. In this sense we may make a distinction – a distinction which Gadamer's analysis has the effect of preventing us from perceiving – between cultural reproduction and tradition.

The third point concerns one particularly important way in which such foreclosures take place. Here the instance of mimesis in pre-Socratic poetic utterances may be seen as illustrative of a type of behaviour which is encountered much more widely – for instance, in all ritually commemorative acts. Here we are concerned with acts which are articulated not exclusively through the shaping of words (that is, by using texts in vocal contexts) or through the shaping of music (that is, by using instrumental resources), but also through a dimension that from many points of view is more important: the dimension of ritual gesture. The movements of the body often express more of the totality and background of life than words alone are able to do. The re-situation of traditional understandings in what might be called the grammar and the pragmatics of performative acts entails the recognition of this dimension, which plays a crucial part in the social formation of memories. This is the level of transmission carried by bodily performances, the elaborate repertoires of culturally specific kinesic actions.

Long before the level of 'tradition' in Gadamer's sense is reached, therefore, the body must be operative in the dynamics of oral speech and the actual pronunciation of words; in the continual re-enactment of certain basic motions of the tongue, lips and hands. In this sense, at least, tradition is more a matter of bodily re-enactment than it is a matter of conducting a conversation with texts of the past.

NOTES

1 P. Bourdieu, *Outline of a Theory of Practice* (Cambridge, 1977), p. 94.
2 H-G. Gadamer, *Truth and Method* (New York, 1975), pp. xviii, 465–6. Henceforth this work will be referred to as *TM*.
3 *TM*, p. xxi.
4 *TM*, p. xviii.
5 *TM*, p. 240.
6 *TM*, p. 244.
7 E. Gombrich, *Art and Illusion* (London, 1960), pp. 170–1.
8 *TM*, pp. xxi–xxii, 268.
9 *TM*, p. xxii.
10 *TM*, p. 251.
11 *TM*, p. 272
12 *TM*, pp. 419–20.
13 *TM*, p. 258.
14 *TM*, p. 258.
15 *TM*, p. 360.
16 *TM*, p. 354.
17 *TM*, p. 354
18 *TM*, p. 331.
19 *TM*, p. 337.
20 *TM*, p. 340.
21 *TM*, p. 327.
22 *TM*, p. 327.
23 *TM*, p. 327.
24 *TM*, p. 309.
25 *TM*, pp. 324–5, 327.
26 *TM*, p. 266.
27 *TM*, p. 332.
28 *TM*, p. 330.
29 *TM*, p. 326.
30 *TM*, p. 329.
31 *TM*, pp. xvii–xviii.
32 H-G. Gadamer, *Kleine Schriften. Vol. II* (Tubingen, 1972), p. 22. Gadamer might wish to reply to this by saying that, although the subject of Plato and the poets is not treated in *TM*, the argument of that book assumes – even though it does not explicitly cite – the conclusion reached in a much earlier article of 1934 in which the subject is addressed; this is his 'Plato und die Dichter', now reprinted in H-G. Gadamer, *Platos dialektische Ethik* (Hamburg, 1968). Gadamer there makes the point that Plato's attack on the poets occurs in an historical context in which traditional poetry can no longer retain its earlier function, because the shared ethos on which the educational significance of poetry was based had been eroded. When the consensus now holds that no one does what is just voluntarily, Homeric poetry is exposed to misuse by those who seek to exploit it in their pursuit of political power. In the hands of the sophists, traditional poetry is made to contribute to the dissipation of the souls of the citizens. In this sense Plato's extreme critique of the poets must indeed be understood as an ironical reply to the opposite extreme of

sophistic misappropriation. Yet even if we concede Gadamer this, his account of mimesis still lacks the recognition that familiarity with a shared tradition is more than the inheritance of a common set of ideas. His concept of mimesis as presented in *TM* (see especially pp. 102ff.) fails to give an account of what I call below the 'mechanics' or 'forms' of mimesis.

33 See E.A. Havelock, *Preface to Plato* (Cambridge, MA, 1963).

34 *TM*, pp. 102, 118, 371.

35 Havelock, *Preface to Plato, passim.*

36 *Ibid.*, pp. 307ff.

37 See A.B. Lord, *The Singer of Tales* (Cambridge, MA, 1960).

38 See J.B. Hainsworth, *The Flexibility of the Homeric Formula* (Oxford, 1968).

39 M. Detienne, *Les Maîtres de vérité dans la Grèce archaïque* (Paris, 1967), pp. 9ff.

40 *TM*, pp. 432–3.

41 *TM*, p. 304.

42 *TM*, p. 304.

43 *TM*, p. 304.

44 M. Bloch, 'Symbols, Song, Dance and Features of Articulation: Is Religion an Extreme Form of Traditional Authority?', *Archives Européennes de Sociologie*, xv (1974), pp. 55–81.

45 P. Ricoeur, *Hermeneutics and the Human Sciences* (Cambridge, 1981), p. 91.

46 P. Abrams, 'The Sense of the Past and the Origins of Sociology', *Past and Present*, 55 (1972), pp. 18–32.

6   Tattoos, masks, skin

I begin with two citations, one from a nineteenth-century traveller, the other from a twentieth-century novelist.

Dr Clavel wrote an article in 1885 on tattooing in the Marquesas Islands. Tattooing had been developed there to a higher degree of elaboration than that exhibited in many societies, so ornately, indeed, that the first European travellers mistook the tattoo-marks they saw there for a form of clothing. Dr Clavel describes his encounter there with a man of awful aspect, a tribal chief who proudly displayed his body on which no visible part remained unmarked. His lips, his tongue, his gums, his palate and his genitals were all entirely tattooed. These marks the chief displayed with pride, because he considered them signs of honour.[1]

In his well-known short story *The Penal Colony*, Franz Kafka describes a particularly excruciating form of punishment. A 'drawing machine' is strapped to the prisoner's body and fitted with a needling device, the purpose of which is to inscribe onto the body of each convict the article of the law which he has infringed; the inscription is driven into the skin ever more deeply, until the tortured man can read it in his own flesh. These marks are the signs of the prisoner's shame.[2]

I shall return to this distinction between marks of honour and marks of shame; but for the moment we need to note the etymologies which have come down to us for the practice of tattooing.

We know of at least three of these. We owe the best-known, of course, to the Polynesian root *tatu* or *tatau*, which gave Europe the word 'tattoo'. Captain James Cook observed the practice of 'tattowing' on Tahiti in July 1769, and his description, although not published until 1893, is the first appearance of the word in the English language; he returned from his South Sea Islands voyage in 1774 with the tattooed Tahitian known to the British as Omai.[3] Polynesians used the vocabulary of tattoo to make sense of European writing, and Europeans understood tattoos as a kind of writing;[4] the French fur trader Etienne Marchand pursued the same train of thought when, at Vai Tahu in June 1791, he reported that Marquesan tattoo artists were specialist professionals and that their tattoos resembled 'a species of hieroglyphics or characters of Chinese writing'.[5] A second etymology, though less well known, has an even longer ancestry. Greek texts referring to body-marking often employ the term *stigma*, or cognate words like the verb *stizo*; and the Romans took over the noun *stigma* from the Greeks to denote a tattoo, but not the verb *stizo*, for which they found substitutes such as *inscribo* 'inscribe' and *imprimo* 'imprint'. 'Stigma' has passed into our own language with the sense of 'moral blot' or 'mark of infamy'.[6] A third etymology stems from the Indian subcontinent, where the Hindi verb *godna*, which clearly refers to the same practice, means to prick, puncture, mark the skin with dots; a *godni* is a tattooing instrument and a *godnawali* is a tattooist.[7]

As a technical procedure tattooing entails the puncturing of the skin and the insertion of an indelible dark pigment into the dermis to a depth of between 0.25 and 0.5 centimetres, by means of a needle or other sharp instrument. Instruments may be made of many substances, such as metal, wood, shell or bone; and the dark pigment may be of soot, pine resin or charcoal mixed with walnut oil. When the prickings are clustered together densely enough, they assume the appearance of linear patterns. This basic technique is found throughout the world.[8]

This mechanical process admits of a number of variations.[9] Throughout most of Oceania a small adze-shaped implement with multiple points attached to, or cut into, the blade is rapped with a rod to drive the pigment into the skin. The Maoris gash the skin with a sharp blade to reduplicate the pricked tattooing with raised scars and by this means obtain a relief effect. The Papuans repeat the tattoo operation after a month or so, re-marking all the lines to obtain a more conspicuous pattern. In Japan, in South East Asia, in Western Asia and in North Africa, points set into the end of a rod are pushed directly into the skin. The Eskimos use needle and thread, the latter being coated with soot and passed under the skin. In parts of the Arctic tattooing employs a very distinctive technique; a needle is used to draw a carbon-impregnated thread under the skin to produce linear patterns.

Since tattooing can only achieve its full visual effect on a light skin, it prevails in Oceania, Asia and America, whereas the dark pigmentation of the people of sub-Saharan Africa means that the sculptural quality of scarification, rather than the more graphic medium of tattooing, is the predominant method adopted to achieve an irreversible alteration of the surface of the human body. Scarification consists in marking out the design first of all, then driving a needle or thorn under the epidermis along the line already marked out in order to lift up the skin; the scars may be patterned in relief by raising them, or they may consist of sunken designs with alternating hollows and protrusions.

Tattooing and scarification belong to a much larger class of practices designed to alter bodily appearance, which include plastic surgery, dress, adornment, coiffure, cosmetics, body-building, tight-lacing, and marking the skin with henna and other substances. With the exception of plastic surgery, tattooing and scarification are distinctive, in the sense that their effects are indelible rather than transient. Nicholas Thomas has argued that tattoos are the most immutable of mobile inscriptions; he writes that, 'whereas objects gathered might be lost, broken or sold, and could only ever be tenuously connected with one's person and uncertain in their significance, a tattoo is not only ineradicable and inalienable, it is unambiguously part of you'.[10] In a similar spirit the physician-philosopher François Dagognet has argued in *Ecriture et iconographie* that, for late eighteenth-century analysts, 'inscription guaranteed and guarded immutability'.[11]

Transitory states are also indicated by facial paint. Such transient decoration is known to date from Palaeolithic times. The famous Venus or Woman Holding a Bison Horn carved in the Laussel cave in the Dordogne, the Venus Impudique carved in mammoth ivory in the Musée de l'Homme in Paris, the Willendorf Venus in the Museum of Natural History in Vienna: all of these display bodies painted with red ochre.[12] In ancient Greece, in the Dionysiac cults, adepts smeared themselves in wine lees or coated their faces with clay to simulate the dead.[13] In the kabuki theatre, which arose in the seventeenth century, first at Kyoto, later at Edo, make-up, far from characterising individuals in psychological terms, was designed to free the individual from any naturalistic expression, so that codified designs could fall into place with the structural rigour of body writing.[14] In the Western circus, clowns, with their eccentrically painted faces, play a part similar to that of animal characters in fairy tales, representing a momentary suspension of the constraints of reality, an interspace in which waking dreams can unfold.[15] In Western culture, where anatomical reticence and an obsession with cleanliness and with an unscratched skin prevail, cosmetics are employed to enhance the appearance of the skin; this practice reinforces the conviction that there is a fundamental contrast between an inner and an outer self, an antithesis between, on the one hand, the body which is cosmetically decorated and, on the other hand, the inner and whole person.

All these forms of decoration, with the exception of Palaeolithic red ochre designs, are short-lived. They are designed to meet occasional circumstances, associated with ceremonies of ritual transgression of taboos and with rites of passage: a marriage, a bereavement, a hunting ceremony. Body painting is here a transitory adornment, intended to mark a particular event and signalling an interruption in the course of everyday life. It is not a chronic feature of life.

Of all the forms of body decoration the most culturally important is the mask. As the most direct and most widespread form of disguise, masks play a predominant role in rites of passage, in curative ceremonies and exorcism, in funerary rites and in religious dramas. In Greek antiquity there was no acting without masks. To wear a mask was to act a part, a thought which is retained even today when we refer to the activity of wearing a mask purely figuratively. The thought that it could even be possible to act a part without wearing a mask never occurred to those responsible for the Greek stage. Aristotle assumes that dramatic performances are bound to be masked; he takes masks for granted without discussing them; masks are simply there, a performance feature of the dramatic world.[16]

The word 'mask' comes down to us via two routes, one Arabic, the other Latin. The words 'mask', 'masquerade' and 'mascara' come into European languages from Arabic. The Arabic word for 'masquerade', *maskharah*, stems from the root *skhr*; the Arabic verb from which the noun is derived means 'to laugh, scoff, jeer, sneer, ridicule, mock, deride, make fun'.[17] In ancient Rome the term *persona* referred to the mask worn by an actor in a play. This notion of the Latin 'persona' – a mask, a tragic mask, a ritual mask, an ancestral mask – dates back to the beginnings of Latin civilisation.[18] Masks of ancestors have been found to be particularly prevalent among Etruscan remains, and many effigies of sleeping and seated ancestor masks have been discovered in the excavations made of the vast Tyrrhenian kingdom, as well in excavations found in Rome, in the Latium and in Graecia Magna.[19] All freemen of Rome were Roman citizens and all of them had a civil persona; some masks remained attached to particular privileged families of the religious *collegia*. Only the Roman slave was excluded from the right to be a persona. Slaves did not own their bodies, they had no ancestors, no name and no personal belongings.[20]

In locating the role of masks in a broad historical setting Marcel Mauss has given us some valuable points of orientation.[21] He has demonstrated that the words 'self' and 'category of the self', the 'cult of the self' and the 'respect for the self', particularly respect for the selves of others, were all of recent date. The idea of the person developed only slowly over many centuries. The Greek notion of the person, the Roman notion of the person and the medieval notion of the person were all far removed from our current notion of the person as an individual ego. Our own notion of the human person, which assumes a sharp distinction between self and role, is still basically a Christian one. To paint the history of the development of the person in broad brush strokes, as Marcel Mauss does, we may say that the story leads from a condition in which there is a pure role without self to a condition in which there is a pure self without role.

Martin Hollis has elaborated upon Marcel Mauss' insight.[22] He observes that even if the notion of a role arises from the practice of wearing masks in sacred dramas, the category of role is not so easily separated off from the category of the person or self as might be suggested by the image of the mask in an age of secularisation. Today, one use of the concept of role is in analysing social institutions and practices, another is in analysing more intimate spheres of social life, where it borrows from the dramaturgical analogy of dramatis personae or characters in a play.

If you were to collect illustrations of masks from newspapers and else-where, you would be able to assemble a vast hoard of examples. These would include objects commonly found from the Nootka up to the Tlingit of North Alaska, a form of remarkable shutter mask, which are double or even triple, and which open up to reveal two or three creatures, which are totems placed one upon the other, and are personified by the wearer of the mask. The last shutter opens to reveal, if not the whole face, then at least the mouth, and most frequently both mouth and eyes. Some very fine specimens of shutter masks are held in the British Museum.[23] Then again, in assembling your list of masks, you would be able to cite pictures of Venetian carnival-goers, oxygen masks, welding masks, Arab refugees wrapped up and protected by masks against wind and sand, visors, veils, camouflages. As an expressive action, the wearing of a mask may signify a performer's protection from witchcraft or by witchcraft, and as an instrumental action, the wearing of a mask may have the capacity of defence manifest in oxygen masks, welding masks and gas masks in the material culture of modern Europe. We would need to notice also all those artefacts which establish distance between persons without covering the face as masks do: as, for instance, with the vestments of kings, priests and judges. This suggests that roles, titles and offices may provide dominant or more or les permanent personae.[24]

The use of masks has been found, and their meaning discussed, in a very wide range of societies. To name only some of the areas in which they have been investigated, masks are found in African cultures, in ancient Greek culture, in Rome and in Venice.

In his classic account of *The Mande Blacksmiths* and their place in Mande society in Western Sudan, McNaughton shows that Mande blacksmiths are proficient smelters, metal-workers and wood-carvers.[25] The *kòmò* masks which they construct are potent images, carved of wood and covered with many different animal and vegetable materials, the ostensible purpose of which is that they should function as instruments of divination and destroyers of criminals and sorcerers. The masks are worn by high-ranking officials of the *kòmò* association, who are always men and often leaders of the tribe. Almost invariably the mask wearer will be a member of the profession of blacksmiths; only they can make the masks and dance in them.

In appearance the masks are a manifestation of power. As material struc-tures, they consist of three horizontal units: a dome, horns and a mouth. The wearer's head fits into the dome, or central helmet, which anchors extensions to the front and rear of the face. Large antelope horns protrude from the rear of the dome; these first run horizontally and then curve upwards in an arc which unifies the entire structure while potentiating the suggestion of ominous energy. In front of the dome there is a long, thin, fierce-looking carved mouth, often furnished with a series of paired small antelope horns or wild pig tusks which are attached to the top and face forward. The carved mouth is associated with the hyena, an animal thought by the Mande to be a symbol of knowledge and intelligence. The dancing smith holds in his mouth a whistle-like horn made of bamboo, wood or iron; with this he produces an exceptionally loud bellowing sound which by the force of its aural terror amplifies the visual ominousness of the mask's mouth.

If the appearance of Mande masks makes them a manifestation of power, the process governing their manufacture reinforces this effect. The blacksmith will retreat to the bush to create the mask, returning there day after day until his work is complete; even though the carving of a mask can be completed in less than an afternoon, the mystery surrounding the mask is underscored by the fact that it will be under construction for at least four weeks, and frequently for as long as six weeks.

Kòmò masks are transformative artefacts. They entail thereby not the transformation of inert material from one category to another, but a further transformation in which the material is regarded as something endowed with the power to act: that is to say, the artefact is thought to be imbued with agency. The transformation of wood into mask, and then of the mask into an artefact of power, creates an enduring political legitimacy for those who are entitled to make, to own and to perform with the masks. Taken together with its accompanying costumes and accoutrements, the mask is regarded by the Mande as the acceptable face of something: a power, a kind of energy or metaphysical presence, which otherwise would be too dangerous to see directly.

Of the masks worn in ancient Greek religious ritual three may be singled out: Gorgo, Artemis and Dionysus.[26]

The gaze of Gorgo provokes panic, horror and terror. In the face of Gorgo man faces the powers of the beyond in their most radically alien form: as death and as nothingness. Odysseus, the heroic model of endurance, quails at the thought of encountering Gorgo; panic turns him pale, and he is gripped by the sudden fear that Persephone might send up from Hades' halls some ghostly monster like the head of Gorgo. Gorgo has this terrifying effect because in her countenance the bestial is superimposed on the human. Her broad, round head evokes a leonine mask, her hair is frequently represented as a seething mass of snakes, the skull-like grin across her face reveals the pointed teeth of a wild boar, and her gigantic tongue protrudes grotesquely over her chin. Part human, part animal, Gorgo is also a fusion of genders: her chin is bearded and, when portrayed in a standing position, Gorgo is frequently endowed with male sex organs, while in other representations she is portrayed in the process of giving birth.

Artemis is a goddess of mask because, especially in initiatory rites for young people, over whom she presides, masquerades play an especially important part. The cult of Artemis requires a hyper-feminine demeanour: young boys must walk silently in the streets, never raising their voices, and their eyes must be downcast. Yet the cult of Artemis simultaneously prescribes hyper-virility: its adepts are required to steal from the tables of adults, and to demonstrate a violent brutality in fierce collective fights, biting, scratching and kicking, and exhibiting all the frenzy of a warrior. The mask of Artemis mirrors the contrary attitudes of feminine reserve and male ferocity.

The mask of Dionysus also reveals a creature of opposites. On one vase, for instance, the mask of Dionysus is flanked with maenads and satyrs, the latter themselves being masked, mixed creatures, half men, half beasts.

With masks the ancient Greeks confronted the circumstance of radical otherness. They faced the radical otherness of death in the case of Gorgo, whose gaze plunged whoever beheld it into a state of terror. They faced the otherness situated in the space of civilised society that stretches from the city to the area of the seas and mountains, reaching from the centres of culture to the borderlands of untamed nature, in the case of Artemis. And they faced the otherness of a world of unbridled joy where the constraints of human life faded away in the state of Dionysiac possession. We can see, then, that the masks of Gorgo, of Artemis and of Dionysus expressed the tensions between contraries: in every case it is hilarity that relieves these tensions. Laughter liberates from the terror of death, from the anguish of mourning and from the shackles of prohibition.

The Saturnalia of the Roman carnival survived from ancient times into the eighteenth century. In his account of *The Roman Carnival*, published in 1789, Goethe describes the saturnalian behaviour of masked Roman citizens, in which sexuality and murderous violence were mimed, evoked and otherwise alluded to; a surviving form of pre-Christian festivity, the Roman carnival preceded the Lenten and Easter mysteries of the Roman Catholic church.[27] Throughout the French wars of religion, ritual occasions including carnival also offered circumstances under which religious riots frequently occurred, and they became the most likely forum for the expression of genuine revolutionary sentiments; festive occasions could sometimes turn into occasions for genuine revolts.[28]

The clownish behaviour characteristic of the carnival in Venice was, of course, nothing like the direct, personal role-reversal that slaves enjoyed in ancient Rome, when they wore badges of freedom as well as their masters' clothes and had their owners serve them at table. The Venetian carnival ought to be seen as a ritual of states-reversal, where persons of low rank affected the style of their social superiors and in doing so temporarily inverted a hierarchy they normally accepted.[29] This structured reversal of roles has been classically analysed, of course, by Mikhail Bakhtin and Victor Turner.[30] Most masquer-aders in Venice identified themselves ritually and dramatically with their social opposites: nobles dressed as peasants, men as women, harlots as men, the old became young and the decrepit affected potency. These social rever-sals were all structured. Nevertheless, these forms of structured licence some-times let through the cracks, as it were, some forms of less structured licence. Masks made it possible for prostitutes dressed as men to ply their trade more covertly than usual, and such violations of public peace and morality led to occasional prohibitions against wearing masks during carnival time; after the death of Doge Marino Grimani in 1605, for instance, masquerades were prohibited during carnival in order to discourage outbreaks of violence.[31]

The transient decorations of the mask differ from the indelible designs of tattooing and scarification, which, far from indicating a transitional or episodic circumstance, indicate the embodiment, the incarnation, of an entire system of social organisation. They are the marks upon the body of an institutional and personal permanence. This is because, unlike all other forms of bodily alter-ation, tattoos and scarifications, and these alone, entail a threefold process: an initial wounding of the skin, a subsequent healing of the wounds, and an ultimate residue of durable markings.

But are these markings truly durable? There is some debate on this. The sixth-century doctor Aetius gave directions for the removal of tattoos by using some highly caustic substances; and from this it is reasonable to infer that there was at that time a clientele of ex-convicts and ex-slaves anxious to erase the marks of a painful past from public view. But it is unlikely that the method he proposed was particularly successful, since it must surely have left scars which were almost equally incriminating.[32] Again, seven articles on tattooing were published in the *Scientific American* between 1891 and 1903, four of which dealt with tattoo removal. These discussed the procedures developed by three French physicians, Variot in 1891, Baillot in 1896 and Brunet in 1899, all of which entailed the use of acids to remove tattooed skin. But we may suspect that these methods were relatively unsuccessful from reading an article by T.W. Dodds in a *Scientific American* of 1891.[33] He there writes about the removal of three 'very indelible tattoo marks by applying nitric acid with the stopper of a bottle . . . just sufficient to cover the stain so as to avoid marking a larger scar than needful'. His reference to 'a larger scar than needful' surely indicates the difficulty of securing a successful outcome. On the subject of removing tattoo-markings it may be prudent, there-fore, to leave the last word to a Maori man who told James Cowan in the early twentieth century that 'you may be robbed of all your most-prized possessions but of your moko (that is to say, your facial tattoo) you cannot be deprived'.[34]

Because of their indelibility, tattoos and scarifications, unlike all other forms of bodily alteration, enjoy a unique relationship to the skin. That uniqueness hinges upon the fact that the skin is two-sided. There is an outside-facing skin and an inside-facing skin, and these two sides form an indivisible structure. The outside of the skin creates a boundary between the self and the world, a boundary that is especially sensitive to the world, and one which over time accumulates a complex texture of marks which remain as witness to the ways in which external forces have impinged upon the skin. The inside of the skin holds in the contents of the body and registers the inner state of the cavity, its emptiness, its repletion, its well-being and its malaise. The power of tattoos and scarifications, as distinctive forms of marking, depends upon this double quality of the skin.[35] They are indelible marks that are at one and the same time *on* the surface of the skin and *under* the surface of the skin. The fact of constituting this physical boundary is paralleled by, and makes possible, the capacity to constitute a second, cultural, boundary, one which marks the difference between cultural inclusion and exclusion.

It is this distinguishing feature of shaping a double boundary, one physical, the other cultural, which justifies Didier Anzieu in speaking of the skin ego as 'the original parchment which preserves, like a palimpsest, the erased, scratched-out, written-over, first outlines of an "original" pre-verbal writing made up of traces on the skin'. The skin-ego has the function of registration. The skin is a kind of external biographical memory, a system of inbuilt 'memory places' for reconstructing the history of the person as a locus of remembered events and cultural affiliations.[36]

Tattoos and scarifications may be understood, therefore, as *literalisations* of a circumstance which on other occasions are registered not physically but linguistically, when, as Laura Benthien has shown, the skin is taken to be a metonym for the person.[37] The entry on 'touch' is by far the longest, comprising fourteen columns, in the *Oxford English Dictionary*, and is full of idioms indicating the widespread experience of touch, not only as a straight-forward physical modality, as a physical sensation, but also affectively, as emotion. There is a rich correspondence of semantic fields, of external touching and inner feeling. When we speak of those who have, or who do not have, a delicate sense of what is fitting and proper when dealing with others we refer to them as 'tactful' or 'tactless'. Some people are said to be 'thin-skinned', others 'thick-skinned'. Tactless people are said to 'get under one's skin', while those who are oversensitive or easily prone to anger are spoken of as 'touchy'. We speak of 'rubbing' people up the wrong way, of someone who is 'a soft touch', and of someone as having 'the human touch'. Some people must be 'handled' carefully. A deeply felt experience is said to be 'touching' and we speak of the heart 'being touched'.

The linguistic idiom in which the skin is taken to be a metonym for the person is no idiosyncrasy of English. It has equivalents in French, Italian and German. In the *Grand Robert* French dictionary, the entries for *peau* 'skin',

main 'hand', *toucher* 'touch' and *prendre* 'take' are among the most extensive. *Avoir la main heureuse* means 'to be lucky'; *tu me fais suer* means
'you're a pain in the neck'; *c'est une peau de vache* means 'he's a bastard';
faire peau neuve means 'to turn over a new leaf'; *mon petit doigt me l'a dit*
means 'a little bird told me'; *se lever la peau pour quelqu'un* means 'to
sacrifice oneself for someone else'; *de se faire la peau* means simply 'to lose
one's life', and the saying *avoir quelqu'un dans la peau* means that one
possesses the loved one fully, one has the beloved literally in one's skin.

The Italian language proceeds similarly. Italian speaks of *avere la pelle
dura* for 'to have a thick skin'; contact *fra pelle e pelle*, 'between skin and
skin', means that two people have an external, merely superficial encounter,
whereas *entrare nella pelle di qualcuno*, 'to get literally into someone's skin',
refers to a passionate and inner connection; *lasciarci la pelle* means simply
'to lose one's life'; and 'to provoke someone' is rendered as *mettere in pelle*,
meaning something like 'to get under someone's skin'.

German has similar idioms. Grimm's *Deutsches Wörterbuch* of 1877
contains many adjectives used to characterise a person where that person is
described in terms of skin, as when one describes someone as *verwegene*
('reckless'), *bose* ('evil'), *lose* ('roguish'), *feige* ('cowardly'), *schäbige*
('shabby') and *unbedentende* ('worthless') skin. One finds references in the
same dictionary to *gefällige* ('pleasant'), *lustige* ('merry'), *gute* ('good'),
brave ('decent'), *ehrliche* ('honest') and *gutmütige* ('good-natured') skin.
To provoke someone is expressed as *einen Stachel unter die Haut setzen*
('to put a thorn under the skin'), and a German who wished to express the
thought of putting oneself empathically in someone else's place would say
that it is necessary *sich in die Haut des anderen zu versetzen*.

Nor are the usages of language to speak of the skin as a metonym for the
person confined to European languages. Outside the European context such
usages may sometimes be even more emphatic. In Papua New Guinea, for
example, no dichotomy is thought to obtain between an inside and an outside,
and there is correspondingly no idea of striving to attain some incorporeal
condition of selfhood. The inner self is thought to be manifested, whether for
good or for ill, through the skin, and a person's visible resources, those that
the person allows to be seen, are said to be 'on the skin'. Dancers will speak of
adornments as 'making the skin good' and, if their adornments have been
admired, will say that this is because 'my skin was good'; whereas, on the
other hand, they may express their vulnerability by making statements about
being sorry for their skin.[38]

The distinctiveness of tattoos and scarifications as the only types of bodily
alteration that exist both *on* the skin and *under* the skin, taken in tandem with
the widespread linguistic practice of referring to the skin as a metonym for
the person, puts us in a position where we are able to understand how these

forms of bodily decoration operate, as no others do, as a form of powerful mnemonic code. We can now return to the distinction I introduced at the outset between marks of honour and marks of shame.

Honorific tattoos are known to us in the Middle East from ancient times. In Egypt, in the period dating from 4000 to 2000 BC, tattooing has been found on certain female figures, generally those believed to symbolise fecundity.[39] Keimer tells us that in Egypt tattooing was reserved in particular for prostitutes, dancers and singers, as indicated by the frequent use of the symbol of their divinity, Bes; a tattoo of this kind has been found on the mummy of a woman named Amunet, who served as a priestess of the goddess Hathor during Dynasty XI, about 2164–1994 BC; the lower abdomen beneath the navel bears an elliptical pattern of dots and dashes, and parallel lines of the same pattern adorn her thighs and arms.[40] Writing around 430 BC, Herodotus says that for the Thracians 'to be marked is considered a sign of high birth, whereas to be unmarked is considered one of low birth';[41] an observation corroborated in the second century AD by the Greek moralist Dio Chrysostom, who remarks that 'in Thrace free women are full of tattoos, and the higher their rank the more they have'.[42] The historian Xenophon, writing in the fourth century BC, makes the same point; when he describes a tribe called Mossynoikoi or 'tower dwellers', who lived on the shores of the Black Sea, he says that they showed their Greek visitors 'children of good families . . . entirely decorated on back and front, being tattooed with flowers'.[43]

The use of scarifications as honorific mnemonics is widely dispersed throughout Africa both historically and geographically. Signs of scarification have been discovered on Saharan wall paintings dating from as far back as the fifth millennium BC, as, for example, on the famous Horned Goddess of Inaouanrhat, who bears unmistakable signs of body decorations on shoulders, breasts, thighs and calves.[44] European explorers' accounts written in the 1880s and photographs taken at the end of the nineteenth century show the incidence of scarification among the Tabwa of the southeastern Democratic Republic of Congo and northeastern Zambia, who at that time covered themselves with body decorations from head to foot, and whose term for the practice, *Kulemba*, in addition to meaning 'to scarify', also meant to succeed, to reach a goal and to catch hunted game.[45] Women of nomadic tribes in Yemen and the Maghreb still practised facial and hand scarification in the early twentieth century with the intention that this should ensure fertility and bring good fortune.[46] We can infer a similar intention among the Tiv of Nigeria, where the most characteristic scars are those on the bellies of women which are said to promote fertility. Yoruba consider elaborate body-markings visible proof of strength and courage; a Yoruba woman displaying such marks exhibits her willingness to bear pain and demonstrates that she possesses the necessary fortitude to endure the pains of childbirth.[47]

The fact that scarifications are understood to be marks of honour is corroborated when we find the absence of scarification regarded with disdain, as among the Bafia of Cameroon, who say that a man who is not scarred looks like a pig or chimpanzee.[48]

Similar honorific markings are found in Asia, the only fundamental difference being that tattoos rather than scarification prevailed there. Marco Polo, reporting on his travels in Central Asia in the late thirteenth century, observes that the men of the province of Zardandan considered as a mark of distinction the dark stripes tattooed around their arms and legs, and records that in the province of Kaugigu both men and women had their flesh covered with tattooed pictures of lions, dragons and birds, which they took to be marks of gentility, so much so, indeed, that the more elaborately anyone was decorated, the greater they were considered to be.[49] The people of Borneo, especially the Kayans, had complex beliefs regarding the spiritual significance of tattoo-marks as a passport to the land of the spirits.[50] Among the Long Glat women, where an elaborate system of tattooing began at the first menstrual period, it was believed that after death those who had been tattooed with orthodox designs on hands, feet and thighs would be able to bathe in the heavenly river and gather pearls which lie in its bed, that partially tattooed women would be required to remain on the banks of the river to observe their more fortunate sisters, and that untattooed women would not even be permitted to approach the banks of the mythical treasure stream.[51]

Beliefs about what was implied by the absence of tattoo-marks, as in this case, corroborate the honorific significance assumed to obtain when such marks were present. It was said in nineteenth-century Bengal that a respectable Hindu would not accept water from the hand of a girl who did not wear a tattooed *bindi*, the inference being that such a woman would be amoral;[52] among the Hindus of Bengal in the early twentieth century there was a widespread idea that an untattooed person would encounter considerable difficulties on the journey from this world to the life beyond;[53] and in Kerala, the absence of tattoos on the thighs of a young man was thought to be so emasculating that it was said that such persons would as soon think of wearing a woman's skirt as of omitting to be tattooed.[54]

When Europeans travelled to the Americas they found the practice of exhibiting tattoos as marks of honour just as they did in Oceania. Among the tribes of the lower Mississippi, warriors displayed decorations composed of a great number of parallel red and blue lines on the abdomen when they were renowned because of having killed some famous enemy.[55] In Louisiana, killing an enemy or other war honours entitled a man to have a tomahawk or war-club tattooed on his shoulder above a symbol identifying the nation against which he had accomplished this deed.[56] The Eskimos tattooed a whale's tail on their forehead for each one they had killed.[57] The earliest travellers to Virginia, Carolina and Ontario reported observing extensive representational tattoos on the bodies of women, which were understood to be signs of high status.[58] Dobrizhoffer, an eighteenth-century traveller in Paraguay, writes that 'those that are most painted and pricked you may know to be of high rank and noble birth'.[59] The Caduveo, who believed that unless one's body was marked one was not properly human, had a saying that 'an unpainted body is a stupid body'.[60]

Oceania is, of course, the area where honorific tattooing was most widely found. In the Arioi society in Tahiti the seven classes of society were marked by distinctive tattoos; chiefs usually displayed more extensive tattooing; and chiefly women commonly had their feet tattooed to an inch above the ankle.[61] Tongan men were under much pressure to be tattooed in order to exhibit their courage;[62] Samoans highly value the qualities of heroism and endurance which their tattoos were believed to demonstrate;[63] and in Melanesia the men who belonged to the secret Sokapana society took pride in displaying the long symmetrical gashes inflicted with a curving thorn on their backs.[64] There was only one exception to the rule according to which Mangarevan males were tattooed at puberty; this was the presumptive heir to the position of high chief, who was tattooed shortly after birth with marks on the dorsal surface of the feet.[65]

It is among the Maoris that tattoo designs have been most extensively studied.[66] Among them to have a *papatea*, or a plain face, is considered a matter for reproach. All ranks, for the rest, are ornamented with a facial tattoo or *moko*. The face is divided down the median ridge into equal halves. The right side conveys information about the father's rank; the left side provides information about the mother's rank. For the chief the distinctive mark called *puhoro* is placed on the inside of the thigh and descends towards the knee in varying degrees according to the greater or lesser ranking of the chief; for high-ranking women the distinctive mark called *kawatore* is placed upon both upper and lower lips. Two triangular areas on either side of the centre line of the forehead, above the centre of the eyebrows, mark a zone reserved for indications of rank; a person lacking status inherited from either patrilineal or matrilineal line will have no tattoo in this area. It will be seen that in all these cases tattoos create and mark social differentiation and identity.

At the opposite pole from honorific mnemonics stands the tattoo as a mnemonic of shame. There are forceful material reasons why tattooing lends itself to such a signification. Marks of servitude have customarily been inscribed on the face, and the face is the worst place to receive a tattoo imposed against one's wishes. Marks on the face defy most attempts at concealment, and the gaze of the onlooker is inescapable. Marks on the face, moreover, will be felt to be particularly incriminating because the face is generally viewed as the reflection or mirror of one's person, self, soul.

Ancient texts abound in references to tattoos imposed as marks of shame. They were imprinted primarily on convicts, slaves and prisoners of war. Plato recommends that a temple robber, if a slave or alien, should have his offence marked on his forehead.[67] Cicero reports that the letter K, short for *kalumnia*, was the mark printed on the head of those found guilty of having made a false accusation.[68] Herodotus, writing about the time when Xerxes was imposing tattoos on Greek prisoners of war, remarks laconically that 'the Thebans who deserted to the Persians did not entirely prosper, since the barbarians killed some of them, and marked most of them with the royal tattoo'.[69] The Persian Emperor Darius is known to have branded cuneiform letters on the brows of some 4,000 Greek prisoners.[70] Plutarch, writing centuries after the event, tells us that, after Samos revolted against the Athenian empire in 440 BC, the Athenians imprinted upon the foreheads of their Samian prisoners of war a representation of a Samian ship, while the Samians reciprocated by tattooing their Athenian prisoners of war with an owl, the emblem of Athens.[71] The Cynic philosopher Bion laments that his father was a freed slave 'who instead of a face had a document on his face, the mark of his master's harshness'.[72] Several sources report that the Emperor Theophilus, who reigned between AD 829 and 842, ordered that two monks charged with idolatry, the Graptoi brothers, should have twelve lines of iambic verse tattooed on their foreheads.[73] But the Theodosian Code, a collection of imperial legislation published in AD 438, preserves an edict of AD 316 issued by the Emperor Constantine urging clemency; 'if someone', it states, 'has been condemned to a gladiatorial school or to the mines for the crimes he has been caught committing, let him not be marked on his face, since the penalty of his condemnation can be expressed both on his hands and on his calves, and so that his face, which has been fashioned in the likeness of divine beauty, may not be disgraced'.[74]

The face was repeatedly disgraced by the micro-physics of power imposed through the administration of the early modern state. The Portuguese, Spanish, French, Dutch and English were all engaged in the slave trade and regularly branded slaves with their owner's initials so that they could be identified if they tried to escape; sometimes it would happen that slaves changed hands and a new mark would be imprinted on them with each change of owner, so that in the course of time they might acquire an overlay of enforced marks as a kind of palimpsest of servitude.[75] Marks of shame were imprinted on convicts too. Examples abound in England, France and Russia of abbreviated names indicating the form of a punishment being imposed as a punitive mark on the body of convicts. In England, where as late as the 1890s senior policemen believed that tattoos provided an invaluable weapon in the campaign against recidivism, V = vagabond, M = malefactor, B = burglar, SL = seditious libeller, D = drunkard, and

AD = adulterer were tattooed on the bodies of those held to be guilty of these things.[76] In France GAL signified those condemned to the galleys (*aux galères*) and TP indicated those condemned to perpetual hard labour (*aux travaux forcés à perpétuité*).[77] In Russia, where the autocracy applied the same terminology – *kleimenie* 'branding' – to the branding of convicts and to the imprinting of official documents and coins, exiles at resettlement were branded with the letters SB (*ssylno-brodiag* 'vagrant exile'), those condemned to hard labour with the letters SK (*ssylno-katorzhnik* 'exile at hard labour'), and those condemned to hard labour in Siberia (*katortga*) were tattooed on the cheeks and forehead with an abbreviation indicating that punishment.[78]

When, in the nineteenth century, many medical and psychiatric works came to be devoted to the subject of tattooing, and when the functionaries in police and prison administrations of Europe collated and published data based upon the classificatory zeal which sought to demarcate the boundaries of abnormality, the proposition came to be generally accepted that deviant identity could be read off from physical characteristics. The danger posed to civilised society was conceptualised in the concept of 'degeneration', and the model of such degeneration was read in particular onto two sets of bodies: the male tattoos of criminals and the female tattoos of prostitutes. Lombroso and Lacassagne were in agreement in linking tattoos to criminality. Lombroso believed that 'tattooing assumes a specific character, a strange tenacity and diffusion among the sad class of criminals . . . locked in combat with society', among whom 'the tattoo can be considered, to use the medico-legal term, as a professional characteristic'. Lacassagne, more cautiously, concluded that a 'large number of tattoos are the measure of the tattooed man's criminality, or at least the number of his convictions'. Since access to female prostitutes was guaranteed in continental Europe by their compulsory inscription on official registers, and since signs of venereal disease were deciphered from symptoms on the skin, Parent-Duchâtelet was able to record in detail, in his two-volume work *De la prostitution dans la ville de Paris, considérée sous le rapport de l'hygiène publique, de la morale et de l'administration*, how the skin of prostitutes was exposed to regular and detailed scrutiny which rendered their tattoos particularly conspicuous.[79]

Apart from this, there is what might be called the internalisation of infamy. By this I mean to refer not to the imposition of punitive marks by governing agencies onto the bodies of subalterns, but to the imposition of marks onto subaltern groups by members of those groups themselves. Maertens suggests that the permanent inscription upon their bodies of the hostile attitudes towards them entertained by the dominant group meant that these hostile attitudes became absorbed, and were intended to be absorbed, into the very substance of their bodies: they came to embody their own subjection.[80] The spaces where European tattooing most flourished were those in which the expanding powers of the nation-state's will to impose regulative order upon male bodies held greatest sway: the prison, the armed forces, the labouring population. This is, as it were, the point of departure from which tattooing in modern Western cultures became characteristic of marginal subcultures: criminals, soldiers, sailors, prostitutes. Soldiers and sailors, especially in old-style armies and navies where enlisted men had little chance of marrying and having families, frequently covered themselves with national flags, regimental badges, and female figures identified as mothers, girlfriends and wives. More blatant still, prisoners might adopt the oppositional practice of inscribing the words 'born criminal' upon their bodies; in this way they accepted definitively that they were indeed criminals and tried to construct their cultural world on that very basis, by a passive proclamation of destiny which became a symbolic equivalent of exercising mastery over it. In all these cases the effect, and most probably the intention also, was to create a social envelope, a protective carapace, which provided a symbolic substitute for the domestic envelope that their personal circumstances made it impossible for them to develop.

Life is too diverse, too protean, to fit neatly into the procrustean bed of a binary opposition. The distinction between marks of honour and marks of shame needs to be modified and supplemented, therefore, by a further opposition: that between, on the one hand, honourable degradation, and, on the other hand, honourable stigmatisation.

I am indebted to Alfred Gell for the paradoxical term 'honourable degradation'.[81] The term is obviously puzzling, for how can what is honourable be at the same time degrading? Gell introduces this concept to explain the fact that in Polynesia it was characteristic of persons of particular sanctity or nobility that they might not bear any tattoos at all.[82] We find that the supreme Maori leader during the critical phase of the Maori wars, and the one judged by both Maoris and whites to possess the greatest skills as a political negotiator, Tarapipi, is known not to have been tattooed.[83] There were paramount sacred chiefs in Western Polynesia, Tui Manu'a and Tu'i Tonga, who were not tattooed.[84] In their report of 1844 on the islands of Tahiti, Vincendon and Desgruz tell us that the chief of the Ua Pou 'differed from his subordinates in that he was not decorated with any tattooing'.[85] Salmond reported in 1975 the story of Mihi, a young woman of very high birth; when she was a girl, some Arawa experts had come along the coast to give selected local girls the facial tattoo, but when Mihi was presented to them they refused to tattoo her on the grounds that her ancestry was too exalted.[86] We know that the paramount 'sacred' chiefs of Hawaii also belonged to the category of those deemed too noble to be tattooed. Even though it was a socially approved practice in Polynesia generally, including among the nobly born elite, tattooing represented an unacceptable degradation for all these people. Such pre-eminent individuals were not numerous; but they were distributed widely over the whole of Polynesia. Gell presents a clinching argument in support of his concept of honourable degradation. Throughout Polynesia there is found the premise that, whoever else might be tattooed, the gods themselves are not.[87] To be tattooed was always to bear the stigma of humanity.

I mean the term 'honourable stigmatisation' to be counterposed to that of honourable degradation. The activity to which it refers was originally practised by early Christians. Living in an ancient culture where gross physical marks were imposed for punitive purposes, Christians reconfigured the significance of such markings by taking them instead to be an indication of their allegiance to a culture that was initially a persecuted minority; they affirmed that allegiance, rather than denying it. In so doing they could appeal to the authority of St Paul. When St Paul says 'I carry the *stigmata* of Lord Jesus on my body' he is referring, most probably, to marks such as bruises and welts, the visible signs of the ill-treatment he has endured as a 'slave of Christ'. From this source there developed the later conception of *stigmata* as the marks borne by the body of Christians though their participation in Jesus' suffering.[88] We know that Armenian Christians who made the pilgrimage to Jerusalem were tattooed with their name and the date of their journey, and that they considered these signs of great honour.[89] The Christian practice of tattooing was recorded in the fifth century by the Greek historian Procopius of Gaza, and there is abundant evidence that early modern European pilgrims to Palestine were tattooed with Christian symbols which they acquired in Jerusalem.[90] The English traveller George Sandys recorded in 1615 having seen the arms of pilgrims marked with 'the names of Jesus, Maria, Bethlehem, and the Jerusalem cross; and seventeenth century travellers to the Holy land, such as Fynes, Moryson and Jean de Thevenot, observed the same practice'.[91]

The strategy of reconfigured significance practised by early Christians is exemplified too by Russian prisoners both before and after the October Revolution. In taking over control of practices otherwise associated with the exercise of official power, they inscribed their opposition to officialdom by assimilating its technologies for their own ends. The criminal sphere in late imperial Russia meticulously regulated the use of tattoos in the belief that only those convicts who had distinguished themselves by virtue of their crimes and bloody deeds had earned the right to display their regalia on their breast, and that only the most fearless vagrants could enjoy the right to reward themselves with tattoo-marks; and much later some prisoners are reported to have tattooed their own foreheads with letters signifying 'prisoner of Brezhnev'.[92]

The same category of honourable stigmatisation may be assigned to the *demi-monde* in the West. This took two forms, one aristocratic, the other déclassé. There is a distinction between the kind of tattooing an aristocrat might acquire, which incorporated discrete reference to low-life practice, and genuine subcultural tattooing. Aristocrats might acquire tattoos while travelling abroad as young men, or, in the last decade of the nineteenth century, by flocking to MacDonald's Jermyn Street studio, where the tattoo craze had its origins in the patronage of Edward, Prince of Wales. Among the famous tattooed personages were Czar Nicholas II of Russia, King George of Greece, King Oscar of Sweden, Kaiser Wilhelm of Germany and most of the male members of the British royal family.

The same category of honourable stigmatisation may be assigned to those members of the *demi-monde* in the West who exhibited their elaborately tattooed bodies as showmen at fairgrounds. Notable among these were the Greek Alexandrino, the most celebrated tattooed man of the nineteenth century, known in Germany as 'the tattooed man of Burma' and in America as 'the living Picture Gallery', who bore some 390 images tattooed in Burmese style from the soles of his feet to his hairline;[93] La Belle Irène, who exhibited herself at the Panoptikum in Berlin at about the same time, and was decorated with some 400 images, including butterflies, insects, flowers, eyes, rattlesnakes, eagles and suns;[94] and, perhaps most extraordinary of all, the Great Omi, the most celebrated tattooed showman of the early twentieth century, whose tattooist, George Burchett, estimated the number of pricks he had had to endure on his face and head at around 15 million, with 500 million being required to cover the rest of his body, a process which took in all seven years to complete between 1927 and 1934.[95]

It is tempting to conclude by viewing tattoos and scarifications as examples of what Bourdieu identified as bodily habitus. But a word of caution is in order. The reason for that caution emerges from close attention to the terms in which Bourdieu defines habitus. Bourdieu, it will be recalled, states that if all societies safeguard the principles they most urgently wish to transmit by placing them beyond the grasp of consciousness, so that they cannot be touched by voluntary, deliberate transformation, nothing seems more precious than the values made body, incorporated, which instil the whole cosmology, ethic and political philosophy through injunctions as apparently insignificant as 'stand up straight' or 'don't hold your knife in your left hand'.[96]

Tattoos and scarifications *transgress*, rather than exemplify, the category of the habitus as described by Bourdieu. They do not embody principles that are placed beyond the grasp of consciousness. They owe their existence to voluntary, deliberate transformation; and it is of their essence that they are made explicit. It is by virtue of transgressing, rather than exhibiting, these features of bodily habitus that tattoos and scarifications operate with such palpable and evocative force, both for those who wear them and for those who observe them.

Frances Yates' *Art of Memory* therefore provides a more appropriate model than does Pierre Bourdieu's concept of bodily habitus for thinking about the efficacy of tattoos as memory codes. Frances Yates has explained how, for the ancients, the *loci memoriae* were a necessary mnemotechnics in a society without modern media. They were practical mental tools, heuristic devices. Their usage was based on the assumption that the best aid to clarity and persistence of memory is orderly arrangement in space. As Cicero says, 'persons desiring to train this faculty select localities and form mental images of the facts they wish to remember and store those images in the localities, with the result that the arrangement of the localities will preserve the order of the facts, and the images of the facts will designate the facts themselves'.[97] Quintilian elaborates the same point in greater detail. 'When we return to a place after considerable absence,' he says, 'we do not merely recognise the place itself but remember things that we did there, and recall persons whom we met and even the unuttered thoughts which passed through our minds when we were there before.' It follows that, once we have chosen our memory building,

the first thought is placed, as it were, in the forecourt; the second, let us say, in the living room; the remainder are placed in due order all around the impluvium and entrusted not merely to bedrooms and parlours, but even to the care of statues and the like. This done, as soon as the memory of the facts requires to be revived, all these places are visited in turn.[98]

As memory codes, tattoos obey the same principles as the *loci memoriae* of which Cicero and Quintilian speak, the difference being that the places of the latter are found upon stone whereas those of the former are found upon flesh. Moreover, they are *political* loci. Condillac and Rousseau argued that the coming of graphism accompanied the institutions of political and pedagogic power;[99] and it has been persuasively argued that Marquesan tattoos are signs that 'multiplied vision and knowledge', and that they are part of the technology for the creation of political subjects and so for the reproduction of political relations.[100]

This is what makes tattoos and scarifications so powerful as mnemonic codes, both for the group and for the individual. For the group: because as Claude Lévi-Strauss says, writing of the Maori people, the purpose of these markings was 'to stamp onto the mind all the traditions and philosophy of the group'.[101] And for the individual: because, as the Seattle tattoo artist Vyvyn Lazonga says, 'getting pierced and tattooed tends to develop a person's awareness of *memory*: the piercings or tattoos become points of reference that reinforce the self and its history'.[102]

NOTES

1 Dr Clavel, 'La tatouage aux îles Marquises', *Revue d'Ethnographie de Nancy* (1885), pp. 133ff.
2 F. Kafka, 'In der Strafkolonie', in W. Kittler, H-G. Koch and G. Neumann *Schriften, Tagebücher, Briefe: Kritische Ausgabe* (Frankfurt, 1994), pp. 201–48.
3 J. Caplan, 'Introduction', in *Written on the Body: The Tattoo in European and American History* (London, 2000), p. xv; C.P. Jones, 'Stigma and Tattoo', in Caplan, *Written on the Body*, p. 1; M. Thévoz, *The Painted Body* (New York, 1984), p. 40.
4 S. Schaffer, 'On Seeing Me Write: Inscription Devices in the South Seas', *Representations*, 97 (2007), pp. 96–122.
5 J.R. Forster, *Observations Made During a Voyage Round the World*, eds. N. Thomas, H. Guest and M. Dettelbach (Honolulu, 1996), p. 157.
6 Jones, 'Stigma and Tattoo', pp. 1, 2, 4, 11.
7 C. Anderson, '*Godna*: Inscribing Indian Convicts in the Nineteenth Century', in Caplan, *Written on the Body*, p. 108.
8 Caplan, *Written on the Body*, p. 255; Thévoz, *The Painted Body*, p. 38.
9 Thévoz, *The Painted Body*, p. 39; A. Rubin, ed., *Marks of Civilization: Artistic Transformation of the Human Body* (Los Angeles, 1988), p. 15.
10 N. Thomas, 'Introduction', in N. Thomas, A. Cole and B. Douglas, eds., *Tattoo: Bodies, Art and Exchange in the Pacific and the West* (London, 2005), p. 20.
11 F. Dagognet, *Ecriture et iconographie* (Paris, 1973), p. 15.
12 Thévoz, *The Painted Body*, p. 12.
13 *Ibid.*, p. 85.
14 *Ibid.*, p. 90.
15 *Ibid.*, p. 91.
16 A.D. Napier, *Masks, Transformation and Paradox* (Berkeley, CA, 1986).
17 J. Picton, 'What's in a Mask?', in F. Harding, ed., *The Performance Arts in Africa: A Reader* (London, 2002), p. 52.
18 M. Mauss, 'A Category of the Human Mind: The Notion of Person; the Notion of Self', in M. Carrithers, S. Collins and S. Lukes, eds., *The Category of the Person* (Cambridge, 1985), p. 13.
19 *Ibid.*, p. 15.
20 *Ibid.*, p. 17.
21 *Ibid.*, pp. 1–25.
22 M. Hollis, 'Of Masks and Men', in Carrithers *et al.*, *The Category of the Person*, pp. 217–33.
23 Mauss, 'A Category of the Human Mind', p. 9.
24 See Picton, 'What's in a Mask?'; J.P. Mitchell, 'Performance', in C. Tilley, W. Keane, S, Küchler, M. Rowlands and P. Spyer, eds., *Handbook of Material Culture* (London, 2006), pp. 384–401; E. Tonkin, 'Masks and Power', *Man*, n.s. 14.2 (1979), pp. 237–48.
25 See P.R. McNaughton, *The Mande Blacksmiths: Knowledge, Power and Art in West Africa* (Bloomington, IN, 1988).
26 J-P. Vernant and F. Frontisi-Ducroux, 'Features of the Mask in Ancient Greece', in J-P. Vernant and P. Vidal-Naquet, *Myth and Tragedy in Ancient Greece* (New York, 1990), pp. 189–206.

27 N. Boyle, *Goethe: The Poet and the Age. Vol. 1: The Poetry of Desire* (Oxford, 1991), pp. 556–7.
28 N.Z. Dayis, 'The Rites of Violence: Religious Riot in Sixteenth-Century France', *Past and Present*, 59 (1973), pp. 51–91.
29 E. Muir, *Civic Ritual in Renaissance Venice* (Princeton, NJ, 1981); E.O. James, *Seasonal Feasts and Festivals* (New York, 1961).
30 M.M. Bakhtin, *Rabelais and his World* (Cambridge, MA, 1968); V. Turner, *The Ritual Process: Structure and Anti-Structure* (Ithaca, NY, 1977).
31 Muir, *Civic Ritual*, p. 175.
32 M. Gustafson, 'The Tattoo in the Later Roman Empire and Beyond', in Caplan, *Written on the Body*, p. 24.
33 T.W. Dodds, 'To Remove Tattooing', *Scientific American* (2 May 1891), p. 273.
34 J. Cowan, 'Maori Tattooing', *Journal of the Polynesian Society*, 30 (1921), p. 242.
35 A. Gell, *Wrapping in Images: Tattooing in Polynesia* (Oxford, 1993).
36 D. Anzieu, *The Skin-Ego: A Psychoanalytic Approach to the Self* (New Haven, CT, 1989).
37 L. Benthien, *Skin: On the Cultural Border between Self and the World* (New York, 2003).
38 M. Strathern, 'The Self in Self-Decoration', *Oceania*, LVIX (1979), pp. 241–57.
39 W.D. Hambly, *The History of Tattooing and its Significance with Some Accounts of Other Forms of Corporeal Marking* (London, 1925), p. 34.
40 L. Keimer, *Remarques sur le tatouage dans l'Egypte ancienne* (Cairo, 1948).
41 Jones, 'Stigma and Tattoo', p. 4.
42 *Ibid.*, p. 14.
43 Ibid., pp. 5–6.
44 Thévoz, *The Painted Body*, p. 19.
45 A.F. Roberts, 'Tabwa Tegumentary Inscription', in Rubin, *Marks of Civilization*, pp. 41–56.
46 Hambly, *The History of Tattooing*, p. 109.
47 H.J. Drewal, 'Beauty and Being: Aesthetics and Ontology in Yoruba Body Art', in Rubin, *Marks of Civilization*, pp. 83–96.
48 Thévoz, *The Painted Body*, p. 50.
49 Rubin, *Marks of Civilization*, p. 107.
50 Hambly, *The History of Tattooing*, p. 57.
51 *Ibid.*
52 Anderson, '*Godna*', p. 104.
53 *Ibid.*, p. 102.
54 *Ibid.*
55 Hambly, *The History of Tattooing*, p. 221.
56 Rubin, *Marks of Civilization*, p. 179.
57 Thévoz, *The Painted Body*, p. 48.
58 *Ibid.*, p. 91.
59 Hambly, *The History of Tattooing*, p. 40.
60 Thévoz, *The Painted Body*, p. 50.
61 W. Ellis, *Polynesian Researches*, 4 vols (London, 1831).
62 Gell, *Wrapping in Images*, p. 102.
63 *Ibid.*, p. 51.

64 Thévoz, *The Painted Body*, p. 48.
65 Gell, *Wrapping in Images*, p. 225.
66 P. Gathercole, 'Contexts of Maori Moko', in Rubin, *Marks of Civilization*, pp. 171–8.
67 Gustafson, 'The Tattoo in the Later Roman Empire and Beyond', p. 25.
68 *Ibid.*, p. 26.
69 Jones, 'Stigma and Tattoo', p. 7.
70 Thévoz, *The Painted Body*, p. 64.
71 Jones, 'Stigma and Tattoo', p. 8.
72 *Ibid.*, p. 9.
73 Gustafson, 'The Tattoo in the Later Roman Empire and Beyond', p. 20.
74 Jones, 'Stigma and Tattoo', p. 13.
75 Thévoz, *The Painted Body*, pp. 64–5.
76 J. Bradley, 'Body Commodification, Class and Tattoo in Victorian Britain', in Caplan, *Written on the Body*, pp. 136–55.
77 Gustafson, 'The Tattoo in the Later Roman Empire and Beyond', p. 58.
78 A.M. Schrader, 'Branding the Other/Tattooing the Self: Bodily Inscription among Convicts in Russia and the Soviet Union', in Caplan, *Written on the Body*, pp. 174–92.
79 J. Caplan, 'National Tattooing: Traditions of Tattooing in Nineteenth Century Europe', in Caplan, *Written on the Body*, pp. 156–73.
80 J-T. Maertens, *Le Dessein sur la peau: essai d'anthropologies des inscriptions tégumentaires* (Paris, 1978).
81 Gell, *Wrapping in Images*, esp. pp. 210, 211, 259, 262, 265, 296.
82 *Ibid.*, p. 55.
83 *Ibid.*, p. 262.
84 *Ibid.*, p. 210.
85 C. Vincendon and C. Desgruz, *Les Isles Taiti* (Paris, 1844).
86 Gell, *Wrapping in Images*, p. 265.
87 *Ibid.*, p. 314.
88 Caplan, *Written on the Body*, p. xvii.
89 Hambly, *The History of Tattooing*, p. 75.
90 Caplan, *Written on the Body*, p. xviii.
91 *Ibid.*, p. 79.
92 Gustafson, 'The Tattoo in the Later Roman Empire and Beyond', p. 30.
93 S. Oettermann, 'On Display: Tattooed Entertainers in America and Germany', in Caplan, *Written on the Body*, p. 202.
94 *Ibid.*
95 *Ibid.*, p. 211.
96 P. Bourdieu, *Outline of a Theory of Practice* (Cambridge, 1977), p. 94.
97 Cicero, *On the Orator*, Books I–II (tr. E.W. Sutton and H. Rackham, Cambridge, MA, 1967).
98 Quintilian, *The Institutio Oratoria of Quintilian. Vol. 4* (tr. H.E. Butler, London, 1961).
99 Schaffer, 'On Seeing Me Write', pp. 96–122.
100 N. Thomas, *Discoveries: The Voyages of Captain Cook* (London, 2003), p. 227.
101 C. Lévi-Strauss, *Structural Anthropology* (New York, 1963).
102 S. Benson, 'Inscriptions of the Self: Reflections on Tattooing and Piercing in Contemporary Euro-America', in Caplan, *Written on the Body*, p. 246.

7   Bodily projection

By speaking of bodily projection I mean to refer to the fact that buildings around us and other features of our habitat are not regarded as entirely external to and wholly separate from us, but that the body-subject 'reads' features of the human body onto the habitat around us and within which we conduct our lives. This reading, or projection, can be accomplished in a number of different ways. It might be done by projecting onto the features of the habitat aspects of human bodily *states*. It might be done by projecting onto features of the habitat particular bodily *attributes*. Or it might be done by projecting bodily features in a form of cognitive mapping onto *elements of nature*.

I shall speak of these three types of projection as, respectively, empathic, mimetic and cosmic. All of these different types of reading or projection entail different modes of emotional or affective memory being applied to the habitat.

The distinction I make between empathic, mimetic and cosmic projection is intended as both a logical and a historical distinction. As a logical distinction its aim is not to indicate mutually exclusive or watertight categories, but rather to highlight degrees of emphasis as to where the priority lies. As a historical distinction it indicates the broad sweep of a historical narrative, and this narrative is an explicitly and admittedly Eurocentric one – and as such is subject to the objection of being what Jack Goody would describe as yet one more 'theft of history'[1] – although the varieties of projection to which it draws attention might be applicable, with modifications, beyond that limited historical frame.

I shall consider these three modalities of projection in reverse chrono-logical sequence. I have chosen to investigate the three modalities in this particular sequence – a decision which might appear puzzling or even perverse – because empathic projection may be reasonably assumed to be that mode with which we are now most familiar, whereas mimetic projection is one with which we are less familiar, and cosmic projection is the one with which we are now least familiar.

In empathic projection, spectators identify with parts of a building or with areas of unbuilt terrain by projecting onto them an experience of aspects of their own bodily states. Buildings or other topographical features are conceived as an amplification of the body's experience, as opportunities for the trans-position of our interior states onto inanimate forms. An array of vertical lines will arouse in us a sense of upward direction, whereas horizontal lines will convey suggestions of rest. A hundred yards of even ground could never have the same effect upon us as a tower a hundred yards high, or a rock of that altitude; and a perpendicular has more force in evoking in us a sense of the sublime than has an inclined plane. A straight line conveys a sense of sharpness and speed. The very idea of flexibility we derive from our body; by virtue of its tensile strength we are able to adapt to circumstances, most immediately in a physical sense, and then by extension figuratively speaking; and we can observe this same quality of flexibility, and so empathise with it, when we see a tree whose branches, while they bend in the wind, spring back to their original position.

Certain architectural forms will incite us to bodily movement: as when we enter the nave of a cathedral, and begin to walk forward; and, even if we stand still, our eyes will be drawn down the perspective, so that, in imagination at least, we will move forward. Or again, if we encounter a pronounced top-heaviness or disproportion in a building, we will experience a corporeal discomfort from that space; if, for example, we were to find ourselves in a room whose ceiling was seven feet high, the space provided would be quite adequate, functionally, for most movements we would need to make, yet that space would undoubtedly feel experientially bizarre and would occasion a sense of cramped discomfort. Some spatial features yield a sense of bodily comfort: from corners in a house, or alcoves in a room, or any area of secluded space where we feel free to withdraw into ourselves, we derive a sense of desired solitude. And sometimes we want more than comfort, we want intimacy, secrecy; a desire to a degree satisfied, as Bachelard has noted, by the chests of wardrobes, by the drawers of desks and by small boxes.[2] Such objects provide us with models of intimacy.

Many turns of phrase express this projection of bodily states onto what we would now understand to be inanimate topography. We speak of inanimate topography as if it were animate. Classical European languages are rich in such terms. The Latin verb *ambire*, from which is derived 'ambience', also possessed connotations of protection, of warm embrace; the Roman word for 'continent', *terra continens*, meant 'that which holds together'; and the expression *air de cour*, which was current in the sixteenth century, and has its analogues in the German terms *Hofluft* and *Klosterluft*, was used figuratively to suggest the spiritual atmosphere, the moral climate, emanating from a certain place.[3] And of course many turns of phrase now familiar to us in everyday speech make us aware of the projection of bodily states onto our life-spaces: as when we say that hills roll, that mountains rise, that belfries

point, that spires soar, that domes swell, that vistas stretch; and as when we
speak of lines and surfaces, which are in fact motionless, as if they were
moving, flowing, bending and twisting. Many of these metaphors are 'dead',
taken for granted, simply lying around in ordinary linguistic usage; no special
imaginative gift is required to employ or comprehend them, so that when we
say that a tower is standing or rising, we use metaphors that are easily
understood and we feel no need to argue that they are apt, for the aptness of
the phrase is something of which we are immediately aware, and only
subsequently, if at all, do we reflect on the metaphorical component: that
metaphorical component which is drawn from the states of our body. We are
able to employ language so unreflectingly, to think of lines and surfaces,
which we consciously think of as inanimate, as doing what we would feel
ourselves to be doing if we were, so to speak, inside them, because, in a sense,
we are inside them, for we have felt ourselves into them, we have unconsciously invested our life-spaces with the attributes of our bodily states,
recognising lines and surfaces as having particular qualities, as soaring or
swelling or stretching, by unconscious analogy with our bodily movements.

This is not to say that physical states enter substantially into the subjects'
consciousness. Quite the reverse: the conscious physical element in such forms
of pleasure or unpleasure is in fact slight. But the body participates in the
activity of empathic projection in the sense that the physical states of our body
are a necessary precondition of the pleasure or unpleasure that architectural or
other topographical features precipitate in us; for particular acts of empathic
projection depend, in fact, upon what might be called the condensation of past
bodily experiences which still act in the present, on the residue or sedimentation of motor-conditions which in the process of bodily repetition have lost the
marks of their particular origin. The projection of our inner bodily experience
onto the outer bodies of buildings or other topographic features necessitates
the revival, even if that revival is unconscious, implicit and untheorised, of
subjective bodily states in our memory. We find here no overt reference to, no
explicit memory of, the body; rather, there is an implicit reference to, an
evocation of, the body's memories – the body's memories of pointing, or
stretching, or flexing.

Elizabeth Behnke has made some particularly astute observations on the
condensation of past bodily experiences.[4] She makes these observations in
the course of a minute analysis of certain nuances of bodily movement that
are usually taken for granted. In doing this she is following Husserl's
analysis of the way in which, when we bring about certain changes in the
surrounding world of nature, we do not necessarily have any immediate
awareness of the bodily movements which our aims and activities entail;
and equally she is following through Merleau-Ponty's observation that it is
far from easy to lay bare pure motor intentionality, which, so to speak, hides

behind the objective world that it contributes to constituting. Behnke shows how, in laying bare such motor intentionality by a process of subtle and painstaking analysis, we would need to make explicit, for instance, the way in which our steps adjust to a terrain, how the gestures of opening a door must adjust to the kind of door it is, how giving a hug must adjust to the size and condition of the person being hugged as well as to the ambient social situation.

Although the visible moves I perform will vary with the circumstances – we might consider the kinds of movements typically involved in doing research in a library, or in running to catch a bus – these overtly visible moves always presuppose what Behnke calls a 'deeply sedimented kinaesthetic style', that is to say, an ongoing and persistent constellation of micromovements. The bodily 'sedimentation' that is operative here is the effective presence of the past; it relates, for example, to a general having access to certain skills and capacities, as for instance the capacity to breathe whilst giving birth, or the capacity to play the organ. If we observe attentively a musician's hands, for example, we may become aware of how they subtly embody the requirements of the instrument concerned, even when that instrument is not at present being played, so that, for instance, after decades of playing the violin, a violinist's left hand is somehow always inwardly curving around the neck of the fiddle in the way prescribed by the first violin teacher.

Behnke calls these micromovements 'ghost gestures'. Such gestures are related to socially contextualised, 'appropriate' expressions: for instance, heterosexual desire in the micromovements manifesting modesty on the part of a woman, and respectful restraint of passion on the part of a man. Women, in particular, may detect the ghost gesture of the ever-ready social smile, meant to be graciously produced on virtually any occasion; while men may detect ghost gestures relating to the assumption of an appropriately serious facial expression which is meant to indicate that they are capable of shouldering responsibility.

Behnke's analysis of ghost gestures is particularly luminous and affecting when she discusses the case of disoriented elderly persons, especially those confined to institutional settings.[5] In this context, ghost gestures have, as it were, escaped from what is elsewhere their relative invisibility. They have become visible rather as an X-ray renders the inside of the body visible. The elderly person may seem to have withdrawn from current reality and to have become engaged in apparently mindless repetitive motor actions. Their eyes blink, focus and unfocus, and their fingers pat, fold or trace a line along the surface of a chair. We can best make sense of such gestures, Behnke suggests, as – literally – the ghosts of what once were meaningful actions performed by these persons in the past: perhaps of milking cows, or shovelling dirt, or hammering nails. Or they may represent the ghosts of emotionally meaningful movements – movements of cradling, or caressing, or rocking – which were far more vividly meaningful in past situations than they are to the person in present reality.

The point of this detailed excursion into Behnke's refined analysis is to remind us of the *implicit* reference to, and evocation of, the body's memories. All progress in scientific physics, that is to say in exact measurement, seeks to eradicate these anthropomorphic elements of our immediate sensory perception. Admittedly, the idea that the new sciences sought to eradicate all anthropomorphism and qualitative discourse is a feature of some strands of the early Royal Society rhetoric, but not of its practices. Moreover, the more cosmobiological and causally holistic world of the Renaissance *épistème* arguably survived strongly enough in a whole range of fields of natural philosophy far beyond the so-called 'scientific revolution'. Nonetheless, we should not underestimate the enormity of the repercussions which flowed from the opening pages of the *Principia*. When Newton announced that the geometricising of space belongs to the province of mathematics, he meant it to be understood that measurable spaces must be conceived as homogeneous, and that places are to be understood as mere parts, or mathematically determinable positions, in space.

Whether he was writing in English or in Latin, Newton used the term 'medium' to refer to space. In classical Latin the substantive term *medium* contained a twofold spatial reference: it referred to the midpoint of an object, and it referred to the intermediate point between two or more objects. Although Newton frequently speaks of the 'ambient medium', the term 'ambient' here is entirely devoid of the connotation of 'all-embracing' which had been present in the classical Latin *ambire*. When he speaks of an 'ambient medium', the phrase contains no overtones of warmth or beneficence; in Newton's description of the universe humankind is alone in an infinite space run according to rigid laws; and even though these are conceived of as being ruled over by a God, Newton pointedly says that such a Being should be called Deus, not Dominus, since the latter term would imply reference to human subjects and human worshippers.[6]

This concept of an infinite space comprehensible in terms of measurable magnitudes reappears in Pascal and in Leibniz. Pascal speaks of the position of the human person as an isolated one, excluded from the two extremes of the 'infiniment grand' and the 'infiniment petit'. Leibniz develops Pascal's thought when he writes that 'Il est raisonnable aussi, qu'il y ait des substances capables de perception au dessous de nous, comme il y en a au dessus; et que nostre Ame, bien loin d'estre la dernière de toutes, se trouve dans un milieu dont on puisse descendre et monter.'[7] When Karl Jaspers in 1931 defined the 'spiritual situation of the age' as essentially 'ungeborgen'[8] – 'unprotected' – he was re-echoing Pascal's more celebrated dictum of three centuries earlier: 'le silence Eternel de ces espaces infinis m'effraie!'

In this new spatial discourse, geometrical space is characterised by the basic attributes of continuity, uniformity and infinity; all these run counter to the space of immediate sensory perception, and can be arrived at only by a systematic negation of what seems immediately given in sensory perception. This new discourse about space affords no purchase for empathic projection. Confronted with this predicament, answers were found in what may be called a twin strategy of *empathic compensation.*

The first consisted in the cultivation of the interior milieu of the dwelling. The emerging private sphere of bourgeois culture, with its attendant exploration of aspects of subjectivity – the conventions of the diary as a letter addressed to the sender, for instance, and the first-person narrative as a conversation with oneself addressed to another person – requires a particular disposition of interior spaces as the scene of a form of psychological emancipation;[9] the interiorisation and cultivation of family life entailed a culture of life in the home that depended on the conscious physical shaping of the most intimate material environment. 'Se trouver en hiver, dans un endroit ami, entre des murs familiers, au milieu de choses habituées au toucher distrait de vos doigts, sur un fauteuil fait à votre corps': in this invocation of domestic space from the Goncourts' *Journal* there is expressed a mode of thinking about the individual as surrounded by familiar things, each of which makes up the quality of the individual's milieu, and on each of which the individual has left some imprint.[10] Familiar things are at once part of the domestic whole and part of the individual.

This milieu is suffused with a sense of contact. We find this idea of a domestic milieu already in seventeenth-century Dutch paintings, with their interiors which are enclosed and filled in.[11] Mid-seventeenth-century Dutch still-life paintings depict the comfortable cosiness of well-furnished human dwellings, a tremendous pride in possessions – a 'milieu' far removed from the 'infinite spaces' that terrified Pascal. Expelled from the closed cosmos to an infinite universe, some sought a cultural counterweight in the experience of an immediate physical environment filled with things. There is a sense, then, in which the domestic interiors of Vermeer – his *Soldier and Laughing Girl*, or his *Woman Playing a Guitar* or his *Woman Reading a Letter* – may be viewed, in their concentration on the domestic world of women attended by men, which excludes the public stage on which 'history' is thought to take place, as an early painterly riposte to the transformation of the world from an organism to a mechanism at the hands of Gassendi, Descartes and Newton.

The second strategy of empathic compensation creates the idea of landscape, not as nature but as a piece of nature. When natural forces first became the 'object' of the natural sciences nature was represented in pictorial art as an 'aesthetic' object; scientific objectification and aesthetic representation proceeded simultaneously. Once nature is objectified by science and technology as 'the other', the modern relationship to nature acquires a dual disposition: both towards increasing instrumentalisation, and towards increasing non-instrumentalisation. Descartes' distinction between the 'small sun' accessible to sense perception and the 'great sun' subjected to astronomical observation anticipates Kant's remark that aesthetic imagination inherits the residual task of presenting to the sentiments the starry heavens 'simply as one sees them' and the ocean 'simply as it appears to us'.[12]

The mechanisation of the universe, however, was no monopoly of philosophers. When the world was conceived no longer as an organism but as a machine, sixteenth- and seventeenth-century Europeans were becoming familiarised with newer and more efficient kinds of actual machinery whose proliferation was compatible with the image of a mechanical universe: in navigational techniques, in the refining of metals, in the development of mining technology, and in advances in ballistics machinery. Renaissance engineering treatises – Biringuccio's *Pirotechnica* of 1540, for instance, or Agricola's *De Re Metallica* of 1556, or Besson's *Theatrum Instrumentorum et Machinarum* of 1569 – exhibited accurate representations of machines employed in the mining, metallurgical and gun-making industries.[13] Once the relationship to nature came to be mediated by machines which acted as distancing devices by which body-contact with the earth and elements became slowly attenuated, the concept of nature acquired a double-edged connotation of destruction and sentimentalisation. Land was devalued by mechanical exploitation and valorised as an object of longing. Independence *from* nature was compensated by a beautiful *image* of nature. Empathy for nature was a counter-weight to separation from it. But the destruction of nature preceded the yearning for it; the pastoral idyll was rooted in human violence against nature.

After the twin strategy of empathic compensation found in the interior milieu and the exterior landscape, the *theory* of empathy was formulated mainly by late nineteenth-century German philosophers and art historians. The resources of the German language were particularly apt for articulating the thought. The term 'empathy' is a rendering of the German world *Einfühlung*, which was formed from the reflexive verb *sich einfühlen*, 'to feel in, or into'. *Sich einfühlen* contains a sense of apperceptive activity not present in the verb 'to feel'; it means something like 'to transport oneself into something in feeling', a sense which can be adequately conveyed in English only with the aid of a verb such as 'to project, to transport, to enter into'. Vischer in 1872 introduced the word *Einfühlung* to refer to the process, whose basis he saw as 'the pantheist desire toward a union with the world', by which we project our emotions onto artefacts and natural forms: a thought which implied, with respect to architecture, that feelings of the inner self might be projected, for example, onto walls or doorways or domes; and which described a projective contact with natural forms that 'may be so intimate that even a lifeless form – the contour of a rock, for instance – may awaken and guide the transformation of feelings'.[14]

Lipps developed the thought by arguing that, in so far as any sensuous object exists for me, it is suffused with the activity of my inner life, and then, on this assumption, he distinguished between two types of empathy: positive empathy, where I succeed in transposing my inner states into an object through an apperceptive activity which I experience as a pleasurable expenditure of my own life-force, an ease with which the soul – Lipps compares it to the strings of an instrument – will vibrate in response to aesthetic stimuli; and negative empathy, where I find an external form repellent such that, in contemplating it, I feel myself to be inwardly impeded and subjected to a more or less obscure sense of coercion.[15] Wölfflin, in his study of Renaissance and Baroque art, argued that we relate to architecture, an art of corporeal masses, as corporeal beings, with our structurally particular habits of movement, and that we interpret the outside world according to the range of possibilities made available to us by the expressive system with which we are familiar from our own bodily resources; so that, for example, there may be said to be such a thing as a Gothic deportment, with its tense muscles and precise movements, in which figures are slim and extended, and appear as it were to be on tiptoe.[16] And Worringer, building on the insights of Lipps, located the crucial feature of empathic identification in an aesthetic pleasure which always entailed a feeling of free self-activity, an experience attainable only when there prevailed a relationship of intimacy, of untrammelled well-being, a primary trust vis-à-vis the outer world, a capacity to experience joy in the power of organic forms through which one could enjoy an enhanced sense of one's own organism: a condition which he found fulfilled, pre-eminently, in the art of classical Greece and the Renaissance.[17]

The citation of classical Greek and Renaissance art as the prime exemplars of empathic projection signals the retrospective character of this theory. In fact the theory of empathy is doubly retrospective. It is retrospective in a literal sense, because it expounds a conception of beauty from the point of view of the spectator; in an act of *post facto* identification, spectators are envisaged as engaging in an act of apperception in which they identify themselves with parts of a building through the experience of aspects of their own body or bodily states; the theory is not in the least concerned with architectural forms as seen from the outlook and intentions of the maker of works of art or architecture. It is retrospective also in a historical sense. A few dates will indicate this: Robert Vischer, *Über das optische Formgefühl*, 1872; Heinrich Wölfflin, *Renaissance und Barock*, 1888; Theodor Lipps, *Ästhetik*, 1903 and 1906; Wilhelm Worringer, *Abstraktion und Einfühlung*, 1908; Vernon Lee, *The Beautiful*, 1913; Geoffrey Scott, *The Architecture of*

Humanism, 1924; Adrian Stokes, *Smooth and Rough*, 1951.[18] If the proponents of this position take their primary examples, aside from the occasional reference to natural beauty, from ancient classical and Renaissance art and architecture, that is a revealing historical delimitation; for what they are reacting against is a context in which, for the first time, built topography is dominated by steel and iron: materials which make such structures particularly unamenable to interpretation by means of a theory of empathy.

Almost none of the theorists of empathy acknowledges or reflects on this fact. But one of them does. In Adrian Stokes, who has dealt with empathic identification in much of his writing, the hidden polemical intention of the theory of empathy becomes overt. 'Today, and not before', he writes in *Smooth and Rough*, we are beginning to 'emerge from the Stone Age'; 'for the first time on so vast a scale throughout Europe', hewn stone gives place to plastic materials, and, with this momentous material transformation, 'an attitude to material', an attitude which amounts to 'far more than the visual-aesthetic basis of Western civilization, can hardly survive long'.[19] Modern building materials are essentially plastic. The organisation of rooms will be simply a matter of design; 'with an armature of steel, Le Corbusier can make you a room of any shape you like'; and 'millions of jerry-built buildings' are 'moulded like cheap tea-cups'. But brick cannot be a substitute for stone, because 'the essence of stone is its power to suggest objectivity', to be 'more or less immovable'. This shift from hewn stone to plastic materials, Stokes concludes, entails a new affective disposition, one 'unrestricted by so deep an imaginative communion with the significance of the material itself'.

Stokes' insight was essentially correct, even if his dating for the end of the Stone Age was a trifle inaccurate; he might have chosen to locate it about a century earlier. For the theory of empathy was at the same time a celebration of that protracted Stone Age and a covert protest against the Iron Age inaugurated by the production machines of the nineteenth century. It was only because of iron that mill factories could be articulated with new spans in novel ways: with the substitution of cast iron for timber columns at Strutt's six-storey cotton mill in Derby in 1792–3; with the replacement of timber beams by cast iron at Benyon's Shrewsbury flax mill of 1796–7; with Bage's construction of the first all-iron mills at Leeds in 1802–3 and at Shrewsbury in 1803–4; and with the Stonehouse woollen mill in Gloucestershire in 1813, when, developing beyond its initial utilitarian forms, Tuscan columns made of iron and painted to look like marble supported elaborate iron tracery.[20] As an artificial building material, iron received a decisive advance when it was discovered that locomotives could only move on iron rails; the rail was the first iron unit of construction, the forerunner of the girder. Riveted wrought iron box and tubular beams for the Conway and Menai bridges then demonstrated an excellent strength-to-weight ratio.

These were the roots of the iron technology which shaped the railway stations, the arcades and the great exhibition spaces of the nineteenth century: all buildings which, as Walter Benjamin remarked, served *transitory* purposes. Transitory too was the Crystal Palace of 1851, the first cult iron object of the century: made from highly flexible parts, mass produced and systematically assembled, it was constructed of the same iron and glass that had been used in the Paris arcades, but in monumental proportions, its 112-foot-high roof covering over entire trees.[21] The international exhibitions held in Paris in 1855, 1867, 1878, 1889 and 1900 all followed this manufacturing scheme. But of course the most famous cult iron object of the nineteenth century, and the one most frequently photographed, was the Eiffel Tower of 1889, constructed from some 7,000 tons of iron. Commenting on the Paris exhibition of that year, Gauguin observed the same material mutation which Stokes was to inveigh against over half a century later; 'this exposition', he wrote, 'marks the triumph of iron, not only from the standpoint of machinery, but from the standpoint of architecture', since 'engineer-architects have a new kind of decorative art all their own', 'a kind of Gothic tracery in iron'.[22] The mostly unspoken opponent of empathic projection, its almost unmentionable historical taboo, was the age of iron and steel.

Whereas the mnemonic function of empathic projection is implicit, the mnemonic function of mimetic projection is explicit. For the mimetic mode, unlike the empathic, is a projection not of bodily *states* but of bodily *attributes*. In mimetic projection, the human body and its parts provide an overt system of reference, a set of organisational terms for what is not the body; the image and organisation of the human body provide a set of coordinates for thinking about other articulated wholes, a system of spatially distributed attributes which can be transferred to other spatial distinctions.

Where contemporary European languages tend to use prepositions to express spatial relations, in many preliterate societies spatial relations are expressed by means of concrete nouns which are words designating parts of the human body.[23] Mandingan languages express our prepositional concept 'behind' by an independent substantive meaning 'back' or 'rear end', our prepositional form 'in front of' by a word meaning 'eye', our preposition 'on' by 'neck', and our preposition 'in' by 'belly'. In South Sea languages such words as 'face' and 'back', head' and 'mouth', 'loin' and 'hip' perform the same function. Though the Egyptian language developed prepositions, an etymological analysis of these prepositions often leads back to names for parts of the body.

Well-known anthropological research has demonstrated this principle of mimetic projection in operation among the Hausa and the Dogon. Among the Hausa[24] the body is conceptually divided into a male right and a female left, and a male front and female back, which correspond to a division of a person's body and their parents' clans, such that the right side is held to belong to the paternal clan and the left to the maternal. This identification of one's own body with clan divisions is extended to the configuration of the total settlement in which the human body, or a substitute animal, is identified with an orthogonally quartered world. Among the Dogon mimetic projection is even more exuberantly elaborated. Marcel Griaule[25] was told by his informant Ogotemmêli that the Dogon believe that their village should extend from north to south like the body of a man lying on his back: the housing is the chest and belly of the village, the communal altars at the south end are its feet, and the mill for crushing fruit, at the village centre, is the female genitals. This mimetic mapping of body onto topography applies equally, as Calame-Griaule[26] has shown, to the individual house; where the vestibule represents the male partner, the outside door being his sexual organ; where the big central room represents the female partner, the storerooms on either side being her arms and the communicating door her sexual parts; and where the central room and storeroom, considered as an ensemble, represent the woman lying on her back with outstretched arms, the door open and the woman ready for intercourse.

The search for mimetic identification need not necessarily lead to preliterate societies. Nowhere, in fact, was the mimetic projection of bodily attributes onto topographical features more elaborately developed, more geographically diffused, or more long-lasting in its historical influence than in the case of the classical Roman city, where architectural method was conceived of as the transposition into stone of the body's favourable states, its balanced articulation, its symmetry and its standards of proportion.[27]

The Roman city was a total mnemonic symbol. At its foundation, the Romans would first establish the point they called the umbilicus, the centre of the city conceived in explicit analogy with the navel of the body. Given this centre, they would then define the city's boundary, the pomerium, where they tilled a furrow in the earth; every fifth year, every May and every 2 February, sacrificial rites were dedicated to the protection of the boundaries. The demarcation of the boundary was thought to be a matter of crucial importance; Livy wrote that to violate the pomerium was like deforming the human body by stretching it too far. Having now established a centre and a boundary, the Romans would draw the two main right-angle streets, the decumanus and the cardo, so creating a space with four symmetrical quarters, and they would place the forum just to the north of the crossing, at the central intersection or umbilicus; this rectilinear pattern is observable even today in old imperial lands as far distant as Scotland and the Sudan. The projection of human attributes onto the configuration of the city went further still: the mundus or world was conceived as female, and its deities were Vesta, Tellus and Ceres; the pomerium was conceived as male, and its deities were Deus Fidus, Mars and Terminus.

The same principles of construction were applied to the Roman encampment. The fact that the term for military camp, *castrum*, was insinuated into place names, as with Chichester, Cirencester and Winchester, contributed to the later mistaken assumption that the Roman town was a more formal version of the military camp. But the truth is quite the reverse: the Roman military camp was in fact a diagrammatic evocation of the city of Rome, a mnemonic of the imperium; Polybius writes that when the Roman army entered the site selected for their military encampment, it was as though citizens, returning to their native city, each sought out his own house.[28] The Roman temple, like the encampment, was divided into four quarters by cardo and decumanus according to the same diagrammatic principles and employing the same terminology. In the book *On Symmetry: In Temples and in the Human Body*, Vitruvius stated his conviction that the architect must derive the scale and proportion of his buildings from the scale and proportions of the human body and its parts; 'nature has designed the human body', he wrote, 'so that its members are duly proportioned to the frame as a whole', and it is this model that the builders of temples should emulate, so arranging 'the members of the works that the separate parts and the whole design may harmonize in their proportions and symmetry'.[29]

The Roman city, military camp and temple all instantiate the classical theory of proportions, whose principle of beauty required consonance of the parts with each other and with the whole: a principle announced by Vitruvius when, writing of symmetry, he referred to 'the appropriate harmony resulting from the members of the work itself, and the metrical correspondence resulting from the separate parts in relation to the aspects of the whole configuration'. Vitruvius expressed human proportions as fractions of the total length of the body, and envisaged the 'appropriate harmony' of the dimensions, through which the members should be beautifully and suitably related to each other, in terms of relations which derive from the organic articulation of the body. He made the analogy between bodily attributes and architectural components more explicit still when, in *De architectura*, he presented a narrative to account for the architectural orders, according to which the Athenians first created Doric sanctuaries, which used a system of proportions based on the male human body; then invented a column of the same type, but built according to the proportions of the female human body; and finally produced the Corinthian column, created in imitation of the body of a young girl.[30]

Interest in Vitruvius enjoyed a reflorescence during the Renaissance. Though his text was known, copied and used from the High Middle Ages onwards, his specifications regarding proportions were neglected. But after Poggio Bracciolini's rediscovery and critical edition of the *De architectura*, the re-reading of Vitruvius stimulated a preoccupation with the theory of human proportions as expressing the harmony between microcosm and macrocosm. The proportions of the human body come to be so far valorised that they were conceived of as a visual realisation of musical harmony; they were formulated in terms of arithmetical and geometrical principles; and, explicitly connected now with various gods of classical antiquity, they were invested with mythological and astrological significance.

The valorisation of bodily proportions was now extended beyond the position adumbrated by Vitruvius. Alberti,[31] developing his argument from Vitruvius' statement that the foot is equal to one sixth of the total length of the body, devised a new system of measurement. The traditional units employed by Vitruvius were too large for detailed measurement; but by dividing the total length of the body into six *pedes* (feet), sixty *unceolae* (inches), and six hundred *minuta* (the smallest units), Alberti was able to tabulate accurately the measurements from the living model. Leonardo,[32] developing his insight from Alberti's observation that the breadth and thickness of the arm changes in the course of moving it, investigated the mechanical and anatomical processes through which the objective dimensions of the quietly upright human body are modified; and by this means he was able to determine the expansion and contraction of muscles while bending or stretching knee and elbow, and so to combine the theory of human proportions with a theory of human movement.

The valorisation of bodily proportions led to new attempts to demonstrate the architectonic 'symmetry' of the human body and the anthropomorphic character of architecture. The first and greatest of these was Alberti's *De re aedificatore*, produced in 1452 and continually reworked until his death in 1472. Shortly afterwards two other treatises on architecture were composed: Filarete's *Trattato d'architettura*, written between 1451 and 1465; and Francesco di Giorgio's *Trattato di architettura civile e militare*, completed between 1481 and 1492. Both Filarete and di Giorgio are explicit about adopting the approach proposed in *De re aedificatore*. All three treatises are dominated by the axiom that the building is a body.

Alberti takes it as a given that 'the building is a form of body', and he makes it clear that by 'body' he means a living body; 'the building', he writes, 'is in its entirety like a body composed of its parts'.[33] He believes this analogy to hold both between bodies and individual buildings, and between bodies and cities; and the axiom permits him to introduce a new metaphor to guide spatial division, one which is organised around a central organ of privileged status analogous to the heart: the atrium for the house, the forum for the city. He presses the analogy further by distinguishing the supporting skeleton (*ossia*), the connective elements, nerves and ligaments (*nervi, ligamenti*) and the panelling (*complementa*), that is to say the infill and skin of the edifice. In two passages that introduce, respectively, the rules for the construction of walls, and those for the construction of the roof, he develops the *idée maîtresse* of the body as skeleton and ligaments that structure infill panelling. Here he designates the supporting elements as bones and explicitly names them as such, and he envisages these bones as playing different roles: the columns which bear the roof he speaks of as the spinal column, and the angles of the walls he speaks of as the arms.

On one crucial point Alberti leaves us in some doubt about the precise amount of weight we are being asked to place on the proposed analogy between a building and a human body. The creature whose organisation he most readily compares to that of a building is in fact the horse; 'the parts of buildings should be arranged', he writes, 'similarly to those of an animal; as is seen, for example, in the case of a horse, whose parts are equally beautiful and efficient'.[34] Di Giorgio and Filarete leave us in no such doubt. For them the body referred to can only be the human body. For them the analogy is unequivocal, and it is both more insistent and more elaborated. Di Giorgio develops the analogy in anthropomorphic drawings of columns, churches and towns which are explained with the precise anatomical correspondences specified organ for organ; his drawings include, for instance, a human figure superimposed on the plan of a cathedral, and on that of a city with the navel at the point of the main square; and he declares that 'basilicas have the shape and dimensions of the human body' and that 'cities have the qualities, the dimensions and the shape of the human body'.[35] Filarete introduces into the analogy the further metaphor of engendering, when he sees the privileged relationship between the client and the architect as two protagonists who, as he explains it, form a couple, where the male is the client unable to conceive on his own, and the female is the architect who carries within her their common project before bringing it into the world, like a living body. Filarete also observes that just as the body 'contains cavities, entrances and deep spaces which lead to its proper functioning, so too a building has orifices in the form of doors and windows', and that 'just as the eyes, ears, nose, mouth, veins and viscera, the organs are arranged in and around the body as a function of its needs and necessities', so too 'one should do likewise in cities'.[36]

There came a time when it was no longer thought that one should do likewise with cities. The reflorescence of the classical Roman interest in projecting the theory of human proportions onto the larger morphology of cities was, after all, the product of a particular historical moment, when the dialogue between architects like Alberti, Filarete and di Giorgio and their princely patrons was conducted in the setting of the city-state, where one party to the dialogue held the political power while the other enjoyed the new parallel power of a creator. Later, as architects were excluded practically from the problem of large-scale city planning, they increasingly lost interest in the theoretical level of discussion about the projection of a scheme of human

morphology onto the life-spaces which people inhabited, and the city envisaged as a comprehensive edifice disappeared from architectural treatises
from the late Renaissance onwards. In so far as the city retained a presence
in architectural treatises, it was primarily as a support for the process of
circulation – of pedestrians, vehicles and water, by means of its streets,
bridges, aqueducts and sewers. 'What bonds link the two million inhabitants
who crowd into Paris?' asked Haussmann in a speech of 1864.[37] His answer:
Paris is a great consumer's market, a vast workshop, an arena for ambitions. The
metaphoric transfer between attributes of the human body and architectural
features was at best impoverished, at worst eliminated.

When the city is still given metaphoric attributes, it is spoken of mainly as a
piece of pathology. For Le Corbusier Paris is a 'sick' realm, 'crammed to
bursting', 'becoming impotent and senile'.[38] Frank Lloyd Wright sees modern
cities as cancerous growths and 'the cross section of any plan of a big city' as
like 'the section of a fibrous tumour'.[39] For Cerdà the image of dissection recurs
throughout his treatise on the theory of urbanisation, the city being for him a
pathological body, with its disgusting and unhealthy slums, its streets which
obstruct communication by their layout, size and surfacing, unhealthy because
of their narrowness and the excessive height of buildings, the overcrowding, the
deprivation of sunlight.[40] The idea of the city as a pathological body implies,
of course, a norm against which this depleted condition might be measured,
but that norm is no longer provided by a theory of human proportions. Cerdà
refers to the city as an inanimate object, a container, an instrument; and Le
Corbusier speaks of it as a machine. It was no longer the *proportions* but
the *maladies* of the human body that were felt to offer an analogy between
the body and its surrounding topography. A *permanent* feature is replaced by a
contingent feature as the possible source of metaphoric transfer.

When occasionally a reference to the human body is pressed into service
to celebrate some felicitous aspect of city space, it is now but a husk or
remnant of a formerly coherent system of metaphors, a fragmentary metaphor. When Marina Warner, describing Paris, speaks of it as quintessentially
feminine, its buildings having 'bosomy and vaginal contours, pillowy roofs
and open-mouthed entrances';[41] or when Rem Koolhaas speaks of Coney
Island, at the entrance to New York harbour, as a 'clitoral appendage';[42] or
when Jean-François Lyotard writes that 'the blindness of the eye in the
labyrinth of Los Angeles is none other than the blindness of the palm as it
traverses the length of thighs, the span of shoulders, of groins';[43] then, in all
these cases, even though they are no doubt aware that their words echo an
ancient symbolism, we may confidently conclude that they have chosen to
deploy such turns of phrase, which might strike us as somewhat mannerist,
because they lie outside or near the margins of the expected horizon of
discourse, by virtue of the titillating transgressiveness which may attract the

attention, precisely because the theory of human proportions as a normative reference can be assumed to be *absent*.

It was not only to polemicise against the new architecture of iron and steel, but to fill the felt absence left by the disappearance of the theory of human proportions from all considerations of urbanism, that the theory of empathy was elaborated in the late nineteenth and early twentieth centuries, as a method of reinstating a modality of bodily memory into the relationship between bodily projection and the body's surrounding topography. But the attempt was only partially successful; for with the disappearance of explicit reference to the theory of human proportions in the idea of mimetic projection, what was also lost was a sense of the way in which *architecture is an ingredient in cultural memory*. Françoise Choay reminds us that 'Alberti's contemporaries could believe that the builder labors to assemble a treasure for society – an *indefinitely* extendible architectural patrimony in which to anchor social memory'; and she is surely right to infer from this that with the effacement of this mimetic assumption the intuition of a relationship of scale between body and building is lost; as she says, 'having assumed a planetary scale, the built environment has ceased to serve memory, which now relies on other means'.[44]

In passing from empathic and mimetic to cosmic projection we pass from one type of memory to another: from the implicit workings of habitual bodily memories and the explicit workings of mimetic bodily memories to the explicit organisation of cognitive memories. Cosmic projection operates as a memory schema not by producing a narrative of past events which can be stored and so retrieved by association with particular places, but by taking the elements of nature as the leitmotif for encoding the experience of place, for a mode of cognitive mapping.

If we find difficulty in envisaging what cosmic projection might be, that is because of the categorical distinction between society and nature which we now take for granted. Modernity distinguished between the laws of external nature, which no one has constructed, and the conventions of society, which are of our own making. That distinction was not always an obvious one. In the wonder-cabinets of Renaissance princes we can observe, as in a chemical experiment, a residual collection of hybrids which demonstrate that this work of conceptual purification, the total separation of culture and nature, has yet to be accomplished. Rare fish, ostrich eggs, uncannily large bones and stuffed crocodiles were there displayed side by side with antique busts and Chinese porcelain, and goblets fashioned out of shell or worked coral tested to the limit the supposed border between the craft of culture and the craft of nature.[45]

But once that conceptual border had been firmly installed, the categories of society and nature were clearly distinguished and, as Horkheimer and Adorno demonstrated in *Dialectic of Enlightenment*, humanity set about eliminating the basic principle of myth: anthropomorphism.[46] To eliminate the remaining vestiges of anthropomorphism, external nature had to be stripped of qualities; the dissimilar had to be made comparable by reducing it to abstract quantities; whatever could not be reduced to numbers became illusion. The rational subject confronted the unity of inanimate nature, in a relationship between the subject who bestows meaning and the meaningless object. This entailed the elimination of mimetic or imitative actions, in which the forces of nature were viewed as possible partners in interaction, where a form of communicative dialogue was thought possible enabling persons to open themselves up to the other subjectivities contained in nature by ritualised *assimilation.*

It would be anachronistic to think of such ritualised assimilation as an identification with nature, since the concept of nature did not yet exist, nor, in consequence, was there any 'environment' in the sense in which we would now understand it. It is the power within or behind what we would speak of as natural phenomena that was identified with; and we therefore need to make a special imaginative effort to conceive of existential experiences in which the emotion felt at merely seeing or feeling natural elements could be as strong as what our contemporaries might regard as the most intimate 'personal' experiences. Instead of speaking of nature we should refer rather to the elements: to earth, water, air and fire. We need to envisage a situation in which the imagination is attuned to specific *material qualities* of these elements and valorises them. For it is the elements that provided a *mnemonic system*, a systematic device for grouping together and recalling whatever belongs within specifiable categories. And this puts us in a position to understand how cosmic projection works as a mnemonic method, and to see how this applies in turn to the four elements of earth, water, air and fire.

The primary intuitive feeling we have about earth is as the foundation of every manifestation of what exists, an intuition expressed in many words for earth whose etymologies have the primary sense of that which is 'firm', that 'which stays'.[47] Because of this we are able to imagine a sense of solidarity between persons and plants as a continuous circulation of life-force between human and plant life, a sense of what has been called 'conjoined growth'[48] whereby certain trees, for example, are endowed with the status of religious objects, an attribution stemming from a double feature of trees vis-à-vis persons: for their life-span is, so to speak, both before that of persons, and beyond that of persons. Before them, because trees are always anterior to the life of persons and human generations, whereas the life of fields, with their different phases of tilling and harvesting, accompany the phases of a person's life-history; and beyond them, because, though persons, like trees, grow, they cannot continue to grow through a series of apparent deaths, through a constantly repeated defeat of death.

This sense of conjoined growth linking the life of persons and the life of the earth figures most prominently in the widely asserted analogy between the fertility of land and the fertility of women:[49] as when Aeschylus in the *Choephori* speaks of the earth that 'gives birth to all beings, feeds them, and receives back from them the fertile seed'; or when the *Satapatha-Brahmana* identifies the furrow in the soil with the vulva and seeds with semen; or when Paracelsus writes the 'woman in her own way is also a field of the earth and not at all different from it', since 'she is the field and the garden mould in which the child is sown and planted'.[50] This presumed analogy between the earth and the womb reappears in the widespread belief that children abandoned at birth, because they have been in a sense entrusted to the earth, have by virtue of that fact been given the opportunity of achieving a condition beyond the merely human, so that, protected by the earth, the abandoned child may become a hero, king or saint; Zeus, Poseidon, Dionysus, Attis, Oedipus, Romulus and Remus, and Moses all, in this sense, share the same fate.[51] But since the earth is valorised as a womb, admonitions are laid upon those who would devalue it. This is why a number of Roman writers deplore mining as an abuse of the earth:[52] as when Pliny, warning against mining the depths of the earth, speculated that earthquakes were an expression of her indignation at being violated; or when Seneca pointed to the defiling of the earth's waters as her retribution for the quest for metals. As late as 1556 Georgius Agricola, a proponent of mining, marshalled the beliefs of its detractors before seeking to refute them, beliefs which consisted in the conviction that nature did not wish to have discovered what she herself had concealed; for 'the earth' – so he paraphrased their case –

does not conceal and remove from our eyes those things which are useful and necessary for mankind, but, on the contrary, like a beneficent and kindly mother she yields in large abundance from her bounty and brings into the light of day the herbs, vegetables, grains, and fruits, and trees. The minerals, on the other hand, she buries far beneath in the depth of the ground, therefore they should not be sought.[53]

On the subject of water we have many intuitive feelings. At the sight of water we discover an image of clarity such that the idea of purity is not arbitrarily attributed to this substance but imputed to it by virtue of its intrinsic material properties, an attribution whose imperative motivation, far from being qualified, is only confirmed by the automatic repugnance we feel at the sight of a polluted river. At the touch of water, unless it is fiercely cold, we encounter a gentleness which prompts us to attribute to it healing properties; for when applied at moderate heat to the most sensitive parts of the body, such as the cornea of the eye, it causes no pain, and when applied to nerves distended by inflammation, far from causing irritation, it alleviates pain. Since flowing water is cool, it awakens and rejuvenates. Touch also reveals water's transitoriness, a flowing quality and a changeableness which are shared by persons. Transitoriness and coolness combined cause immersion in water to yield the most apt image we are able to envisage for the dissolution of forms and the experience of regeneration. All these valorisations – purity, healing, dissolution, regeneration – flow from the material attributes of the element.

Water is therefore a figure of regeneration and fertility.[54] In Christian theology the descent of Christ into the river Jordan was interpreted as the pattern of baptism; 'when we plunge our head into water as into a tomb', writes John Chrysostom, 'the old man is immersed, wholly buried; when we come out of the water, the new man appears at that moment'. In ancient Greece statues of goddesses of fertility such as Cybele were immersed in springs; and when Hesiod enjoins his readers never to urinate at the mouths of rivers which flow into the sea, or at their source, he is to be understood as thinking of the difference between pure and impure water not in purely rational terms, as would a modern chemist or hygienist, but in terms of ritual purification.

Nowhere perhaps is the veneration of water as the female element more widely elaborated than in the cult of shells.[55] Nourished in water, and so thought to be suffused with the germinating force of that element which was the origin and remains the sustenance of life, shells symbolised creative femininity by virtue of the morphological analogy between the shell and the female genitalia. Hence the regenerative potentialities widely attributed to shells in funerary ceremonies. De Soto's soldiers discovered in Florida, in one of the temples which formed the graves of Native American kings, enormous wooden coffins, in which small baskets filled with pearls were placed beside the embalmed bodies. These findings have frequently been replicated in deposits of oyster shells or other marine shells discovered in many prehistoric settlements very far distant from one another: as in a famous necropolis north of the Caucasus, or in Scythian tombs near Kiev, or in Chinese settlements where shells have been discovered in funerary rooms decorated in the 'cowrie pattern'. Or again, in a grave in the Indre-et-Loire department a coffin has been found to contain 300 small shells placed about the skeleton from the feet to the waistline. The eighteenth-century naturalist Robinet was not being merely fanciful but was formulating a variant on a recurrent theme when he stated that 'nature has multiplied models of the generative organs', and that shells were attempts on her part to prepare forms of different parts of the human body.[56]

If water is a figure of regeneration and fertility, air is a figure of freedom and transcendence. This is why we speak of being as free as a bird, why we talk of aspirations, why we refer to constraining circumstances as ones in which we feel unable to breathe freely, why the term 'most high' is universally taken to be an attribute of divinity, and why high places are universally felt to share in this transcendence and to be impregnated with sacred forces. As with water and earth, all these intuitions and valorisations derive from the material properties of the substance in question.

A popular prayer, which begins 'Our Father who art in heaven', states an identification re-echoed in multiple forms: in Yahweh, who displays his power in storms, whose voice is thunder, and who has at his disposal lightning, his 'fire' and 'arrows'; in Zeus, archetype of the patriarchal head of the family, who governs the sources of fertility and is master of rain; in the Vedic god Indra, who covers the sky, sends thunderbolts, storms and rain, and fertilises the fields; in the Iranian sky god Ahura Mazda, who has for his clothing 'the steadfast vault of heaven'; in the ancient German sky god Thor, who, like Indra and Jupiter, is the god of tempest; in the Celtic god Taranis, whose name is formed from the Celtic root *taran*, meaning to thunder; in Olorun, god of the Yoruba, whose name means 'owner of the sky'; in Iho, supreme being of the Maoris, whose name means 'raised up, on high'; in Puluga, supreme being of the Andaman archipelago, who dwells in the sky, whose voice is thunder, whose breath is the wind, whose anger is hurricanes, and who sends thunderbolts to punish those who infringe his commandments.[57] Then again, all over the world there are to be found sacred mountains, remote, standing apart from quotidian topography, incorporating the power of the 'wholly other': as Japan has its sacred Fujiyama, so Greece has its Olympus, Yahweh appears on Sinai, mounts Tabor and Gerizim in Palestine were thought to be unaffected by the Flood, the sacred mountain Haraberazaiti was thought of in traditional Iranian belief as being at the centre of the earth and fastened to the sky, and the temple of Borobudur was built in the shape of a mountain.[58]

About the fourth element, fire, we have a number of intuitive feelings. Even in the act of kindling fire its sexual connotations become self-evident; the rubbing motion of sliding a stick up and down a groove in a piece of dry wood, if sufficiently gentle and prolonged, evokes, if only subliminally, the experience of a more gentle kind of rubbing which excites the body of the beloved. Once the fire is kindled, these connotations persist; for whereas light plays upon the surface of things, heat penetrates; and whereas flowing water conveys a certain monotony, fire suggests the desire to bring things to finality. But fire incarnates ambivalent values, since it is a figure at once of resistance and of nourishment. It resists human designs; for not only is it difficult to kindle, it is also hard to extinguish, as anyone knows who has tried to put out a candle flame from even a short distance. Yet fire also nourishes; whether through the immediate warmth of alcoholic stimulant, or the slower action of comforting hot soup, the inward heat of a well-digested meal depends on fire.

Again it is from fire's material attributes that its valorisations are drawn. The assimilation of its action with human digestion remains an undercurrent: as when Fabre writes in 1636 that fire leaves behind ashes which are its excretions,[59] or when Boerhaave speaks in 1752 of the 'aliments of fire', the substances 'that really do serve as food for Fire', which through its action are converted into the substance of fire.[60] But the association of fire with human sexuality is more culturally ubiquitous. Hesiod devotes two long passages, in the *Theogony* and in *Works and Days*, to the episode in which Prometheus steals hidden fire from the gods;[61] and Palladas of Alexandria, in a gloss on Hesiod, writes that as a ransom for the human theft of fire 'Zeus made us the gift of another fire, woman', and that 'fire can at least be extinguished but woman is an inextinguishable fire', since 'she burns a man up with worries, she consumes him and changes his youth into premature old age'. The Roman foundation legend of Praeneste,[62] which relates how a girl sitting by the hearth was impregnated by a spark from the flame, and so bore the founder of the city, finds a distant echo in the Australian legend of a totemic animal which was said to have carried fire within its body, and which, once killed, cut open and examined, was found to contain very red fire in the male organ of generation;[63] and a variant of this motif recurs in the widely perceived symbolic homology between alchemical containers and the sexual parts of the human body, as when Nicolas de Locques, describing the unmistakable sexual shapes of alchemical furnaces and retorts in 1665, reports how alchemists 'take a recipient in the form of the Breasts or in the form of the Testicles for the production of the masculine and feminine seed in the Animal'.[64]

The repeated association of fire with human generative capacity yields the thought that, since fire – unlike earth, water or air – regularly dies, the regulated extinction and rekindling of fire is a ritual figure for the renewal of life: as when the sacred fire on Lemnos was extinguished every ninth year and a fresh one brought from the island of Delos, at which point, it was said, 'a new life began'; or as at the commencement of the Roman year, on 1 March, when the fire, deposited in the temple of Vesta as a pledge of the continuance of the Roman Empire, was extinguished and promptly rekindled;[65] or as in the ceremony of the seeding of the new fire among the Natchez, described in detail by Chateaubriand in his *Voyage en Amérique*, when, on the night preceding the ceremony, the fire which had been burning for a whole year was allowed to die, and before dawn on the following day the priest, in kindling the new fire, ritually 'gives a new seed to the extinguished hearth of the village';[66] or as in the ancient ecclesiastical rite in which the Easter candle is thrust into the baptismal water, to the accompaniment of benedictory textual incantations suffused with explicit sexual expressions – *regenerare, admixtio, foecundare, concipere, uterus*.

Whenever we speak of the elements of earth, water, air and fire, we are speaking not of objects but of substances. A mirror is an object; a fountain contains substances. Rather than speaking of the arbitrariness of the sign, we should speak of the way in which imagination seizes upon the specific material qualities of the elements of nature and metaphorically valorises them. The metaphors are not *arbitrary* but *motivated*. And the mnemonic systems of cosmic projection are always characterised by one distinctive feature: they point attention to a process of *transformation*. This process can occur only if it is assumed that inherent in natural substances there resides the paradoxical power of ceasing to be only themselves, as natural substances, even while they remain unchanged in their sensuous appearance. In this symbolic transform-ation substances are transmuted into something other than they appear to be, so that everything can signify both itself and something else as well.

In speaking of empathic, mimetic and cosmic projection I have sought to highlight the significance for cultural memory of the affective investment in life-spaces. But, as I indicated earlier, the distinction between empathic, mimetic and cosmic projection was not intended to suggest the existence of mutually exclusive categories, but rather to signal where, in any particular instance, the *priority* lay.

Thus we may expect to find elements of cosmic or mimetic projection present where the empathic modality has priority, and elements of empathic projection where the cosmic modality has priority. Pearls, for instance, were once thought to be endowed with magical, medicinal and funereal signifi-cance. Formed in water, they were found in a shell, which widely symbolised creative femininity, by virtue of the morphological analogy between the shell and the female genitalia. The pearl was therefore believed to have generative properties. But what was at one time taken to be a metaphysical symbol – something which fully represented itself, while pointing towards something else – ceased eventually to be thought of as an object rich in beneficent sacred powers, and came to be reduced to the status of an ornamental feature, appreciated, consciously at least, for its aesthetic attributes and economic value.

Again, even when an explicitly mimetic theory of building no longer holds sway, we will still usually find that the most important place on the house façade is the front door, towards which, quite frequently, there is an arranged stepping up, while in the case of grander houses we may find that the entrance is set under a roofed porch, which draws even more emphatic connotations of 'upness' to the approach and entrance. And on the contrary, it is unlikely that symmetry will have been sought at the rear of the house, in the shape of any formal arrangement of windows or doors; the attention at the back of the house, as with the human body, is to privacy and the removal of waste. Again, when we think of fire as an element in a system of cognitive mapping, and therefore as part of the cosmic cognitive ordering of a memory scheme, its role as such is partly explicable by virtue of the feature of empathic projection which is also involved: that is to say, the intuitive feeling that fire has sexual connotations, that it suggests the desire to bring things to finality, and that it incarnates ambivalent values, since it is a figure at once of resistance and of nourishment. The distinction between the empathic and cosmic modes is a matter of priority, not of exclusivity.

That said, empathic and cosmic projection may be viewed as being situated at two opposite ends of a continuum. In empathic projection, topographical features are conceived, not as the site of a basic assimilative oneness, but as an amplification of the body's experience, as opportunities for the transposition of our interior states onto the inanimate. In empathic projection the existence of an inanimate sphere is presupposed; in cosmic projection the existence of an inanimate sphere is unthinkable. In empathic projection an evocation of subjective bodily states sedimented in habitual bodily memory is presupposed, even if there is no explicit memory of the body's past states; in cosmic projection an explicit cognitive mnemonic system based on a categorical distinction between the elements is presupposed. The essence of empathic projection is an act of trans-position; the essence of cosmic projection is an act of trans-formation. The theory of empathy occupies the gap which opens up when the idea of cosmic projection is hardly any longer conceivable.

NOTES

1 J. Goody, *The Theft of History* (Cambridge, 2006).
2 G. Bachelard, *The Poetics of Space* (Eng. tr. Boston, 1964), pp. 74–89.
3 L. Spitzer, '*Milieu* and *Ambience*: An Essay in Historical Semantics', *Philosophy and Phenomenological Research*, III (1942–3), pp. 1–42, 169–200; see esp. pp. 2, 13, 17, 22.
4 E. Behnke, 'Ghost Gestures: Phenomenological Investigations of Bodily Micromovements and their Intercorporeal Implications', *Human Studies*, 20 (1997), pp. 181–201.
5 *Ibid.*, pp. 196–7.
6 Spitzer, 'Milieu and Ambience', pp. 36, 40, 41.
7 *Ibid.*, pp. 11, 33.
8 *Ibid.*, p. 200.
9 J. Habermas, *The Structural Transformation of the Public Sphere* (Eng. tr. Cambridge, 1989), esp. pp. 45, 49; H.P. Bahrdt, *Die moderne Grossstadt* (Hamburg, 1961), pp. 36ff.
10 Quoted in Spitzer, 'Milieu and Ambience', p. 186.
11 On Vermeer's domestic interiors see S. Alpers, *The Art of Describing: Dutch Art in the Seventeenth Century* (Chicago, 1983), pp. 31, 100, 118, 166, 203.
12 Quoted in J. Ritter, *Landschaft: Zur Funktion des Ästhetischen in der modernen Gesellschaft*, Schriften der Gesellschaft zür Förderung der Westfälischen Wilhelms-Universität zu Münster, 54 (Munster, 1978), pp. 24–5.
13 C. Merchant, *The Death of Nature: Women, Ecology and the Scientific Revolution* (San Francisco, 1990), p. 220.
14 R. Vischer, *Über das optische Formgefühl* (Leipzig, 1872). On the theory of empathy see A. Vidler, 'The Building in Pain: The Body and Architecture in Post-Modern Culture', *AA Files* (1990), pp. 3–19.
15 T. Lipps, *Raumästhetik und geometrisch-optische Täuschungen* (Leipzig, 1897).
16 H. Wölfflin, *Renaissance and Baroque* (Eng. tr. Ithaca, NY, 1966), p. 77.
17 W. Worringer, *Abstraction and Empathy* (Eng. tr. New York, 1963).

18 H. Wölfflin, *Renaissance und Barock* (Hamburg, 1888); T. Lipps, *Ästhetik* (Hamburg, 1903, 1906); W. Worringer, *Abstraktion und Einfühlung* (Munich, 1908); V. Lee, *The Beautiful* (Cambridge, 1913); G. Scott, *The Architecture of Humanism* (London, 1924); A. Stokes, *Smooth and Rough* (1951), in *The Collected Writings of Adrian Stokes. Vol. II: 1937–1958* (London, 1978).
19 Stokes, *Smooth and Rough*, pp. 213–56.
20 T.A. Markus, *Buildings and Power* (London and New York, 1993), pp. 270–3; A.W. Skempton and H. R. Johnson, 'The First Iron Frames', *Architectural Review*, 131 (1962), pp. 175–86.
21 Markus, *Buildings and Power*, pp. 222–8.
22 P. Gauguin, 'Notes sur l'art à l'Exposition Universelle', 1889, quoted in R. Brain, *Going to the Fair: Readings in the Culture of Nineteenth-Century Exhibitions* (Cambridge, 1993), pp. 52–3.
23 E. Cassirer, *The Philosophy of Symbolic Forms* (New Haven and London, 1955), vol. I, p. 207. On the theory of mimetic projection see Vidler, 'The Building in Pain', pp. 3–19.
24 G. Nicolas, 'Essai sur les structures fondamontales de l'espace dans la cosmologie Hausa', *Journal de la Société des Africanistes*, CXXI (1966), fasc. I, p. 101.
25 M. Griaule, *Conversations with Ogotemmêli* (London, 1965), pp. 96ff.
26 G. Calame-Griaule, *La Parole chez les Dogon* (Paris, 1965).
27 J. Rykwert, *The Idea of a Town: The Anthropology of Urban Form in Rome, Italy and the Ancient World* (Cambridge, MA, 1988), p. 59.
28 Cassirer, *The Philosophy of Symbolic Forms*, vol. II, p. 103.
29 E. Panofsky, 'The History of the Theory of Human Proportions as a Reflection of the History of Styles', in *Meaning in the Visual Arts* (New York, 1974), pp. 96–7.
30 J. Rykwert, *The Dancing Column: On Order in Architecture* (Cambridge, MA, 1996), pp. 122, 237. 'Recognition, together with the separation that it entailed – the primary estrangement – is the condition of my *knowing* the world outside myself at all, which I can only grasp, only comprehend (if you will forgive the truism) *out* of my body, since that is what I am and that is also all I have for a map or model of my exterior. Perhaps the only possible answer to the primal estrangement is re-presentation.'
31 Panofsky, *Meaning in the Visual Arts*, p. 125.
32 *Ibid.*, p. 128.
33 F. Choay, *The Rule and the Model: On the Theory of Architecture and Urbanism* (Cambridge, MA, 1997), pp. 74, 77, 90, 106, 328.
34 *Ibid.*, pp. 99, 328, 374.
35 See Vidler, 'The Building in Pain', p. 4.
36 *Ibid.*; Choay, *The Rule and the Model*, pp. 177, 178, 374. The return of classical ideas about the mimetic equation between a building and a body in the Renaissance was subject to a miscegenation, as a result of which the accreted layers of meaning inherent in the term 'body' – the body of Christ, the king's two bodies – make any analogy between a body and a building potentially multilayered.
37 After Haussmann 'a metaphoric understanding of the city structure is impossible': Rykwert, *The Idea of a Town*, p. 190. Haussmann's hidden logic was that of an economic system. 'It is not by his writings, but rather by their result – the transformation of Paris – that Haussmann influenced all organized urbanization

at the end of the nineteenth century, furnishing a structural model that imposed itself even as far away as the United States, and fascinated in equal measure the emperor Franz-Joseph, the engineer Cerdà, and the architect Daniel Hudson Burnham': Choay, *The Rule and the Model*, p. 29.

38 Le Corbusier, *The Radiant City* (New York, 1967), denounces the suburbs as 'the broken, dislocated limbs of the city [which has] been torn apart and scattered in meaningless fragments across the countryside'. See pp. 92, 99, 107, 140.

39 F. L. Wright, *The Living City* (New York, 1958), p. 33.

40 Medical terminology relating to the pathology of the city is at work throughout I. Cerdà, *Teoría general de la urbanización: y aplicación de sus principios y doctrinas a la reforma y ensanche de Barcelona*, 2 vols (Madrid, 1887).

41 M. Warner, *Monuments and Maidens: The Allegory of the Female Form* (London, 1985), pp. 36–7.

42 R. Koolhaas, *Delirious New York: A Retroactive Manifesto for Manhattan* (London, 1978), p. 23.

43 J-F. Lyotard, 'Passages from *Le Mur du Pacifique*', in A. Benjamin, ed., *The Lyotard Reader* (Oxford, 1989), p. 64.

44 Choay, *The Rule and the Model*, p. 280.

45 S. Alpers, 'The Museum as a Way of Seeing', in I. Karp and S. D. Lavine, eds., *Exhibiting Cultures: The Poetics and Politics of Museum Display* (Washington, DC, and London, 1991), p. 26. On hybrids see B. Latour, *We Have Never Been Modern* (New York, 1993), pp. 10, 30, 34, 41–3, 78, 112, 131, 142.

46 M. Horkheimer and T.W. Adorno, *Dialektik der Aufkärung* (Amsterdam, 1947).

47 M. Eliade, *Patterns in Comparative Religion* (tr. R. Sheed, London, 1958), pp. 239–64.

48 On the idea of a circulation of life flowing between persons and plants see G. Van der Leeuw, *Religion in Essence and Manifestation* (London, 1938), vol. I, p. 56; Eliade, *Patterns in Comparative Religion*, pp. 266, 269, 273.

49 Eliade, *Patterns in Comparative Religion*, pp. 164, 239, 242, 245, 247–50, 253, 254, 256–60, 333, 334. It might be objected that this manner of interpreting the concept 'earth' is a means of legitimating and so perpetuating a particular apportioning of power relations which is gender-laden. I would not wish to deny this; but that particular decoding is not, I think, inconsistent with the claim that to interpret 'earth' in this way is, as is the case with all four elements, *also* a particular modality of cosmic projection.

50 Merchant, *The Death of Nature*, p. 26.

51 Eliade, *Patterns in Comparative Religion*, pp. 166–7.

52 Merchant, *The Death of Nature*, p. 3.

53 *Ibid.*, p. 3.

54 On water cosmogonies see Eliade, *Patterns in Comparative Religion*, pp. 190, 191, 192, 194, 195.

55 M. Eliade, 'Observations on the Symbolism of Shells', in *Images and Symbols* (London, 1961), pp. 125–50; Bachelard, 'Shells', in *The Poetics of Space*, pp. 105–35.

56 Bachelard, *The Poetics of Space*, p. 114.

57 On the symbolism of sky see Eliade, *Patterns in Comparative Religion*, pp. 39–41, 43, 45, 47, 53, 59, 60, 62, 64, 73, 75, 76, 79, 81, 82, 84, 85, 87, 91, 94, 95.

58 On the symbolism of sacred mountains see *ibid.*, pp. 99, 100, 101, 376; Van der Leeuw, *Religion in Essence and Manifestation*, vol. I, p. 55.

59 Van der Leeuw, *Religion in Essence and Manifestation*, vol. I, p. 48.

60 *Ibid.*, p. 65.

61 J-P. Vernant, 'The Myth of Prometheus in Hesiod', in *Myth and Society in Ancient Greece* (New York, 1990), pp. 183–201.

62 Van der Leeuw, *Religion in Essence and Manifestation*, vol. I, pp. 61–4.

63 G. Bachelard, *The Psychoanalysis of Fire* (London, 1964), p. 36.

64 *Ibid.*, p. 73.

65 Van der Leeuw, *Religion in Essence and Manifestation*, vol. I, pp. 61–4.

66 Bachelard, *The Psychoanalysis of Fire*, pp. 31–2.

Name index

Addison, Joseph 65
Adorno, Theodor W. 162
Aegisthus 5
Aeschylus 4, 28
Agamemnon 5
Aguilar, Paloma 36
Ahura Mazda 166
Akhmatova, Anna 4, 75
Alberti, Leon Battista 159, 160
Alexandrino 142
Alstyne, Richard W. Van 77
Angelou, Maya 70
Anzieu, Didier 133
Apollo 10
Arendt, Hannah 73
Aristotle 93
Atget, Eugène 27
Augustus, Emperor 71
Austen, Jane 77

Bachofen, Johann Jakob 18
Bage, Charles 155
Bakhtin, Mikhail 54
Balzac, Honoré de 89
Barakat, Robert 57
Barnes, John 45
Battaglia, Debbora 43
Beckett, Samuel 55
Behnke, Elizabeth A. 149
Benjamin, Walter 156
Benthien, Laura 133
Binswanger, Ludwig 88
Bion 138
Boerhaave, Herman 166
Böll, Heinrich 43, 75
Bollas, Christopher 70
Bourdieu, Pierre 104, 142
Brezhnev, Leonid 141
Buddha 60
Burke, Edmund 65
Burrough, Edward 55

Caesar 19
Calame-Griaule, Geneviève 157
Calvin, John 71
Camus, Albert 22, 73
Casey, Edward 84
Cassandra 7
Castiglione, Baldassare 70
Caxton, William 55
Cerdà, Ildefons 161
Charles II, King 35
Chateaubriand, François-René de 167
Chesterton, G.K. 53
Choay, Françoise 162
Chrysostom, John 165
Church, Frederic Edwin 65
Cicero 85, 138
Claude 65
Clavel, Dr Charles 125
Clytemnestra 5
Cole, Thomas 66
Conklin, Beth 43
Conwill, Houston 5
Constantine, Emperor 60, 138
Cook, Captain James 125
Corbusier, Le (Charles Edouard Jeanneret-
  Gris) 155, 161
Cortés, Hernando 27

Dagognet, François 127
Dante Alighieri 89
Darius 138
Derrida, Jacques 32
Detienne, Marcel 117
Dobrizhoffer, Martin 137
Domitian, Emperor 70
Dostoyevsky, Fyodor 89
Dubiel, Helmut 24
Du Bosc, Jacques 55

Electra 10
Eliade, Mircea 64

Subject index

above 86–90
acoustic ecology 52–3
affective investment in life-spaces 86
apology *see* culture of public apology 16
archivalisation 39
archives 3, 4

behind 92–4
below 86–90
bilaterality 90
bodily attributes 147
bodily habitus 132
bodily states 147–56
body as gendered 95
body as memory 104
body's topography 85

ceilings 88
cinema 26
circus 127
city
  as pathology 162–8
  classical Roman 158
  walls 98
conversation 109
cosmetics 127
cosmic projection 163
culture of public apology 17–18

Dionysiac cults 127
disorientation 104
Dogon 157
doors 98–9

earth 164
elements of nature 147–56
empathic compensation 152
empathic projection 151
empathy, theory of 155
Enlightenment 105
ethereal world 88
ethics of memory 33

falling 87
fire 1
forgetting
  and annulment 38
  and art galleries 42
  and *damnatio memoriae* 41
  and discarding 40
  and food consumption 42–3, 44
  and formation of new identity 36–8
  and the French Revolution 41
  and humiliated silence 46–8
  and information technology 39
  and named ancestors 44
  and parliamentary debates 41
  and planned obsolescence 45–6
  as prescriptive 34–6
  as repressive 41
  as structural amnesia 45
formulaic utterance 122
Fortunoff Video Archive 26
front 92–4

geometrical space 84, 151–2

Hausa 157
hermeneutic circle 108
historical writing 3

inside 94–9
interfaces 97
interior milieu 152
interiors 98
internalised objects 95
Israel, state of 28

kabuki theatre 127

landscape 65–6, 152–3
lateral space 91
law as authorised force 28
legitimation thesis 1
lips 96